STRANGERS AND FRIENDS

INTERNATIONAL SECURITY SERIES

This new series attempts to clarify some of the most important issues which are likely to shape the Western alliance over the next fifteen years. It will seek to affirm the political relevance of some of our present institutions such as NATO, explain the differences between the allies that frequently give rise to public misunderstanding while maintaining throughout an objective evaluation of issues which will make the books of empirical relevance to those responsible for shaping public policy.

These convictions will not make the series unique but certain aspects of its approach will hopefully set it apart from series by other publishing houses.

First, the books will deal openly and explicitly with the values of the Western alliance, looking at the differences that inform European, American and Japanese views of the world. Second, it will focus on the public policy positions of the Soviet Union under its new leadership, testing the credibility of the new reformist approach, its realism and whether the initiatives that will come out of the Soviet Union in the Gorbachev period offer more of an opportunity than a threat.

Third, it will strive to broaden the public debate especially in areas where the position of public lobby groups and the media have received inordinate attention in scholarly and political circles.

It is hoped that the authors of the books, American and European, will contribute major works that will raise as many questions as they answer in the hope of continuing a debate which has often become sterile and stale. While most books will be commissioned directly from authors, those interested in contributing should write directly to the Series Editor.

Christopher Coker, The London School of Economics

Titles in the series:

STRANGERS AND FRIENDS

The Franco-German Security Relationship

Edited by
ROBBIN F. LAIRD

This book was published under the Auspices of the Central Research Program of the Institute for Defense Analyses

Pinter Publishers, London
in association with John Spiers

© Pinter Publishers, 1989

First published in Great Britain by
Pinter Publishers Limited
in association with John Spiers
25 Floral Street, London WC2E 9DS

British Library Cataloguing in Publication Data
A CIP catalogue record for this book is available from the British Library

ISBN 0–86187–014–X

First published 1989

Printed by
Billing & Sons Ltd., Worcester

Contents

Notes on contributors

Robbin Laird is Director of European Studies at the Institute for Defense Analyses in Alexandria, Virginia. Dr. Laird, whose books and articles on European and Soviet Affairs include *The Soviet Union, The West, and the Nuclear Arms Race* (1986), has extensive experience in military, economic and political affairs.

Dr. Barry Blechman is President of Defense Forecasts, Inc., and an expert on European and arms control issues. He served as Deputy Director of the Arms Control and Disarmament Agency during the Carter Presidency.

Robert Grant is a Washington consultant on European economic and security issues and has previously published several articles on French security issues. He received his PhD from Science Politique in Paris.

Cathleen Fisher is a member of the European Institute at Harvard University and is co-author of a recent study on West German arms control issues with Barry Blechman.

Jorg Baldouf is a specialist on Western security policy issues, and a member of the Stiftung Wissenschaft und Politik and staff member of Scientific Consulting in Koln, West Germany.

To my parents,
Bradley and
Miriam

Franco-German security cooperation: an overview
Robbin F. Laird

The purpose of this study is to assess the evolving Franco-German security relationship. In 1982 the French and West German governments decided to activate the security cooperation components of the Elysée Treaty signed in 1963. This study provides a description and analysis of this revitalization process.

The study consists of five chapters. The first chapter identifies and assesses French policy initiatives and approaches to West Germany. The second chapter analyzes the West German response to the French effort to revitalize the bilateral security relationship. Chapter three explores the interaction between French and West German forces in conventional force planning. The fourth chapter analyzes the pattern of armaments cooperation which has developed over the past twenty years. The final chapter provides a summation by a West German security analyst of what the Franco-German security effort has yielded to date.

This overview provides an assessment of the major thrust of the current evolution of the Franco-German security relationship. It does not attempt to summarize the findings of the individual chapters of the project, but rather examines the major factors affecting the development of this relationship in the years ahead.

GENERAL PERSPECTIVE: THE FEDERAL REPUBLIC OF GERMANY

For the West Germans, the Franco-German relationship has become more salient due to concerns about the trans-Atlantic relationship as well as about the evolution of intra-European relations. There has been growing German concerns over the past decade about the uncertainties of American leadership, although this does not extend to serious doubts about the US commitment to Europe. German governments have sought to accentuate their European relationship in order to more effectively steer the American leadership on a steadier course. The Germans have also been concerned with the need to increase the European role within the Alliance in order to bolster pro-defense attitudes in Europe. In part, the government has sought to increase that role through the revitalization of the Western European Union, as well as through such bilateral means as the Franco-German relationship.

The German government has also sought to promote more effectively its national perspectives, interests and priorities in an Alliance context, namely through a greater Europeanization of the Alliance. The bilateral Franco-German relationship is seen as one of the best ways to pursue this Europeanization.

The relationship with France is also perceived to be a critical component of the overall European diplomatic environment. The French and the Germans have a privileged relationship within the European Community, and the activation of the security dimension of the Elysée Treaty has been seen partly as a 'normal' extension of the consultative process which exists with the French on other European issues. This sense of 'normalcy' of consultation on non-security issues has had an important effect of the desire to have an extension of consultation on security issues equally for both the French and the Germans.

The Franco-German relationship in security matters is limited, however, by two critical aspects of the German approach to national security. First, the German government sees its security as best guaranteed by its continuing relationship with NATO, and any Franco-German relationship must be developed within the context of the former relationship. Second, the German government perceives that its relationship with the United States is the most significant dimension of the Alliance relationship whereby German security is ensured in a divided Europe. In other words, although the Franco-German relationship is emphasized within the context of a Europeanization designed to improve the structure of the trans-Atlantic relationship, it is limited by the desire to maintain a strong trans-Atlantic relationship.

From the German point of view, the American attitude toward Europeanization and the bilateral Franco-German relationship is critical in affecting how far the process of Europeanization can go. If the Americans oppose Europeanization then the Germans are placed in a position of making a painful choice, which almost inevitably will be made in favor of the American relationship. If the Americans support Europeanization, then the Germans have more room to pursue the Franco-German dialogue.

In addition to Alliance considerations, there is growing interest within the German government over developments in French security policy. For many German governmental analysts of France, there is strong perception that serious change is underway in France. The French are seen to be interested in strengthening their military relationship with the Alliance through the German connection. The Germans hope to involve the French more in West Germany's defense, and thereby draw the French into greater involvement in NATO in the years ahead. Although some analysts recognize that the price of this might well be less orientation by the Germans to the integrated command, others hope that in 20 to 30 years the French will re-enter the integrated command structure in some way.

There is a special interest on the German side to draw France into a more specific set of commitments with regard to French conventional forces and their role in German defense. This interest cuts across the political spectrum in Germany and reinforces the trend in Germany of emphasizing a greater role for conventional forces and a reduced role for nuclear forces in Alliance strategy.

The Germans view French nuclear forces as a complicating factor, however, because those forces remain outside the NATO context and its formal planning arrangements. None the less, some members of the German government increasingly appreciate the important deterrent role French nuclear forces play, especially after the ratification of the INF agreement.

GENERAL PERSPECTIVE: FRANCE

For the French, the Franco-German security dialogue has been a critical component of their general effort to revitalize their security relationship with the Alliance. Over the past fifteen years the French have sought to reconcile their policy of independence in nuclear matters with interdependence in conventional forces. The Franco-German dialogue is perceived as an important means for pursuing a diplomatic policy of interdependence in conventional forces which, at the same time, can be pursued in the French domestic context emphasizing national independence.

For the French policy-maker, there can be no question of compromising French independence in the public debate. The Franco-German relationship is perceived to be the privileged relationship in France's European policy of economic interdependence. It is deemed increasingly legitimate to pursue interdependence in security affairs by means of this privileged relationship.

In other words, the Franco-German relationship has a more important symbolic role in French security policy than it does in German security policy. For the French, the Franco-German relationship is an important means for reconciling the polarities of independence and Alliance solidarity. For the Germans, the Franco-German relationship is a means for pursuing greater independence within a clearly circumscribed policy of emphasizing solidarity with the Americans and the Alliance. The Franco-German dialogue, then, is pursued by the French to emphasize Alliance solidarity through greater Europeanization while the Germans are pursuing greater independence through greater Europeanization in order the shape the Alliance more to their own liking (i.e. a strong American commitment with less American dominance).

For France, its relationship with West Germany is a privileged one in the EEC and within European diplomacy more generally. The extension of the dialogue to security affairs has been seen as an obvious enhancement of this privileged relationship. The goal is to have something akin to the American special relationship with the British with the two sides pursuing interests in common within the Alliance.

The French have also been deeply concerned with the emergence of negative trends in West German security policy. For some, it is a fear of neutralism which will lead the Germans to trade reunification for demilitarization. The Soviets are perceived to be interested in such a trade-off. For others, it is a concern with Germany's pursuit of *Ostpolitik* whereby the Federal Republic might emerge as the European superpower blending elements of West and East in Middle Europe. For still others, it is a concern that the Soviets are seeking to become the primary arbiter over the fate of Germany, and some French officials fear that West German arms control policy and the pursuit of *Ostpolitik* may allow the Soviets to succeed in this aim.

The French government has perceived it to be necessary to emphasize a more assertive policy of interdependence in security policy in order to check such negative trends in West Germany. Mitterrand's speech in January 1983 in the Bundestag supporting NATO's deployment of the American Euromissiles was viewed by French officials involved as an important step in France's effort to focus West German governmental policy in a more responsible direction.

Finally, the French have a clear sense of historical mission when it comes to European security. French officials have sought for a long time to encourage the emergence of a responsible form of Europeanization, in which the Alliance becomes less dominated by the Americans, and the Europeans take more responsibility for their own security. Through the Franco-German relationship the French seek to inspire the Germans with some of their sense of mission in order to achieve a greater sense of national pride but in a European context. Without such a sense of mission, French officials fear that the Germans will drift east or decay into a form of virulent, anti-Americanism. The French fear that the Germans may confuse concern with the US's role in the Alliance with the necessity for a strong Alliance more generally.

THE CONSULTATION PROCESS

The Franco-German security consultation process occurs against the background of semi-annual summits between the heads of state as mandated by the Elysée Treaty. The summits address the whole spectrum of issues confronting the two states, ranging from economic to security issues. The summits provide an opportunity for the heads of state to talk privately in a direct manner without the presence of numerous aides. In fact, the two heads of state meet much more frequently than the regularly scheduled summits. For example, in 1985 Kohl and Mitterrand met ten times.

Obviously, personalities have an important effect on the quality of interactions between the heads of state. The excellent personal relationship between Chancellor Schmidt and President Giscard d'Estaing was a critical accelerator of the relationship in the 1970s. Also, because the two are fluent in English, they could speak directly to one another frequently on the phone. The relationship between Mitterrand and Kohl has been less warm, but in spite of personal differences, the two heads of state have frankly discussed a wide range of issues. The dialogue is, nevertheless, limited by the need to work through interpreters, and communication except in face-to-face situations is limited.

While personalities certainly facilitate the interaction, the relationship has become deeply institutionalized. Frequent meetings between foreign and economic officials within the EEC and bilaterally have been the rule. The activation of the security clause of the Elysée Treaty has led to an intensification of interaction on security issues. For example, the Ministers of Defense and Foreign Affairs meet regularly just prior to the semi-annual summits prescribed by the Elysée Treaty.

In addition, before and after the semi-annual summits, there are meetings of the

Franco-German Commission on Security and Defense which is composed of ten to twelve high-level civilian, military, political and administrative officials from the defense and diplomatic fields. The high-ranking level of these officials allows the Commission not only to work effectively with a range of subjects, but also ensures that bureaucratic implementation of their decisions will occur. Below the Commission, three working groups have been established which are composed of several defense and diplomatic personnel. The three groups deal respectively with weapons development, military cooperation and political-military affairs. In addition, *ad hoc* groups have been established for a limited duration in order to address specific issues.

The Franco-German consultation process has built in an orientation toward a specific intra-Allied consideration to national decisions. As the French and Germans develop or present policy, they take into account the European dimension (by which they mean in large part each other's perceptions) of that policy. By so doing, both sides believe they enhance the acceptability of their position within the Alliance.

The Franco-German consultative process is perceived by both sides to be a privileged dialogue within an increasingly significant intra-European consultative process. Institutions such as the European Political Consultative Process (where Soviet issues are discussed) and the WEU (where several working groups have been established) are increasingly providing a framework for intra-European consultation. The Franco-German dialogue can provide the impetus for change within this overall European consultative process.

THE CONVENTIONAL FORCE DIMENSION

The West German interest in France's role in the defense of Germany (and Europe more generally) occurs against a background of growing interest in raising the nuclear threshold. The Germans are interested in enhancing conventional forces and in this context an expanded French commitment to German defense and an increased French ability to participate in conventional defense is of growing significance. The capabilities of French conventional forces, as well as the concrete contributions French forces and facilities can make to the conventional defense of Europe is critical to the Germans.

There has been a long-standing interest among German officials in concretizing the French means for central front defense. The withdrawal by France from the integrated military command was a very negative blow to Franco-German relations. The Germans have seen the participation of Allied forces in the integrated command as a critical component in maintaining the Allied commitment to German defense. The Germans are oriented toward procedural detail and ritual as a means of reassurance as well and participation in NATO procedures is perceived as a *sine qua non* of sound defense policy. French unwillingness to participate in many of these procedures has meant that the French have been unable to reassure the Germans of the seriousness of their commitment to defense.

Put in other terms, the French have shifted symbolically and practically toward a more concrete participation in the defense of Germany. The process of reassuring the French public (about its continued independence) has been at odds with what is needed to reassure the German government, namely, participating in NATO exercises and procedures. For the Franco-German relationship in conventional forces to advance, compromises will have to be forged between these two modes of reassurances, but clearly the French must participate in a growing number of German/NATO exercises to demonstrate over time their 'seriousness' with regard to their defense commitments (outside of the defense of the French sanctuary).

The Germans are often impatient with the 'other' missions of French forces, whether conventional or nuclear. This is especially true with regard to France's non-European role. The Germans wish to see France enhance its central front role, and see little utility in the African mission of the French. The French government sees this latter role as a manifestation of its legitimate role in the world as a mini-superpower. Most Germans are skeptical of all Western nations who exercise military power outside Europe, including France.

At the root of the differing perceptions about the legitimacy of France's role out of Europe lie different conceptions about the legitimacy of military power. For the French, military power used by the state is legitimate in almost all circumstances. For the Germans (with the legacy of Nazism), military power is legitimate only if used in a narrow concept of defense, namely defense of the home territory against attack. The French perceive part of their mission as conveying to the Germans the legitimacy of the use of military power in defense of a broader conception of Western interests.

The German desire to engage French forces more effectively in the defense of the Federal Republic has not focused on the German form of national doctrine (i.e. forward defense). Rather, most German officials are more interested in enhancing the effectiveness of the French force's role as NATO's critical reserve. The concern is to ensure that French forces are well equipped and well trained to deal with Soviet breakthroughs in the forward defense. This means that French forces must be upgraded in capability and better coordinated with NATO forces.

The formation of the French Rapid Action Force (FAR) has elicited varying reactions from German officials. Political and diplomatic officials have expressed great interest in the FAR. The formation of the FAR has been seen as an important step forward (quite literally) in the French commitment to Germany. Military officials remain skeptical and critical of the force. Yet even they have grudgingly recognized the potentially positive contribution it might play. The recently completed Franco-German exercise has had an important effect in advancing the interaction between French and German military officials. As the exercise process continues, German military attitudes will undoubtedly be modified favourably from the standpoint of Franco-German relations.

For the French government, the formation of the FAR was designed partly to reinforce its central front commitment in a way consistent with its national doctrine. The FAR was obviously designed to allow the airmobile division to be used in central front defense without France having to say so explicitly. The FAR's creation was also the result of an ongoing debate in the French army over the proper mix of forces. There has been a significant conflict between advocates of heavy versus light forces, and the formation of the FAR represented the success of the advocates of light forces.

For the French government, conventional forces can play a much greater role in the Franco-German and Franco-Allied relationships than can nuclear forces. For French officials and the public, nuclear forces are inextricably interconnected with the notion of French independence. This independence can be modified to some extent, but not to the point of identifying French security completely with the Alliance on the matter of nuclear deterrence. In contrast, the conventional forces can be used better to provide for French security to the extent that the central front is secured from Soviet attack. French security is enhanced by better coordination with Allied forces and it is through the Franco-German relationship that such coordination can be pursued. In other words, by carefully involving the conventional forces in closer relations with the Allies, the French government can reassure the Allies without abrogating its commitment to French independence.

French officials also have a strong incentive to make their conventional forces more effective via better training and exercises with Alliance forces. French officials understand that over time they will have fewer forces available and will therefore seek to deploy these forces more effectively to make up for declining size. Perhaps smaller conventional forces, better armed and better coordinated with Alliance forces, will actually make a more substantial contribution to French security. Put in other terms, the pursuit of French national interests might well be served better by emphasizing the Alliance connection in conventional force deployments.

In addition, there is currently an important generational change in the general officer corps regarding central front operations. The older generation of officers, whose experience was largely in Indochina, is passing from the scene. Increasingly, the new officers think only in terms of a primary central front mission and a specialized mission for French forces in Africa. Also, no responsible military or defense official contemplates a solely national mission for French conventional forces in time of war.

There is an emerging French debate over how to balance conflicting demands on defense resources. The Franco-German priority has become so significant to French officials that one can hear concern voiced lest the nuclear forces or the out-of-Europe forces drain resources from central front conventional missions. It is a measure of how far the Franco-German relationship has gone that French officials can seriously contemplate allocation trade-offs in these terms.

An additional dimension of the conventional relationship will be critical in the years ahead. Although French conventional forces are important in German calculations of how to raise the nuclear threshold, French logistical and infrastructure support is almost as important. Might the French air force allow the Germans to use French airfields? Can the French government acknowledge the role its ports and airfields must play in the American resupply effort to Europe in times of crisis? French geographic depth is critical to any serious enhancement of conventional capabilities in the Alliance and the Germans will undoubtedly pressure the French on these issues in the years ahead.

The developing relationship between Alliance and French conventional forces via the Franco-German connection is being reinforced by another trend in French defense policy, namely, the French are seeking closer military production ties with the Allies rather than promoting national defense industries primarily through Third World sales. The situation in the 1970s which saw French defense industries supported by Middle Eastern sales is viewed increasingly as an aberration.

None the less, the effort to enhance interallied cooperation has not led to an expansion of Franco-German co-production as chapter 4 on Franco-German arms cooperation makes clear, the trend over time has been for less rather than more cooperation. The recently concluded (after much effort) helicopter deal is the exception which proves the rule. To the extent that a special Franco-German armaments axis is considered critical to the broader Franco-German relationship, disappointments are to be expected. Such ties can be successfully pursued only when they are economically and militarily rational. To this extent, the Franco-German armaments relationship can simply be a component of the broader effort to become more competitive in the Alliance and global arms markets.

Finally, some efforts toward inter-operability are either being actively pursued or are the logical outcome of some arms program developments. The joint missile production program means that the FAR will operate with the same anti-tank missiles as the German forces. In addition, the Leclerc tank will use the same ammunition as the *Leopard II*.

THE NUCLEAR DIMENSION

For the West Germans, the French nuclear forces are a complicating factor in the security equation. When French nuclear doctrine is emphasized in the bilateral relationship, the differences between the two sides are more evident. When French officials emphasize a European role for those forces, differences can be muted to some extent.

West German perceptions of French nuclear issues must be understood in the context of the general nuclear angst in the Federal Republic. The general interest among most Germans in raising the nuclear threshold has already been mentioned. The strong desire by most Germans to enhance conventional defense has meant less than open enthusiasm for the priority the French accord to nuclear weapons in the concept of deterrence.

Also, the struggle over INF's double-zero option has enhanced the West German sense of difference with its nuclear allies, including France. The French and British have even developed a growing interest in discussing nuclear issues with each other, in part, as a result of a deeper sense of sharing the important role of being Europe's nuclear powers. The German government has actively sought British and French support for the pursuit of reductions in battlefield nuclear weapons. Senior government officials have expressed disappointment with the lack of French support for their concerns.

The German position on nuclear weapons, however, is never simple. While officials have expressed concern with the reticence of the nuclear allies to handle the battlefield nuclear issue with more vigor, other officials have expressed a growing appreciation of the deterrent role of the European nuclear forces. These officials have sought to obtain some guarantee of a supplemental extended deterrence, especially from the French.

At the heart of German concern about French nuclear weapons is a fear that the French will use their nuclear weapons in a European war prior to the time when the Germans think it would be appropriate. The Germans have sought through various NATO procedures to gain some veto over British and American use of nuclear weapons. Even if these veto power procedures are to some extent illusory, the German propensity toward procedure means that the Germans are reassured because of their participation in a procedural framework.

For the French, there has been growing concern with how to address German nuclear angst. In part, the French seek to convince Germany that nuclear deterrence is a European as well as an Alliance requirement, and thereby to 'de-Americanize' the conflict over nuclear weapons. Yet the French have to balance their concern for reassuring the Germans with the requirements of maintaining national independence. Also, French analysts of nuclear deterrence have insisted for many years that the nuclear decision cannot be shared. To share the nuclear decision with the Germans would mean that deterrence itself would be compromised in both French and Soviet eyes.

The French have, however, shifted the meaning of independence over the past ten years. Increasingly, French officials speak of the need for autonomy in decision-making rather than independence *per se*. The French government wishes to be able to make an autonomous decision on nuclear use, but the effects of this decision clearly could be to extend deterrence beyond the borders of French territory.

The evolution of French thinking about nuclear weapons provides an opportunity for such an extension of deterrence. The French are building a nuclear force structure which will allow for a greater possibility of counterforce strikes, including some limited nuclear options.

In no area is the possibility of rethinking the operational aspects of French doctrine more important than with regard to the so-called pre-strategic or tactical weapons. President Mitterrand's government coined the term pre-strategic largely for cosmetic reasons to try to avoid the embarrassment of tactical nuclear forces. These French forces have been a diplomatic problem with the Germans (the *Pluton* can only be used effectively on German territory) and a strategic problem (in terms of defining their relationship to the SLBM force). Born as a cosmetic change, the pre-strategic concept is now taking on a life of its own.

CONCLUSION

The Franco-German security dialogue has set in motion a process which lacks a definite outcome. It is a dialogue designed to deal with the uncertainties of the evolving European security environment, including the challenge of a fluctuating US role in the Alliance. Much as one cannot confidently predict the future of the Western Alliance, one cannot predict the outcome of the Franco-German dialogue. It is clear, however, the Franco-German security relationship will grow in significance as the American role in the Western Alliance declines. Rather than replacing the American role, the dialogue can help both sides to try to cope with the vascillations in that role.

The main thrust of progress to be made in the relationship will be in conventional forces. Each, for their own set of reasons, seeks to deepen the involvement of French conventional forces in German defense. If this prospect of deepening involvement is handled with some care and political skill, a real change in the role of the French forces in the Alliance can be achieved. None the less, political ineptitude cannot be ruled out, which would eliminate the prospects for change and would lead to bitterness on both sides. In such a situation the Franco-German relationship would become a dialogue of the deaf, precisely at a time when the American role in the Alliance might need to be supplemented.

There will continue to be a clash of two divergent visions. The French seek greater independence for Europe in the Alliance; the Germans seek French integration into the Alliance. The press of events may well move these visions closer to each other, with the French becoming more involved in NATO and the Germans less so. The possible convergence of the two visions – a more independent European role in the Alliance with less dominance by the American command – might well be a critical motor force for change in the Alliance in the years ahead. The key problem will be for the French and Germans to try to engineer such a change while maintaining a serious American commitment to European defense. This juggling act will be central to the evolution of the Franco-German relationship in the years ahead.

1 French security policy and the Franco-German Relationship
Robert Grant

INTRODUCTION

The Federal Republic of Germany is France's leading European partner in the defense field. France has conducted more intensive bilateral discussions, undertaken more collaborative arms projects, and established greater functional and operational military ties with Germany than with any other of its European NATO allies. Although much ambivalence and ambiguity still characterize French policy toward Germany in the defense field, the overall picture just described none the less represents a fairly remarkable evolution in France's defense relations with a country that over the past 100 years engaged France in three major conflicts, all of which were, in different ways, devastating for France, and that Gaullists in the 1960s derisively referred to as 'the best pupil in the Atlantic class' (in contrast to France's 'independent' stance *vis-à-vis* the United States). The current state in Franco-German defense relations is due to a large extent to a strong surge in cooperative activities that has occurred during the 1980s.

The fundamental French goal behind this surge has been the strengthening of European defense cooperation within the framework of the Atlantic Alliance, leading over the long term to a more autonomous European security structure. This goal responds to a complex tangle of near-term fears and long-term aspirations. The French see European defense cooperation, centered on a Franco-German core, as critical in the near term for countering the potential loosening of the FRG's ties to the West under the combined blows of increased pacifist, neutralist and anti-nuclear sentiment in the FRG, and of a weakening of the US defense commitment to Europe, particularly in its nuclear dimension. The French also view European defense cooperation, again pulled along by a Franco-German 'locomotive', as an absolutely necessary component of the long-term endeavor of enabling Western Europe to take greater control over its own destiny. This chapter will examine the nature of the Franco-German defense relationship, the needs it fulfills for France, and the perspectives, from a French standpoint, on its future evolution.

THE HISTORICAL EVOLUTION

Postwar reconciliation and the 1963 defense treaty

During the immediate postwar period, France's overwhelming concern regarding Germany was, of course, that its powerful neighbor should never rise again to present a military threat to France. The March 1947 Treaty that France and Great Britain signed at Dunkirk had as its goal preventing Germany from again becoming a threat to peace. While the Treaty of Brussels, which France, Great Britain and the Benelux countries signed on 17 March 1948 to create the Western European Union (WEU), was inspired by fear of the Soviet Union, its preamble none the less asserted that the five signatories would jointly respond in the event of Germany's readopting 'a policy of aggression'. France also viewed the 1949 Atlantic Treaty as providing a security guarantee not only against the Soviet Union but also against Germany.

During the first half of the 1950s, an agonizing debate took place in France over the question of German rearmament, which the United States was strongly pushing as a condition for reinforcing the American military presence in Europe. France's ultimate disavowal of its own proposal for a European Defense Community (EDC) that would have placed any new German military forces under the control of a fully integrated European army led the way to the 1954 agreements permitting German rearmament within the framework of the NATO integrated command structure.[1] A gradual Franco-German reconciliation then evolved over the latter part of the decade, capped off by the historic meeting in September 1958 between de Gaulle, who had assumed the French presidency several months earlier, and German Chancellor Adenauer.

De Gaulle's return to power not only propelled Franco-German reconciliation forward (de Gaulle and Adenauer enjoyed excellent personal relations), but de Gaulle's international ambitions for France also led in the early 1960s to an initial, far-reaching effort at Franco-German defense cooperation. During the years of the French Fourth Republic that preceded de Gaulle's return to power and the inauguration of the Fifth Republic, there was already a common and obstinate desire on the part of French political leaders to maintain France's international rank, power and prestige to the maximum level attainable. De Gaulle and the Fifth Republic lent both greater force and coherence to French ideology on France's role in international affairs, offering the key concept of 'national independence' in order to restore France to an appropriate world rank. In brief, this concept did not reject the benefits that cooperative endeavours could bring to France, but simply meant that the French government had to be able to decide on its own what policies would best serve French interests; hence de Gaulle's rejection of the principle of integration or of overtly binding relationships.

Upon returning to power, de Gaulle's initial effort at regaining a suitable role for France took the form of reintroducing and amplifying a previous Fourth Republic proposal, the establishment of a tripartite American-British-French directorate at the head of the Atlantic Alliance. This effort failed, and de Gaulle focused his attention toward the organizing of Western Europe (minus Great Britain) under French leadership as the key mechanism for increasing France's international influence.

In late 1961 France submitted a proposal, termed the Fouchet Plan, to its five European Community partners (Germany, Italy and the Benelux countries) to form a union of European states that would have as one of its objectives the adoption of joint foreign and defense policies. The Gaullist conception of the project was that France would dominate the new union, and the weight of its five partners behind it would enhance France's influence and role in the foreign policy and defense spheres. Negotiations on the proposed union stalemated in spring 1962 over the questions of British entry into the EEC and the union (with France adamantly opposed), and of the relationship of the union to NATO.

De Gaulle then turned to the possibility of a bilateral Franco-German agreement that would form the core of an independent European defense entity, both lessening Europe's dependence on the United States and harnassing German power in support of French ambitions. A significant agreement on Franco-German cooperation was signed in January 1963. The agreement, termed the Elysée Treaty, stipulated that cooperation in the defense field would have three objectives. First, in the area of strategy and tactics, the competent authorities of the two countries would attempt to harmonize their doctrines in order to reach joint positions. The two countries' Defense Ministries would meet at least once every three months, and the chiefs of staff at least once every two months. Second, personnel exchanges between the two armies were to be increased, including temporary detachment of entire units. Third, the two governments were to attempt to collaborate on arms production, including the initial stages of the elaboration of weapons projects and the preparation of financing plans. On all important questions of foreign policy, including those discussed within NATO, the two governments were to consult before taking any decision, and, as much as possible, reach a joint position.

De Gaulle's success in forging the treaty was rather short-lived. Several months after the signing of the treaty, the German Bundestag, in ratifying it, added a preamble over the objections of Chancellor Adenauer. The preamble subordinated the application of the treaty to the pursuit of the fundamental objectives guiding FRG foreign and defense policy, notably that of common defense within the framework of the Atlantic Alliance and the integration of the military forces belonging to the Alliance, as well as the unification of Europe through the EEC and with the inclusion of Great Britain. The preamble thus contradicted France's basic reasons for entering into the treaty, and the kind of close defense cooperation the treaty called for was not to be achieved until the 1980s.

There was an interesting footnote to this initial, aborted effort at Franco-German defense cooperation. In order to lure German interest away from the US proposed multilateral nuclear force (MLF), France strongly emphasized during 1963–64 the important role its nascent nuclear force could play in the defense of Germany. From the French perspective, German participation in the MLF would have drawn the FRG even further under the US wing, and German access to nuclear weapons, however circumscribed by the multilateral structure, would have detracted from the political and strategic value of France's independent nuclear force. Consequently, French leaders stressed that the geographic proximity of France to Germany automatically made French nuclear forces of substantial deterrent value to West

Germany as well as France, and Prime Minister Pompidou stated before the French parliament in 1964 that the defense of France was physically inseparable from that of Europe; hence, the French nuclear force would provide insurance that any attack against Europe would meet with a nuclear response on the attacker's homeland. These statements on the role of French nuclear forces are in sharp contrast to those made later in the 1960s and 1970s, and they were more 'advanced' than any pronouncement French leaders have made in the 1980s.

The central role of Germany in French defense policy during the period of the early 1960s was, in summary, to provide key support to France's efforts to promote European defense cooperation and achieve autonomy in the defense field *vis-à-vis* the United States. In this schema, France's nuclear weapons would assure its preeminence within the cooperative European framework over Germany's superior conventional military potential. With the failure of these initiatives, France undertook its unilateral distancing from NATO.

The distancing from NATO and the establishment of 'Gaullist' defense doctrine

The two characteristics of French defense policy most associated with Gaullism are the development of a national nuclear deterrent force outside the NATO framework and the withdrawal from the North Atlantic Treaty Organization's (NATO) integrated military command, both of which fulfilled six broad objectives that still motivate French policy.

Three of the objectives are purely political. The French express near unanimous agreement with the view that a nuclear arsenal brings 'uncontestable prestige' to France across the world. An independent nuclear force is also the condition *sine qua non* of the 'national independence' foreign policy *leitmotif*. Finally, American dominance of the integrated NATO command placed France in an unacceptable and subordinate position *vis-à-vis* the United States.

The two Gaullist defense initiatives also fulfilled three military objectives. First, doubting the long-term credibility of the American nuclear guarantee, the French saw their own deterrent force as the best means of ultimately safeguarding their territory and national sovereignty. Second, de Gaulle viewed integrated military forces as courting potential disaster for France in a war. The French political scientist Alfred Grosser has noted that in terms of psychological consequences the most significant Franco-American confrontation of World War II occurred in January 1945 when General Dwight D. Eisenhower, reacting to the last German counter-offensive in the Ardennes, ordered the French army to evacuate Strasbourg. De Gaulle, fearing massive German reprisals against the Strasbourg population, ordered the French army to remain, and won Eisenhower's acquiescence after threatening American lines of communication in France. For de Gaulle, the incident demonstrated that even the most benevolent of Allied generals could not be trusted to take French interests sufficiently into account.[2] Lastly, an independent foreign policy meant that France had to avoid becoming engaged in armed conflict without making a deliberate and thoroughly considered decision to do so. This 'no automaticity' requirement led to France's removing its forces from front-line positions in Germany in mid-1965, one year before its withdrawal from the NATO integrated military command.

The French elaborated the concept of deterrence 'by the weak of the strong', or 'proportional deterrence', to provide theoretical credibility for French strategic nuclear forces (FNS). In essence, 'The thermonuclear force can be proportional to the value of the stake it is defending.' To meet this requirement, France only needed a second-strike counter-city force.

The deployment of tactical nuclear weapons in the 1970s resulted in the enhancement of French deterrent strategy aimed at boosting the credibility of the strategic forces. French conventional forces would provide a first 'test' of the enemy's intention to attack France by conventional forces on the ground. If the enemy pursued its attack, the use of tactical nuclear weapons would serve as a 'last warning' that France would retaliate massively. Official French doctrine has placed added emphasis in the 1980s on the fact that in order for the enemy to perceive clearly France's last warning, the tactical nuclear strike should have as great a military impact as possible.[3]

In spite of these modifications, the French generally deny that their doctrine bears any relation to NATO's flexible response policy. Most French commentators disregard the ambiguities of flexible response and interpret NATO plans for tactical nuclear weapons use as aimed exclusively at re-establishing a deteriorating battlefield situation. By ignoring the potential political purposes of NATO tactical weapons use, the French are able to indicate a nearly diametrical opposition between flexible response and their last-warning strike concept. The French present their doctrine as a strategy of 'non-war', as opposed to NATO strategy which 'explicitly envisages the possibility of a conflict'. French doctrine only envisages that possibility to the extent necessary to test the enemy's intentions prior to FNS use. Deterrence is consequently equated with the impossibility of war.

French adherence to an almost pure deterrence doctrine has been the result of two factors. First, a more variegated strategy has clearly been beyond French means. The only possibility for an independent defense policy was simply to threaten massive retaliation. Second, France has also maintained its commitment to pure deterrence out of conviction. There is widespread consensus in France that high-intensity conventional war would destroy Europe – and France – just as thoroughly as nuclear war. The marked French preference has been to rely on the dissuasive value of the massive nuclear retaliatory threat.

At all levels of force, French policy emphasized France's own security to the detriment of that of the FRG and its other allies. The only explicit commitment of the FNS was the defense of France's 'vital interests', which were defined as the protection of the 'national sanctuary' and of the *immediate* approaches to it. There has been some broadening of late of this narrow approach to FNS use. But it is still a matter of official ambiguity exactly when an enemy army approaching French territory might trigger the use of the FNS. According to French strategists, the uncertainty resulting from doctrinal ambiguity complicates enemy planning and thus enhances the credibility of France's nuclear deterrent.

The priority generally given in French defense budgets to nuclear weapons has left conventional forces somewhat neglected. Under Giscard d'Estaing, greater attention to European security resulted in additional spending on conventional forces. But well over half of the budgeted funds went into operating expenses, and planned purchases of new conventional equipment had to be stretched out.[4] The Socialist government's 1984–88 defense program allocated 30 per cent of equipment credits to strategic and tactical nuclear forces, as compared with approximately 18 per cent during the presidency of Giscard d'Estaing. Under the current 1987–91 military program law, 32 per cent of equipment credits (almost 152 billion francs) will go to nuclear forces.

Furthermore, the 1972 French defense White Paper cast doubt on the ability of the First Army to fulfill its assigned role as a NATO reserve force. The problem was the role given to the First Army in France's strategic deterrent maneuver. Five regiments of *Pluton* short-range missiles were assigned to be deployed into combat with the First Army. The First Army had to be sufficiently powerful to force the concentration of Soviet troops that would make the tactical strike an effective one. The predominantly political role of the tactical nuclear strike meant that French ANT had to remain under the strict control of the French President. This crucial requirement would be difficult to fulfill if the *Plutons* advanced into the NATO-Warsaw Pact battlefield area.[5] The White Paper added that attrition of French forces in the so-called European battle could leave France without the means to carry out her own deterrent strategy. The practical impact of the White Paper's guidelines was that either NATO would stop the Warsaw Pact without any significant French assistance, or France would be left face-to-face with the Red Army.

Official statements during the presidency of Giscard d'Estaing attempted to dispel Allied doubts concerning French fulfillment of its planned NATO conventional role.[6] However, the operational contradiction between the dual role of the First Army as an integral component of France's national deterrent strategy and as a NATO reserve force remained unchanged.

Thus, on the nuclear level, despite French assertions that the FNS makes a *de facto* contribution to deterrence in the broader European theater (this French argument was accepted by the US and NATO in the 1974 Ottawa Declaration, which stated that the French nuclear force is 'capable of playing a deterrent role of its own contributing to the overall strengthening of the deterrence of the Alliance'), the fundamental French emphasis has been on the strictly national value of its nuclear forces. The government of President Giscard d'Estaing briefly flirted with the concept of an 'enlarged sanctuary', as well as with the assigning of missions related to the defense of Germany to French tactical nuclear weapons (ANT). But these initiatives provoked considerable controversy and the government rapidly abandoned them.

French deployment of ANT in the 1970s, in particular the *Pluton* battlefield missile (range of 110 km), provoked a fundamental, and at times bitter, debate between France and Germany on defense policy. The missile's short range, combined with its being stationed in France, meant that if used it would inevitably fall on German soil, and for the exclusive benefit of the defense of France.

At the conventional level, the overriding impression as the 1960s and 1970s evolved was of increasingly poorly equipped French forces, and, despite increasing cooperation with NATO, of continued ambiguity as to whether the French army would fully fulfill its NATO role or might be held back to some degree to support France's national deterrent strategy. In this intertwined nuclear-conventional Gaullist-inspired defense schema, the FRG played a dual role; still that of an ally, but also that of a French 'security shield'.

The role of French ally remained, because France never repudiated the treaties committing it to come to Germany's defense in the event of a Soviet attack, French forces remained stationed in Germany, and a number of agreements were drawn up between France and NATO to facilitate effective French participation in the defense of Germany once France took the political decision to become engaged. On the other hand, Germany's role as a French security shield was also quite prominent, as France's independent deterrent strategy was only made possible by the interposition of Germany between it and the Warsaw Pact (guaranteeing that the Soviet Union would have to confront the American troop and nuclear presence in Germany before Soviet forces could approach France). The non-automatic nature of the French commitment to West Germany's defense also implied that France, in the event of a Soviet attack on Germany, might attempt to wait and assess the situation before intervening, while German territory was being destroyed in the battle.

Not surprisingly, Franco-German defense cooperation hardly flourished during this period. Although the French point out that Franco-German arms collaboration prospered during the 1960s, when a wide number of successful cooperative weapons projects were launched, practically all of these projects were started in the early 1960s, before the break with NATO and the clear emergence of a defense doctrine that seemed to emphasize Germany's role as a security shield for France.[7] Among projects such as the Transall tactical air carrier, the MILAN and HOT anti-tank missiles, the *Roland* surface-to-air missile, the Breguet Atlantique naval patrol aircraft, and the *Alpha Jet* tactical support and training aircraft, only the last was initiated after 1964. Except for the *Alpha Jet* (1969), it was not until the 1980s that Franco-German weapons collaboration was able to start up again.

CHANGING DEFENSE POLICY ASSUMPTIONS

During the 1980s there has been a broad degree of consensus among the non-communist French political parties that old assumptions about the European security environment were no longer valid. This spurred defense policy innovations, and especially a major rethinking of France's defense relations with West Germany. Two assumptions had been critical to the formulation of Gaullist defense policy.

First, the Soviet Union no longer posed a serious military threat to Western Europe. When US Ambassador Charles Bohlen asked de Gaulle in 1965 whether the less menacing Soviet attitude 'could be regarded as more than transitory', the French President replied that 'prudence was necessary in this regard'.[8] But four factors resulted in a continued tendency on the part of French governments to minimize the Soviet threat. For Gaullists, the belief in the tradition of nations over regimes led to emphasizing the 'eternal Russia' with which France had a long history of relations, as opposed to the more recent 'Soviet' enemy. Gaullists also remained attached to the idea of using good relations with Moscow to enhance France's diplomatic position. Giscard d'Estaing firmly believed that détente and trade could lead to a democratization of the Soviet regime. Harmonious relations with the Soviet Union also attenuated French communist opposition to conservative governments, thus helping to keep the left from assuming power in France. Many French observers believe that Giscard d'Estaing's refusal to support overtly the NATO Euromissile deployment was due to his tacit courting of Communist Party electoral support as well as to a desire to play a central role in relaunching East–West détente in the aftermath of the Soviet invasion of Afghanistan. In both 1974 and 1981, the Soviet Union tacitly endorsed Giscard d'Estaing for president against François Mitterrand.

The second assumption behind Gaullist defense policy was that West Germany would continue to provide a stable security shield for France. This assumption had two corollaries; the United States would maintain a strong commitment to West German security and thus the West Germans would remain relatively content with their security situation. Given this kind of security environment (a relatively benign USSR, a reasonably strong US defense commitment, and a stable Germany), one of France's major preoccupations with West Germany was the maintaining of politico-military superiority over its more dynamic neighbor to the east. The independent nuclear force and a 'privileged' relationship with Moscow were seen as two of the key means of leverage by which France could maintain this politico-military pre-eminence over the FRG.

On all counts, the assumptions that have come to dominate French views of the 1980s indicate serious difficulties in the security field. A perception of the Soviet Union as a significant politico-military threat predominated within the three main non-communist French political formations: the Socialist Party, the neo-Gaullist Réassemblement pour la république (RPR), and the centrist Union pour la démocratie française (UDF), an alliance of three small parties.

The break-up of the Union of the left in 1977 started an anti-Soviet evolution within the Socialist Party that was spurred on by the human rights issue. The growth of Soviet military power and the series of military interventions by the Soviet Union and its proxies in Africa and Afghanistan led to genuine perceptions of a threatened East–West politico-military balance. During the 1981 presidential campaign, Mitterrand was extremely critical of Giscard d'Estaing's '*Ostpolitik*'.

Developments during the early 1980s have strongly reinforced this heightened French threat perception of the Soviet Union. French officials and commentators stress the fact of Moscow's having turned the INF deployment into a crucial test of Alliance cohesion through the pressure it placed on the deploying nations, and in particular on West Germany. The journal *Le Monde* noted that Soviet pressure over the 'Euromissile' question was greater than that of any period since 1954–55, the years preceding German rearmament.

The Gorbachev era, with its change in the Soviet approach to arms control from intransigence to innovativeness, has only heightened French concerns. The French almost unanimously see Soviet strategy as one of 'disarming' Europe, previously by pressuring the Europeans into rejecting new nuclear deployments (necessary in themselves to modernize the West's deterrent posture, and all the more important in view of the Soviet Union's massive nuclear modernization program), and under Gorbachev by pursuing the denuclearization of the continent altogether, leaving Western Europe in a state of vulnerability against superior Soviet conventional and chemical might. While this Soviet policy arouses French apprehension for a number of reasons, the potential 'destabilization' of Germany is one of the major ones. The French are not confident, to say the least, about the policy direction of a Federal Republic bereft of any real nuclear cover yet still confronting Soviet tanks on its eastern border.

The concern over Soviet policy has been paralleled by increasing distress in the 1980s over the direction of US policy. These doubts have resulted from three broad US defense initiatives. The strong French belief in the effectiveness of nuclear deterrence results in a general suspicion of any American-sponsored efforts to raise NATO's nuclear threshold. The marked tendency in France has been to equate the 'no first-use' option with the proposals put forward in the early 1980s by General Bernard Rogers. The formulation may be different but the practical outcome is seen to be identical.[9] Former Defense Minister Charles Hernu warned that the Rogers proposals would 'excessively raise the nuclear threshold' and that they 'ignore nuclear deterrence to a greatest possible extent'.[10] The Soviet Union might thus come to believe that a European war could remain limited to the conventional level for a protracted period, a situation in which the costs to Moscow of an aggression might not outweigh the gains.

Secondly, the Strategic Defense Initiative (SDI) has aroused additional French uneasiness. In the short term, the French feared that President Reagan's 'messianic statements' on the possibility of total nuclear disarmament would further erode public support in the West, and in particular in Germany, for nuclear deterrence.[11] The French saw a dual assault on nuclear deterrence, from 'below' by the Rogers proposals and from 'above' by SDI.

Over the longer term, the prospect of an eventual deployment of extensive ballistic defenses by the United States and the Soviet Union raised a host of concerns over the future credibility of France's independent nuclear force. Although these concerns have abated as the French have concluded that the credibility of their strategic forces would not be threatened until at least well into the next century (2015-20),[12] French analysis has still tended to view SDI as destabilizing for European security.[13] One line of French analysis asserts that Ballistic Missile Defense deployment, by most effectively protecting nuclear forces and other key military assets, would force a US return to deterrence founded on counter-city strikes, thus putting the last nail in the coffin of NATO's flexible response strategy.

Thirdly, the French have been stunned by the evolution of US arms control policy. Reykjavik, with its discussion of eliminating all superpower ballistic missiles, provoked great consternation in France. Views in France toward the 'zero' and then 'double-zero' option were somewhat more nuanced, but they tended to range from only somewhat negative to exceedingly negative. Although the French government ultimately came to accept the double-zero option, it was the object of sharp criticism in France, including within the French government.[14]

This 'very curious dialogue between the United States and the Soviet Union', as an aide to Giraud termed it, provided further confirmation to the French that the US was proceeding towards a denuclearlization of European defense policy. Many French observers expect the US someday to undertake a partial or even total withdrawal from Europe.

Given these French perceptions, it is not surprising that the French have also tended to discern a declining German confidence in the US nuclear guarantee.[15] The outburst of German neutralist-pacifist sentiment in the early 1980s, together with the fear that the continuing evolution of US policy would leave Germany without credible nuclear coverage, has provoked great French concern over whether Germany would maintain a steadfastly pro-Western course in the face of increasing Soviet pressure. While French anxiety over the strength of neutralist-pacifist forces in Germany may have abated somewhat during 1984–85, it was rekindled in 1986–87 by Gorbachev's initiatives and the US and German responses to them.

The French – who themselves place a strong emphasis on the need to be 'vigilant' *vis-à-vis* Gorbachev – see the West Germans as being too susceptible to succumbing to Gorbachev's 'sirens' and to the growing domestic pressure for denuclearization (which, in the French view, can only lead to eventual neutralism and pacifism). France opposes negotiations on battlefield nuclear weapons that are desired by the FRG, and French politicians have voiced fears over potential German support of a 'triple-zero option'.[16]

While the West German SPD comes in for the greatest French criticism,[17] there are also concerns over the view of Foreign Minister Genscher, his liberal FDP, and even some elements of the CDU. Genscher's warm reaction to Gorbachev's initiatives has helped sustain the traditional French fear of a 'deviation to the East' of West German diplomacy. After having feared for Genscher's future before the January 1987 Bundestag elections (Genscher is seen as a strong Francophile), the French have shown concern since the election that Genscher had been too reinforced politically.

Thus, in the 1980s, the French see a menacing convergence of an American strategy lacking coherence, of European nostalgia for an 'unarmed peace', and of a heightened Soviet threat, all pointing toward an eventual 'destabilization' of Germany and the threat of France's finding itself in a much more exposed position *vis-à-vis* the Soviet Union and the Eastern bloc. Even those in France who remained relatively serene during the first wave of French anxiety of the 1981–83 period, appear now to have succumbed to the rekindling of a crisis atmosphere since late 1986. It is difficult to underestimate the impact Reykjavik and the successive post-Reykjavik zero options have had in France. The re-election in 1983 of Chancellor Kohl's coalition in Germany (and that of the Conservative Party in Britain), along with the successful start of the INF deployment at the end of that year may have created some feelings of complacency in France that the worst of the crisis was over. Reykjavik and the subsequent developments in the INF negotiations completely swept aside any such sentiments.

A very prominent example of this phenomenon is former Prime Minister Raymond Barre. Through the early 1980s, Barre continued to find attenuating circumstances for the invasion of Afghanistan and to advocate 'understanding' toward the Soviet Union. He was the leading French mainstream politician to remain relatively unconcerned about the evolution in Germany, and, in any event, viewed it as an American problem and not one for which France had any responsibility. Barre has now greatly changed his tune, and in a speech he gave in late March 1987 before the IISS, he emphasized the gravity of the current European (and French) security environment, including the political and economic weakening of the United States versus the refound dynamism and still increasing military power of the Soviet Union. Barre criticized the zero option as both technically and psychologically favoring decoupling between Europe and the US.[18]

The consequence of these changing assumptions regarding their security environment has been an enormous upsurge of French interest in Allied security issues in European defense cooperation, above all between France and the FRG. The overwhelming view of the French political mainstream was that the 'woolliness' of US policy and the neutralist-pacificist tendencies in Germany (the first feeding the second, as the French saw it) required France to throw its weight into the balance to head off the threat of Germany's 'destabilization' and eventual move eastward.

The tightening of defense relations with the FRG thus fulfills several near-term objectives. It, as well as the broader European defense cooperation it encourages, is seen as a key means of reinforcing NATO and encouraging the US to maintain a strong commitment to the defense of Western Europe (the French are well aware that there is no near- or even medium-term European defense alternative to this strong US commitment). A closer Franco-German defense relation both in itself and as a core of broader European defense cooperation was also seen as the best way of countering the West German temptation to go too far toward the East. It would provide additional security assurances to the FRG, and, in 'Europeanizing' somewhat the defense of West Germany, would give the Germans a greater sense of control over their security environment.

Thus, unlike the early 1960s when de Gaulle conceived the Elysée Treaty as a means of reinforcing Franco-German defense ties at the expense of those between Germany and the US, France's goal in the 1980s has been to draw closer to the FRG and NATO at the same time and to establish a special Franco-German defense relationship as an 'alliance within the Alliance'. Former President Giscard d'Estaing, who is currently chairman of the National Assembly's Foreign Affairs Commission, nicely summed up the state of French thought at the end of June 1987 when he stated: 'the central problem is to anchor Federal Germany to Europe, because the day she deviates – which I don't believe will occur – we would find ourselves in a completely different situation, there would no longer be a European Community and France would find itself on the front line.'[19]

INITIATIVES TAKEN

The first major step taken in the establishment of a deeper Franco-German defense relationship was the formation in October 1982 of the Franco-German Commission on Security and Defense.[20] The Commission was established under the aegis of the Ministers of Defense and Foreign Affairs of the two countries, who meet before each of the regular Franco-German summit conferences. The Commission is made up of approximately five high-level civilian and military officials (divided between the Defense and Foreign Affairs Ministries) from each country. Underneath the Commission, three specialized working groups were formed – on weapons cooperation, military cooperation and politico-strategic affairs.

The politico-strategic area

It was the work of the latter group that was most immediately relevant, as the 'Euromissile battle' was in full swing. The INF deployment was the first major topic of consultation between the two countries that the new Commission took up. While Mitterrand had already declared in July 1980 (almost a year before his presidential election victory in May 1981) that the Soviet SS-20 deployment was creating a serious military imbalance in Europe, and in 1981, immediately after assuming office, that the INF deployment was necessary to restore the European balance, the burgeoning cooperation between the two countries helped lead to Mitterrand's dramatic speech of January 1983 before the German Bundestag. In that speech, he not only reasserted the necessity of the INF deployment in order for the Geneva arms talks to succeed, but also reaffirmed that only nuclear weapons are capable of maintaining peace through deterrence. He thus attempted to undercut the anti-nuclear themes of the West German 'peace movement'. (This broad threat to nuclear deterrence was reportedly a major factor motivating Mitterrand to make the speech.)

Another topic in the politico-strategic area taken up by the Commission concerned the reactivation of the Western European Union (WEU) – the only exclusively European body that is formally competent to treat security issues (and, unlike the EEC, does not have 'problem' countries in the defense arena such as Ireland, Denmark and Greece, among its members). The WEU is consequently an inherently attractive institution for France concerning European coordination of defense policy. In the process of consultations between ministers and also within the framework of the joint Commission, the French discovered that the Germans had no objections to reactivating the moribund institution on condition that the remaining restrictions on German conventional armaments imposed by the 1954 WEU treaty be eliminated. France then played an instrumental role in having the WEU Council cancel these remaining restrictions.[21] The reactivation of the WEU did not go very far for several reasons, one of which was a warning from Washington (in the form of a letter by Richard Burt) that the Europeans should not coordinate policy on SDI (the key topic of the movement) outside the NATO framework.

SDI was also taken up by the Franco-German Defense and Security Commission. Initial Franco-German discussion on SDI led, according to an authoritative French source, to agreement on a number of significant points concerning the US project.[22] These were the importance of nuclear deterrence for European security, the necessity of not weakening nuclear deterrence, and the importance of threats to Europe stemming from sources other than ballistic missiles. The French and German positions on SDI none the less splintered in 1985 following the US invitation to participate in the program.

At the 1985 Bonn summit of the seven industrial democracies, Mitterrand replied with a very irritated rejection of the US offer and pressure thereon to participate in the program, whereas the FRG decided to negotiate an agreement at government level on German participation in the SDI research program. France was the only major European country left in a position of overt hostility to SDI, with its principal European partners following the route of bilateral accommodation with the US. In point of fact, by the end of the year French and German positions on SDI, for all practical purposes, appeared to be quite similar. France on the one hand, left its industrial firms free to participate in the program; and Germany, on the other, decided not to commit any government funding to back up Germany industrial participation in SDI. The convergence seemed even greater when Prime Minister Jacques Chirac and his government assumed office after the March 1986 French parliamentary elections. Although the Chirac government did not modify the substance of French policy on SDI (it would have had trouble doing so even if it had wanted to with Mitterrand still occupying the French presidency), it did contribute to a modification of French rhetoric.

In view of the real similarities between the French and German (as well as other European) outlook on SDI, the absence of any joint European position on SDI was a keenly-felt disappointment to many in France.[23] Various French observers (and, of course, the UDF/RPR parties in opposition at the time) attributed some or much of the blame for the lack of a coordinated European position to the rigid response the Mitterrand government gave on SDI, viewing it as counterproductive from the standpoint of European defense cooperation.[24] However, the French also point to what they perceive as a tendency of their European partners to be in agreement with French analysis but not want openly to express it in order to avoid offending the United States, and cite Europe's bowing to US pressure not to take up SDI within the WEU framework.

According to one line of French analysis, the differences that emerged over SDI (which, again, appeared during 1985 to be much larger than they would actually turn out) played a significant role in the stagnation that occurred in Franco-German cooperation during the period from 1984–86.[25] Some in France saw the German–American bilateral agreement not only as a new reflection on Germany's reflex to align itself automatically on the US, even to the detriment of European interests, but possibly also of a German aspiration to see nuclear weapons eliminated, allowing Germany's superior economic and conventional military power once again to become dominant factors in Western Europe. This latter suspicion seems somewhat far-fetched and was probably not that widely shared in France, but any future use of SDI by Germany to question the validity of nuclear deterrence would undoubtedly have serious repercussions for Franco-German cooperation. (This, of course, has not yet happened.)

The implications of Reykjavik and the post-Reykjavik evolution of US–Soviet arms control developments has been a more recent area of very intensive Franco-German consultations. Although, as already noted, some very critical statements were made by Chirac and other members of the French government regarding the double-zero option, in the end France refused to lend Chancellor Kohl's government formal public support for a rejection of that option. This was due in large part to President Mitterrand's public acknowledgements as well in advance of a German government decision that he harbored a 'favourable prejudice' toward the option. Mitterrand's refusal to throw French support behind the clear reluctance of Kohl and the CDU/CSU parties to embrace the double-zero option was basically due to his perception that in the final analysis German public opinion would force the Kohl government to accept the option.

The shock of Reykjavik led directly to a proposal by Chirac, made in a speech in early December 1986 before the WEU, for a European security charter. Chirac, noting the anxiety that Reykjavik had aroused among the European countries, proposed a five-point charter:

- Nuclear deterrence remains the only means of effectively preventing war in Europe, any any developments arising from technological progress should aim at reinforcing deterrence, not challenging it.
- The threat to Western Europe must be considered in its totality: nuclear weapons of all ranges, conventional, and chemical weapons.
- The European countries must maintain their defense efforts at a level corresponding to that of the threat.
- Deterrence in Europe requires the presence of US conventional and nuclear forces on the continent.
- Disarmament must have as its goal the reinforcement of security at lower levels of weaponry.

The fanfare with which Chirac presented a charter of such banality can only be understood in the context of the challenges the French saw emanating from SDI and Reykjavik to the fundamental precepts of European security. The proposed charter contained several implicit criticisms of US policy, such as the idea of SDI replacing nuclear deterrence, the excessive US focus (in the French view) on European nuclear arms control, and the reiteration that disarmament must be carried out so as to reinforce security (which the Reykjavik deal, if it had gone through, would certainly not have done in the French view). Nothing has yet come of the proposed charter (Giraud resurrected the idea in spring 1987), nor of the reinvigoration of the WEU that Chirac also proposed during his speech.

The definition France gives to its vital interests is a final key issue that has been the object of French initiatives in the politico-strategic area during the 1980s, and unlike the INF deployment, SDI, and the arms control talks, is above all a bilateral Franco-German issue going to the heart of the defense relationship between the two countries. The French in the 1980s have very cautiously but persistently attempted to modify the traditional Gaullist definition of France's vital interests as an important means of demonstrating greater defense solidarity with West Germany.

Some of the more noteworthy official French declarations in this area are as follows.

- Mitterrand, in his 1983 speech to the Bundestag, used the phrase 'the defense of our territory and of our vital interests'. This formulation of 'France and its vital interests' is often resorted to by French officials.
- Hernu, in a speech during Franco-German maneuvers in June 1985, stated that 'France and the Federal Republic share common security interests'.
- Chirac, in a September 1986 speech to the Institute of Advanced National Defense Studies, declared that 'France must possess the means of preserving its independence and of protecting its vital interests . . . if the survival of the nation is at stake at its borders, its security is at stake at the borders of its neighbors.'
- Most strikingly, the 1987–91 Military Program Law calls for a nuclear response on the part of France in order to 'protect the integrity of its territory as well as its vital interests, particularly in Europe'.

In commencing upon this aspect of the new five-year program law, the official report of the National Assembly Defense Commission, drafted by a leading RPR defense specialist, stated: 'It cannot be better stated that the resort to nuclear weapons is not limited to major threats directed against only the territory of the Nation, that our vital interests are not or are no longer reducible to the sanctuary . . . that the security of France, and perhaps its survival, can be at stake at the borders of its neighbors.'[26] Another statement of note (as its author was then a presidential candidate) was issued by Raymond Barre in his speech before the IISS in March 1987. Barre declared that the evaluation of France's vital interests 'can by no means exclude the solidarities stemming from geography and alliances'.

Military initiatives

The major initiatives the French Socialist government took in the early 1980s to manifest greater military solidarity with West Germany (and its other allies) centered on a restructuring of French conventional forces and a modernization of France's tactical nuclear weapons.

France created a conventionally-armed, five-division rapid assistance force (FAR) which, without occupying a front-line position and compromising the non-automaticity of the French commitment, will be able to intervene more quickly alongside NATO forces prior to or at the outset of a European conflict. Official statements confirmed that the major purpose of the FAR is to eliminate all ambiguity concerning the ability of French conventional forces to contribute to West European defense.[27] The restructuring of conventional forces also included a reduction in army manpower of 22,000 and a loss by the First Army of two armored divisions. This reduction did not, however, apply to French forces stationed in Germany, in contrast to an earlier reorganization during the Giscard d'Estaing presidency that reduced those forces from 60,000 to 50,000 men. Remaining French armored divisions, including those in Germany, received additional main battle tanks.

The *Hades* ground-launched missile is the centerpiece of the tactical nuclear weapons modernization. Its significance lies in its range of 350 km, as opposed to

120 km for the *Pluton* missile. The greater range of the *Hades* will enable France to decouple its last warning tactical nuclear strike from the operations of the First Army. According to current plans, the *Hades* will remain in France, facilitating tight political control, and the First Army will acquire greater flexibility to execute its mission as a NATO reserve force.

The *Hades* missile and a new air-to-surface medium-range missile (ASMP) will result in greatly increased tactical nuclear target coverage and firepower. However, the French government has stressed that tactical nuclear weapons will not be used to conduct a 'nuclear battle'. To emphasize this point, Hernu renamed French ANT as 'pre-strategic' weapons. According to official pronouncements, the ANT modernization will bring three benefits:

1.   It will enable France to execute its tactical warning strike without hitting West German soil.
2.   Superior firepower will render the warning strike more devastating and effective.
3.   The decoupling of the tactical nuclear force from the operations of the First Army accentuates the tactical nuclear role of a last warning. This is because decoupling will 'eliminate the ever present temptation to regard tactical nuclear weapons as a battlefield super-artillery that can make a breach in enemy lines, which then leads to an attempted counter-attack. Decided far from the forces in contact, the tactical strike can now only appear for what it is in French strategy: the last warning. . .'[28]

Yet, other statements have hinted at an expanded role for tactical nuclear weapons. Officials noted that the tactical modernization will increase Soviet uncertainty as to when France might cross the nuclear threshold. The added flexibility concerning the moment of use and the targeting of the *Hades*–ASMP duo, will, according to a former head of the French Joint Chiefs of Staff, increase Soviet uncertainty as to exactly where French vital interests begin. Hernu noted that because of the FAR and the ANT modernization, the Soviet Union, in launching an attack in Central Europe, would immediately run the risk of confronting at a 'more or less brief delay the conventional forces and/or the nuclear forces of the only independent nuclear power of the continent'.[29]

A second major development in the tactical nuclear weapons area occurred in March 1986 when President Mitterrand and Chancellor Kohl announced that:

Within the constraints imposed by the extreme rapidity of such decisions, the president of the Republic declares himself disposed to consult with the chancellor of the FRG on the eventual use of French pre-strategic weapons on German territory. . . . The president of the Republic indicates that he has decided, with the FRG chancellor, to set up the technical means for immediate and secure communication in time of crisis.[30]

French sources indicate that the sentence on providing the technical means of communication during a crisis was inserted at France's initiative, reflecting the seriousness of the French intent behind the expressed willingness to consult on ANT use.

In the conventional area, various kinds of cooperation have intensified. Several developments will improve the future ability of French and German conventional forces to work together. The French Leclerc tank and the German *Leopard-3* will be able to maneuver together in Central Europe through the use of a similar 120 mm cannon, the same munitions, the same treads, and the same fuels. In order to enhance further the inter-operability of French and German conventional forces, significant exchanges take place between the two countries' armies. For example, numerous joint exercises are held. These include: exchanges three times a year of basic units, which spend three weeks integrated within the other's army corps; different exercises at the level of combat groups, sections and companies; an officer-exchange scheme which, within a few years, will have resulted in all of each country's officers working with the forces of the other; and various exchanges in the area of officer training. By the year 2000, all French general officers will have undergone a training session in Germany.[31]

The military working group set up under the Franco-German Defense Commission has had the responsibility of improving exchanges, exercises and other contacts between the two countries' armed forces, including the examination of problems raised by the intervention of the FAR on German soil. Scenarios for deployment of the FAR into Germany require considerable German logistical and operational support (fuel supply, provision of spare parts, missiles, telecommunications and transportation assistance). This need has helped lead to in-depth Franco-German discussions regarding the use of the FAR in Germany. Another provision of the March 1986 Kohl-Mitterrand declaration that expressed French willingness to consult on ANT use stated that the French and German leaders were authorizing the pursuit of studies related to the best use of French forces in Germany, especially the FAR.

Following the March 1986 declaration, the two countries concluded bilateral agreements concerning German logistical support for the FAR, and began planning last September's 'Bold Sparrow' exercise. The exercise, the object of a more than one-year's planning effort, was designed to test the ability of the FAR to intervene effectively in Germany. The exercise was consequently structured to demonstrate the capability of rapidly projecting a major segment of the FAR over a large distance and its ability to fight effectively alongside German troops.

The forces deployed by the FAR for the exercise included 20,000 men (roughly half its total manpower), and almost all its armored vehicles (about 550) and helicopters (about 240). Although problems of coordination arose between the two armies, the French view the exercise as a very strong technical success. The elements of the FAR involved in the exercise took less than 48 hours to cover the more than 1200 km from their bases in France and take up their assigned positions in Germany. From the French viewpoint, the exercise thus established the ability of the FAR to participate in the forward defense of Germany.[32]

In addition to these technical considerations, one highly significant political aspect of the exercise was the placing of the French forces involved under the 'operational control' of the German military. Mitterrand's personal attendance at the exercise lent even greater symbolic weight to this development, which in effect resulted during four days in the indirect return of part of the French army to the integrated NATO military command. On the other hand, a political controversy also arose during the exercise when it was revealed that France had apparently vetoed the attendance at the exercise of NATO supreme commander General Galvin as well as that of General Altenburg, the West German chairman of NATO's military committee. This decision aroused negative comment in France, but it was probably due at least in part to the fact that French forces were placed under German military control for the exercise. This novel development undoubtedly made the French feel sensitive toward maintaining a certain distance between the Bold Sparrow exercise and the NATO military command.

Weapons cooperation

The record of Franco-German arms collaboration has been somewhat disappointing for the French, and if not for the agreement that appears in sight on production of a combat helicopter, would be viewed as extremely so. Collaboration with West Germany on armaments projects and also on high-technology civilian projects of special interest (for example, the *Hermes* space shuttle) is a major priority for France. In the armaments area, the realization has gained force that France cannot unilaterally maintain an across-the-board weapons development and production capability. Franco-German collaboration in the arms area is seen as a key element in maintaining a healthy French defense industry and an across-the-board 'European' capability in the weapons area. In the broader high-technology area (which obviously has repercussions for weapons development), France perhaps more than any other West European country has emphasized the dangers of falling hopelessly behind Japan and the United States and the need for a joint European effort to counter this possibility.

The French cite several major 1980s proposals for Franco-German arms collaboration that never got off the ground or were not carried through to fruition. Although they acknowledge that the Germans do not bear the exclusive or even a major share of responsibility for the failure of some of these collaborative efforts, the French none the less tended to discern a pattern of German reluctance to accord political priority to weapons and high-technology cooperation with France. The first unsuccessful project concerned a joint main battle tank, agreed upon in 1980 between Giscard d'Estaing and Helmut Schmidt. Despite a letter from Mitterrand to Schmidt underlining the great interest France attached to collaboration on the tank, the project was abandoned in 1982 due to differences over the characteristics and performance of the tank, the development schedule, and the division of work between French and German industries.

The failure of the tank project was followed in mid-1985 by the inability of France and a number of other European countries (Germany, the UK and Italy) to reach agreement on the development of a European Fighter Aircraft (EFA). France split off from the others to pursue development of its *Rafale* plane. The hostility of the French aeronautics giant, Dassault, to this collaborative project played a significant role in the failure to reach agreement among the four countries.

During this period the French were also disappointed by West Germany's refusal to join France in developing a military observation satellite, a project to which the French attach considerable importance and are now undertaking on their own. Some in France attributed the failure to reach agreement in this instance to German concern over the US reaction to FRG participation in a project of this nature. Others noted the lack of priority of this type of project for the German army.[33]

In the autumn of 1984, Germany broke off discussions with France on development of an anti-air defense system to replace the US *Hawk* network in the 1990s, citing prospective budget difficulties during the latter half of the decade. Lastly, the French have also judged German participation in the Eureka program to be less enthusiastic than desired and, in particular, lacking an adequate financial commitment. This series of failures in the area of Franco-German arms collaboration, which was offset only by several collaborative agreements on anti-ship and anti-tank missiles, appeared to play a major role in a certain souring of the atmosphere in France regarding the tightening of defense relations with Germany that had developed by 1985.

The situation appears to have somewhat reversed itself over the past year, however. In October of 1986 an agreement was announced concerning German participation in the *Hermes* space shuttle project, with the FRG committing to finance 30 per cent of the project and France 45 per cent (with other European countries financing the remainder). The French view *Hermes* as a 'technological locomotive', the benefits of which will go beyond the purely civilian sector.

Of even greater importance has been the agreement in principle reached in July 1987 on joint production of a new combat helicopter. France and Germany actually launched the joint military helicopter program in May 1984, when an agreement was signed to begin development studies on the three versions of the helicopter (a French fire support/escort version, and separate French and German anti-tank versions) that were to be produced from a common cell. Repeated difficulties emerged over the subsequent three years regarding the characteristics and cost of the helicopter. Differences between the two armies concerned the weight and speed of the helicopter, whether the crew would be seated in tandem or side by side, and, above all, whether the helicopter would use an American fire control/night vision system or one of European origin (with France favoring the latter).

After lengthy and arduous negotiations, including a period during the second half of 1986 and into early 1987 when it appeared that the two countries might well abort the project, the tentative agreement reached appears to have resolved the key problems.[34] Notably, only two versions of the helicopter will be produced in order to ease the financial burden of the project, and they will be equipped with European optical-electronics systems. The projected agreement required both the French and German armies to make significant compromises with respect to the desired performance of the helicopter, and even more so concerning the desired entry into service dates of the two models.

Assessment of initiatives taken

The developments of the 1980s have created a profound change in the climate in France regarding European defense cooperation, and above all defense cooperation between France and Germany. The extent of this change is illustrated by two statements that were made in 1980 and 1981. One was a statement of Jacques Chirac, given during a highly publicized press conference of early 1980. In that statement, Chirac gave a very narrow (and simplistic) enunciation of France's defense options: reintegrate into NATO, associate with a common European defense effort, maintain and develop an independent defense. Chirac dismissed the second option as an illusion lacking the interest of France's European partners, and dismissed the first as contrary to French interests, leaving the third option as the only possible one for France to pursue. The most noteworthy point about this statement is not in its representation of Chirac's views of the period,[35] but rather that at a distance of some fifteen months from the May 1981 French presidential elections, a serious contender for the French presidency, during a major foreign policy press conference designed to lend credibility to his candidacy, made the statement at all. Any 'serious' French politician making that statement today would be the object of widespread ridicule.

A second statement indicating the distance that has been traveled in the 1980s was made in September 1981 by former Joint Chiefs of Staff head General Lacaze. Lacaze stated that European defense cooperation 'only concerns conventional forces and excludes any planning concerning the use of nuclear force . . . '.[36] As seen, the early 1986 agreement on consultations on ANT use severely dented (but did not eliminate) this taboo.

The initiatives France has taken during the 1980s to reinforce defense ties with Germany can be placed into two broad categories: changes in declaratory policy on the one hand, and the achievement of more tangible goals on the other (changes in force posture, collaborative arms projects, joint maneuvers . . .). Both categories have been extremely important, and there have generally been significant linkages between the two.

The French consider declaratory initiatives to be in and of themselves an important dimension of policy. At the broad foreign policy level, declaratory policy has been an important tool for a medium-size power that aspires to play an active and influential role in world affairs but lacks in most areas outside Europe (former Sub-Saharan French Africa being a major exception) the tangible instruments to do so. The French thus perceive declaratory policy, such as advising the superpowers on how to pursue arms control or the Arabs and Israelis on how to make peace, as a key means of obtaining international recognition for France as an important power. French intellectual arrogance often attributes to France the ability to perceive what is in the true self-interest not only of France but also of other nations.

This view of France's special ability to articulate what is in the best interests of mankind in general thus lends French declaratory policy a double, synergistic importance; it enhances France's role in world affairs and it contributes to a more stable world order. De Gaulle was particularly adept in using audacious language as a tool for attempting to influence world developments. A key benefit, in the French view, of an 'independent' foreign and defense policy is that it enables France to express publicly, and if need be theatrically, its own views and analyses. The French often contrast this ability to the purported situation of France's European partners, who may agree with a French position but will not openly indicate it for fear of offending other countries, most often the United States.

In the light of this broad context of how the French view declaratory policy, it is easy to understand the great significance they place on the speech Mitterrand made to the Bundestag in 1983, which appeared as a true de Gaullean-style initiative both in its message and in the setting in which it was given. Following Mitterrand's speech, the newspaper *Le Monde* gave prominence to German press reports on the delight of German Conservatives with it and to a projection of Franz-Joseph Strauss that the speech would swing about 3 per cent of the vote to the Conservative/Liberal coalition in the Bundestag election that was to follow in early March.[37] A common French view is that French declaratory policy has contributed to a recentering of the defense debate in West Germany.

The tenor of declaratory policy can have important psychological consequences that affect concrete projects, such as on arms collaboration. The presentation of French defense doctrine in the 1960s and 1970s, with its implicit portrayal of Germany as a buffer-zone at which France would fire nuclear weapons if the Soviet army came too close to French borders, was probably not conducive to Franco-German military and armament collaboration, as evidenced, for example, by the decline in joint weapons projects during this period as compared with the early part of the 1960s. Conversely, the very cautious but persistent French effort to broaden France's definition of its vital interests potentially to include the whole of the FRG rather than a narrow strip of it contiguous with French borders has been an important element in the improved atmosphere of the 1980s.

This broadening of France's definition of its vital interests takes on added significance in the context of the modifications that are being made to the French force posture in Europe. The eventual *Hades*-ASMP deployments will give France the concrete capability to act on the basis that the defense of Germany is a vital interest for France by enabling Paris to use tactical nuclear weapons for the benefit of German defense (and against targets lying outside the FRG) and not just that of France.

The other major modification to the French force posture, the creating of the FAR, is generally seen as a positive accomplishment for Franco-German defense cooperation. As demonstrated by the Bold Sparrow exercise, the FAR – an airmobile division and a light armored division – appears to be capable of military effective action in a Central European conflict. West German military analysis confirms this point, emphasizing the FAR's flexibility and capacity for rapid reaction, particularly the airmobile division with its force of 90 anti-tank helicopters and 35 escort helicopters.[38] Former SACEUR General Rogers has also congratulated France on the formation of the FAR and has expressed appreciation for the additional flexibility it provides France to intervene in Central Europe.[39] The extensive new Franco-German consultations and planning regarding the modalities of the FAR's eventual intervention at the front lines in Germany, has contributed as well to the tightening of Franco-German defense relations.

Yet, an overall assessment of the initiatives taken during the 1980s to strengthen the Franco-German defense relationship leads to a twofold conclusion. Developments such as the creation of the FAR and the agreement to consult on ANT use clearly reflect a new desire on the part of France to respond in a significant fashion to West German security needs and the strong consolidation of the Franco-German defense relationship that has taken place. Given the hitherto great degree of French sensitivity toward any step that could be construed as linking French nuclear doctrine (tactical last warning strike followed by strategic nuclear use) with that of NATO (limited tactical nuclear 'battle'), the agreement to consult with the FRG represents a significant change, and together with the future *Hades*-ASMP deployments and the evolution of the 'vital interests' definition, a clear enlarging of French nuclear perspectives from an almost strictly national to a European dimension. The placing of the FAR under German military command during the Bold Sparrow exercise, and Mitterrand's direct patronage of this development through his attendance (along with that of Chancellor Kohl) at the exercise, have helped to eliminate some of the ambiguities surrounding the mechanisms for French participation in the battle for Germany and the coordination of that participation with NATO's integrated forces.

The recent helicopter agreement should also be seen as a qualitatively new development in Franco-German collaboration. It is probably no exaggeration to say that this agreement would not have been reached at any other time over the past 30 years. As in the case of the joint tank project of the early 1980s, the technical obstacles to agreement were so substantial that a very strong act of political will on the part of both countries was needed to reach agreement. This kind of will was lacking in 1982 when the tank project was abandoned. The new impetus that Reykjavik and the INF developments have given to Franco-German defense cooperation played a major, perhaps leading role, in getting the helicopter project back on track.

In short, France and Germany have, on the one hand, indisputably reached a new apogee in their defense relationship, and under the impetus of the recent Soviet and US policy evolution are spending far more time than ever before in analyzing and working together on defense problems. On the other hand, much clearly remains to be accomplished. As useful as the formation of the FAR is for Franco-German defense relations, it does not modify the contradictory role of the bulk of French conventional forces, namely the First Army, as both the trigger of French nuclear use and the principal NATO reserve force, nor the still 'non-automatic' nature of its intervention. France's conventional contribution to the defense of Germany thus remains well short of what France is capable of doing, and certainly of what Germany would like to see. The targets of the *Hades* missile still lie in East Germany, which is almost as unacceptable for the West Germans as targets in their own territory.

From the French standpoint, the Germans were guilty of infidelity to the Franco–German relationship during the 1984–85 period, when Bonn, seduced by SDI and the apparent resurgence of American technological dynamism, vetoed the series of collaborative proposals arms on space projects already noted, and enlisted only half-heartedly in the Eureka effort. Collaboration on armament, space and high technology is one of three major areas of 'compensation' in which the French are interested in exchange for their increasing contribution to West German security, and it was not until the agreements on the *Hermes* shuttle and the helicopter emerged that the French began to regard the results and perspectives here as more promising.

The other two major areas where the French seek 'compensation' for their increased solidarity are, first, continued German support for nuclear deterrence as well as support for the maintenance of an independent French nuclear force (and its non-inclusion in nuclear arms talks, except under French conditions); and second, the expansion of the Franco-German 'embryo' into broader European defense cooperation that will one day be able to assure a more autonomous West European defense effort. In the first area the German response, at least at the governmental level, has been reasonably satisfactory, although the French are clearly concerned for the future.

In the second area, there is once again a combination of disappointment over past results with, in the wake of Reykjavik and the INF developments, renewed hope regarding the future. Chirac, in his 'European Security Charter' speech before the WEU, issued yet another French government call for enhancing the role and activities of the organization. Nothing has come of this yet, but intra-European consultations on security issues have intensified greatly.

FUTURE PERSPECTIVES

A wide array of proposals have been advanced within France (and outside it) for enhancing still further the French contribution to West German security, reflecting the distance France can still travel in showing solidarity toward her principal ally. Some of these proposals encompass the nuclear area and others the conventional, some remain within the parameters of current French defense doctrine and others go well beyond it, and some require new force deployments while others can be accomplished with no change in force posture. In part reflecting the wide range of possibilities still open to Franco-German defense cooperation, Mitterrand and Kohl announced at the end of the Bold Sparrow exercise plans for the formation of a joint Franco-German 'defense council'. The declared purpose of the proposed council is to harmonize analyses in the different areas of security policy, including research, armaments, and the organization and deployment of joint units. Mitterrand also characterized the council as a potential future 'core' of a European defense entity.

While the composition and exact role of the defense council are as yet undefined, the intent is clearly for it to be organized at the very highest political level (there has reportedly been mention on the French side that the German Chancellor and French President should participate). The defense council would thus preside over the existing Franco-German Defense Commission, and would attempt to provide a far greater impetus to defense cooperation than existing structures are capable of doing. According to Mitterrand, 'there must be at the head of all this a superior level' to oversee consideration of the various initiatives the two countries could choose to take in the defense area.

Nuclear initiatives

One of the most widely discussed initiatives for France to take in the nuclear area involves the extension of French nuclear deterrence to cover Germany. The idea, which the government of Giscard d'Estaing briefly flirted with under the guise of 'enlarged sanctuarization', returned to prominence in the 1983-84 period. In late 1983, Chirac stated that British and French nuclear forces could soon join with American ones to guarantee European security. He rapidly retreated to a more 'orthodox' position, but still implicitly maintained that France and Britain should one day guarantee West Germany's borders.[40] Also in 1983, the French Institute for International Relations and four other European research institutes recommended an explicit extension of British and French deterrence to their allies and the creation of a European nuclear planning group that would provide a framework for joint discussion of nuclear targeting and for an eventual European financial contribution to the modernization of French and British nuclear forces.[41]

The following year former Chancellor Schmidt gave a speech to the Bundestag in which he proposed a joint Franco-German defense initiative that would combine the extension of French deterrence to include Germany with a sufficient upgrading of German and French reserves to enable the two countries to deploy 30 fully-equipped land divisions in the event of mobilization. Germany would largely finance the required conventional improvements. Schmidt has continued to argue in various fora in favor of France's extending its nuclear deterrence to West Germany combined with an ambitious initiative in the conventional area, most recently the integrating of the French and German armies under French command.

Former Socialist Prime Minister Laurent Fabius joined these voices, when he stated that France must consider the protection of Germany to be a vital French interest, and envisage extending its strategic nuclear deterrent to include West German security.[42] The attention that this option has attracted prompted President Mitterrand to write: 'One hears from all sides, of late, calls for our nuclear force to drop the concept of 'national sanctuary' and broaden that of "vital interests", extending to West German territory the norms of strategic deterrence applicable to ours.'[43]

While Mitterrand's characterization of hearing this argument from 'all sides' is undoubtedly exaggerated, there do appear to be some interesting convergences of opinion within the three major non-communist political parties. The Socialist Party Executive Bureau issued a declaration in mid-1985 stating that France will have an increasingly 'essential interest' for its defense and global deterrent to benefit Western Europe and above all the FRG, described as the most exposed and vulnerable territory of Europe. The 1985 UDF defense White Paper advocated substituting the concept of an 'enlarged sanctuary' for that of the 'national sanctuary'. And the Fillon National Defense Commission report, in discussing the question of a French nuclear strike in response to a nuclear attack against one of France's allies, argues quite strongly that France can extend its deterrence on a credible basis to nations sharing a 'common destiny'.

None of these documents actually advocates giving an explicit guarantee of French nuclear use for the defense of Germany. They all reaffirm, in one form or another, the maxim that an imprecise definition of French vital interests reinforces uncertainty and enhances the credibility of France's deterrent posture.[44] However, under these formulations French strategic forces would clearly be far more implicated than at present in contributing to West German security.

French officials have advanced a wide number of arguments as to why France cannot give an explicit nuclear guarantee to the FRG. The substantive deficiencies of some of these arguments is perhaps reflective of increasing French sensitivity over the issue, resulting in a desire to find as many reasons as possible as to why France cannot take this step.

For example, François Heisbourg, a former aide to Charles Hernu and currently the first French director of the IISS, wrote (while still with the Defense Ministry) that extending French deterrent exclusively to the FRG would excessively differentiate between the FRG and France's other neighbors and allies: 'Would Belgium, Luxembourg, and others be excluded?' Since it is extremely difficult to imagine any scenario whereby the Soviet Union attacks Belgium or Luxembourg but leaves the FRG untouched, it is clear that a French nuclear guarantee on behalf of the FRG would extend de facto to these other countries as well.

A second argument is that an explicit guarantee is unnecessary, since, in the words of Chirac, 'even under a strictly national concept, our forces make, in effect, a decisive contribution to deterrence in Western Europe'.[45] This does not appear to be the view of the West Germans, however. None the less, a third French argument states that Bonn has not asked France for a nuclear guarantee. The Socialist, Michel Rocard, opposed providing a French nuclear guarantee to West Germany on the grounds that Germany does not want it for two reasons; it would, according to Rocard, be asking Germany in effect to choose between the US nuclear cover and a French one, and it would be an unnecessary provocation vis-à-vis the Soviet Union.[46] Pro-nuclear Germans, Rocard asserts, prefers the 'American umbrella'.[47] Put in those terms, this is, of course, an accurate statement. However, the question does not have to be one of either the American guarantee or the French one, but of both at the same time, and a recent Le Monde analysis of Franco-German defense relations noted that the German government has not asked for an extension of French deterrence out of awareness that Paris would not be able to respond affirmatively to that request rather than out of lack of interest.[48] Pro-nuclear Germans not holding government office, such as Alfred Dregger, the CDU parliamentary leader, have not shown such reticence and have called repeatedly for an extension of French nuclear deterrence to the FRG.

The most serious French argument against giving a nuclear guarantee to the FRG is that it would lack credibility.[49] It is clearly difficult for France to envisage extended deterrence while possessing what is essentially limited to a massive retaliation capability. However, the future evolution of the French nuclear force posture will bring some important changes in this regard. The planned augmentation of French SLBM warheads, which will rise from 96 to 592, should provide France with some counter-force capabilities,[50] although it is perhaps problematical whether French SLBM could acquire the flexibility from a command and control standpoint to execute many counter-force options. Consequently, ideas that have been put forward regarding the extension of French deterrence in the context of increasing French counter-force capabilities generally focus on projected new and land- and air-launched systems.

The National Assembly Defense Commission report on the 1987–91 military program law asserts that fulfillment of two conditions are necessary in order for France to provide a credible extended deterrent. First, its interests must be clearly threatened, and, the report asserts, can one doubt that this would be the case for France if the contiguous territory of Western Europe were subjected to a serious and deliberate attack. This line of reasoning that the contiguity of territory can make a key contribution to the credibility of extended deterrence recalls that of the early 1960s, perhaps indicating that where sufficient political motivation and will exist the technical requirements for extended deterrence can be downplayed to some extent.

This obviously does not mean they can be disregarded. The report continues that the Mirage 2000N armed with the ASMP will be able to hit military targets deep into enemy territory, and that the projected S4 missile (an intermediate-range ballistic missile whose mode of deployment is still being studied) will have an even greater range and accuracy.[51] According to one report, the S4 will have a counter-force capability similar to that of the Pershing II missile. Thus, as the defense commission report notes, a French nuclear response to a Soviet attack on Germany would not entail massive counter-value strikes but selective ones against the different components of Soviet armed forces – radar installations, airfields, command centers, logistics, etc. Other sources have also written on the role that a significant French counter-force capability with sufficient range to hit targets deep into Eastern Europe and even the Soviet Union could play in the defense of Germany.[52]

Despite the repeated official French statements asserting that France cannot extend its nuclear deterrence to West Germany, it is possible that under the renewed impetus given to Franco-German defense cooperation in 1987, the issue is indeed being brought up in bilateral discussion. Following a mid-May meeting in Germany between Giraud and German Defense Minister Woerner, the latter stated that discussions were in progress at the level of chiefs-of-staff to examine the concrete implications of an extension of French nuclear deterrence to West German territory. When Giraud was questioned on the different potential courses open to the two countries, he did not reject out of hand any possibility, but added that it would be premature to reveal any of the details of Franco-German discussions.[53] An extension of French deterrence to Germany based on long-range French counter-force capabilities is clearly not a near-term option (for one thing, the systems do not exist yet), but nor is it an option that can be discounted for the 1990s.

A wide range of proposals have also been advanced regarding the role of shorter-range French tactical nuclear weapons (both current and future systems) in expanding defense relations with West Germany. These proposals can be divided into three broad categories, although the categories are linked in many ways. They are proposals that would involve the deployment of French ANT into West Germany, that would require modifications to French doctrine concerning ANT use, and that would involve Germany more closely with French decision-making on ANT use.

Some proposals combine all three of these approaches.

Proposals for the deployment of French ANT into Germany can be placed within the framework of current French nuclear doctrine or can go beyond it. Within the former category, the deployment of France's *Pluton* missiles into Germany would enable them to be used against targets beyond the Elbe, while that of the *Hades* could spare the territory of both East and West Germany from being the target of French ANT use, which would still be conceived as the 'last warning' prior to strategic nuclear strikes. However, the mere presence of French ANT on German soil could be seen as providing a greater, albeit still implicit, deterrent benefit to West Germany.[54]

On the other hand, a deployment of French ANT into Germany could be accompanied by doctrinal modifications concerning their use. Former President Giscard d'Estaing proposed in early 1986 the establishment of 'two distinct levels of nuclear deterrence', whereby the 'massive use' of the French strategic arsenal would only occur in the event that France itself were directly threatened with destruction, but other components of the French nuclear panoply could be flexibly employed to counter an attack on France's allies. Giscard d'Estaing considered neutron warheads to be particularly suited for this latter role.[55] At the same time, Chirac also supported relying on the threat of neutron warhead use as a means of providing some French nuclear deterrence benefit to France's allies.[56] The implication of these proposals is that there would be some degree of 'decoupling' of French tactical from strategic nuclear use; the use of ANT would no longer be an unambiguous 'last warning' of forthcoming strategic strikes.

Chirac seemingly attempted to move toward implementation of this approach some six months into his term as Prime Minister. In his speech before the IHEDN, he declared that a French contribution to deterrence in Europe, 'whether one likes it or not, requires coupling between the action of conventional forces and the threat of nuclear weapons use . . . France intends to be capable of delivering to the eventual attacker a nuclear warning . . . this warning will have the objective of not only addressing an unequivocal signal to the attacker, but also to block the dynamics of the attack.'[57] Chirac thus emphasized coupling between French conventional forces and ANT rather than between the ANT and strategic forces, he downplayed the 'last' warning signal of ANT use to that of a warning, and he appeared to stress as well the battlefield significance of French ANT use.

Chirac's speech brought a stern reply from Mitterrand reaffirming established French doctrine. The French President repudiated Chirac's analysis that the ANT are separable from strategic nuclear forces or that ANT use can have a 'battlefield' objective.[58] This exchange, in addition to being seen as a contest over who would have the leading role in determining French defense policy within the context of 'cohabitation' at the top of the government between a president and prime minister of opposing political parties, was also interpreted in various quarters as a debate between giving French ANT a role in German defense (Chirac) versus reserving the ANT force principally for national deterrence (Mitterrand).

However, it is perhaps questionable as to how interested the Germans would be in a French doctrine of fairly widespread battlefield nuclear use largely (in the

Giscard scenario) or somewhat (in the Chirac scenario) decoupled from the French strategic panoply. One of the German concerns over US policy has been the perspective of a limited tactical nuclear battle. In a speech to the February 1985 Munich Wehrkunde Conference, Hernu sought to allay West German fears that their country could become a nuclear battlefield by emphasizing the unacceptability for France of 'any concept of limited [nuclear] war'.[59]

Lastly, various suggestions have also been made as to how France can more closely involve Germany with French nuclear decision-making, at least in the ANT area. These suggestions include the creation of a Franco-German nuclear planning group, joint Franco-German targeting of French ANT, and the resort to a 'dual-key' arrangement over any French ANT eventually deployed into Germany.

The dual-key approach first achieved prominence in 1983 when *Le Monde* specialist Michel Tatu wrote a long analysis advocating it as a relatively painless way (France would not have to make any doctrinal changes regarding ANT use) of reinforcing solidarity with Germany.[60] The concept does not appear to have aroused serious French government interest due to the delays or even paralysis that could result in ANT use from having two separate authorities exercise this right of control.[61] Even in the current atmosphere there does not appear to be any interest on the part of the French government in this option.

The UDF/RPR joint platform for the March 1986 National Assembly elections called for a 'real' defense dialogue between France and its partners, in particular on the conditions of tactical nuclear weapons use.[62] Following the Kohl-Mitterrand agreement regarding consultations over French ANT use, the French government made it clear that these consultations would apply only in 'time of crisis' prior to any ANT strikes on German territory, and that Paris did not consider the agreement to entail the establishment of a consultative framework similar to NATO's Nuclear Planning Group.[63] Thus, France has seemed to exclude peacetime discussions with Germany on targeting scenarios and the other conditions of French ANT use.

French sensitivity over these kinds of consultation stems from the direct link in French doctrine between tactical and strategic nuclear weapons. The fear has existed that involving Germany, a NATO integrated nation, too closely with French nuclear planning (even at the exclusive ANT level) could threaten the credibility of French doctrine by appearing to dilute it within NATO's flexible response concept.[64] Doubts have been expressed that an ANT strike executed on the basis of a Franco-German targeting plan would carry the same threat of escalation to the strategic level as an exclusively French one.[65] None the less, these objections are perhaps not insurmountable given a sufficient degree of political will. Furthermore, since the Germans are not enamored with the prospect of limited tactical nuclear engagements, it should prove possible for France and Germany to find common ground regarding nuclear planning, especially as longer-range French systems become operational.

The linkages between these concepts are apparent. Any stationing of French ANT in Germany would necessarily entail consultation with Bonn regarding their use. Any doctrinal shift decoupling to some extent tactical from strategic weapons should logically entail deploying ANT into Germany, thereby making them more readily available for use in German defense. The combination of increased consultations on ANT use (which could conceivably be already taking place to some degree within the framework of the joint defense commission – there is perhaps no need to set up a separate Nuclear Planning Group unless it is desired to give visibility to the process) along with some French nuclear deployments (perhaps initially the Mirage 2000N armed with ASMP temporarily landing at German air bases) into Germany is perhaps the more likely near- or medium-term scenario. A decoupling of tactical and strategic weapons use, as suggested by Giscard d'Estaing and seemingly implied by Chirac, is perhaps not the most fruitful way to pursue Franco-German nuclear cooperation, although as French counter-force capabilities emerge the tactical 'last warning' could become the prelude to selective strategic strikes on Soviet territory rather than massive counter-value ones.

Conventional initiatives

As is the case in the nuclear area, a wide variety of potential initiatives have emerged for reinforcing Franco-German conventional defense ties. Again, these proposals range from changes in French declaratory policy to significant modifications in force posture. They include as well pragmatic ideas for expanding operational cooperation between the armed forces of the two nations, and for deepening the Franco-German relationship in the area of arms development and production.

One of the foremost suggestions concerning enhanced conventional defense cooperation would entail an explicit French renunciation of the option of neutrality in the event of a Central European conflict, contravening the 'non-automaticity' shibboleth of French defense doctrine. French declaratory policy has evolved in this direction. Mitterrand has written, for example, 'I conceive with difficulty our troops, stationed in the Federal Republic as they are today, and, at the first alarm, turning around to go home.'[66] At the conclusion of the Bold Sparrow exercise, Mitterrand was somewhat more explicit, stating that 'in a conflict, where there would be an immediate peril, the duty of France would be to come to the aid of its allies and of Germany.' Chirac has indicated that the non-automatic nature of France's commitment to West German defense 'in no way means that France would seek to escape from its responsibilities', and Raymond Barre has asserted that 'for France, the battle begins from the moment Western Europe, and in the first instance the Federal Republic, is the object of an attack.'[67]

Despite statements of this nature, some French observers acknowledge that German opinion does not perceive that 'reality' of France's 'immediate engagement' in the event of an attack on Germany.[68] The deployment of French forces in a front-line position, coupled with an unambiguous declaration indicating France's intent to intervene immediately in any Central European conflict, is one of the more frequently suggested means of dispelling all doubts regarding the French commitment to the defense of Germany.

The 'traditionalist' argument against this opinion is two-fold. First, it would be tantamount to a *de facto* return to the integrated NATO command. It is not completely clear why this would be the case. Concerns along these lines have tended to stem from the enhanced coordination that would be required between

France and the NATO command structure.[69]

The second traditionalist argument is that this option would undermine the independence of French policy. One French analyst has disputed this conclusion, maintaining that any conflict would necessarily be preceded by a period of crisis that would allow France to make adjustments if it decided that becoming involved in the conflict would be contrary to French interests.[70] This argument has also lost prominence since a major motive for it, namely the fear of an aggressive America leading France into conflict that would be contrary to her interests, has become somewhat implausible given French analyses of US policy. A principal remaining motive for maintaining a neutrality option is to guard against Germany itself undertaking an 'adventurist' policy contrary to French interests. This also appears as rather implausible as well as contrary to French analysis of the trends in Germany, and, in any event, is not a scenario worthy of public consideration in the current atmosphere, even if France may privately give it credence.

Thus, arguments against new deployments of French forces designed to render France's participation in the European battle automatic are currently based largely on pragmatic grounds. Chirac has maintained that given the unpredictable nature of future crises, France must preserve its liberty of action and not rigidly commit the use of its forces to 'automatic engagements' that could turn out to be an inappropriate means of meeting the situation. This seems a rather weak argument, as is one put forth by Mitterrand to the effect that a French forward deployment is irrelevant given that less than 200 km separate the Rhine from the Thuringe salient, and the flying time is 45 minutes for an airmobile division and six minutes for a formation of planes.

More substantial arguments against redeploying French forces to the front evoke the considerable expense that such a redeployment would entail, as well as the fact that even before France left the integrated NATO command the principal role of the French army had been one of a reserve force in Central Europe.[71] The substantial financial cost of a French redeployment to the front would thus be disproportionate to the limited or even non-existent military benefit of such a move.[72] The question also remains of whether France's allies would accept a significant deployment of French troops at the front outside of the NATO integrated command. The value of a deployment of a purely symbolic nature is perhaps questionable since, as one French analysis points out, France already has 'a very far forward' symbolic deployment in the form of its garrison of some 2,700 soldiers stationed in West Berlin.[73]

One measure of that could be of considerable military significance and go a long way toward visibly eliminating the non-automatic character of France's commitment to the defense of West Germany would be for France to allow its territory once again to provide peacetime logistic support to the Alliance. When France withdrew from the integrated NATO command, NATO lost the use of French territory for logistic support of the forward area. Agreements exist concerning wartime use of French territory, facilities and lines of communication, but the French have long maintained that pre-established logistical use of French territories and facilities for support of the forward area would make French participation in any conflict as inevitable as if French forces were deployed at the front lines.[74] One could thus argue that, for example, fully reopening NATO supply lines across France and allowing the US to pre-position supplies and equipment at French airfields for use by American reinforcements would provide an important additional guarantee to West Germany of France's immediate participation in a Central European conflict. These steps would also be of military significance for the Alliance.

One problem with this option is that it would entail enhanced direct cooperation with NATO and the US rather than with the FRG. It would obviously fall well short of reintegrating French troops under NATO command, and France has increased its cooperation with NATO during the 1980s. None the less, as illustrated by the Bold Sparrow exercise, and the controversy over the attendance at the exercise of the two NATO generals, there is still far more political sensitivity in France regarding defense relations with NATO than with West Germany. However, reopening French territory for logistical support could perhaps come to be seen in France as a necessary step for preparing the 'inevitable' future of a reduced American military presence on the continent and a more autonomous West European defense. This reduced permanent American presence would need to be offset by greater facilities and means for accommodating the US reinforcements that would be required in a time of crisis.

Another important category of proposals in the conventional area involves the continued deepening of the functional and operational ties between the two armies. Efforts will be required, for example, to remedy the coordination problems revealed by the Bold Sparrow exercise.

Helmut Schmidt's idea of integrating the armed forces of the two countries (under French command) and establishing a joint defense budget will obviously not be achievable in the foreseeable future, but Kohl's more modest suggestion regarding the formation of a totally integrated brigade appears to be a quite plausible candidate for implementation. Kohl made the suggestion at a press conference on 19 June.

The response from the French government was immediately and unanimously favorable, with Mitterrand, Chirac, Raimond and Giraud all stating their support for the idea, although indicating at the same time that serious questions had to be resolved before the integrated brigade could be set up. Among the mainstream French political parties, only the 'traditionalist' elements of the RPR voiced hostility to Kohl's proposal. Mitterrand characterized the proposal as an 'embryo' of European defense.[75]

The major difficulty regarding implementation of the proposal relates to the problem of command. The 1954 agreements permitting German rearmament stipulate that all German armed forces, with the exception of twelve territorial brigades, must come under the integrated NATO command. If the brigade were under French command, this obligation would be violated, while if the brigade were under German command the French forces within it would be effectively reintegrated within NATO. However, the two countries appear possibly inclined simply to ignore the command problem. German Defense Minister Woerner indicated that he sees no problem in having the brigade initially commanded by a French officer outside of the NATO command structure. It is planned that units of Germany's territorial forces would be used in the brigade.

The initial reaction to the integrated brigade proposal was to regard it more as a symbolic gesture than as a truly substantive aspect of Franco-German defense cooperation. However, the military cooperation working group of the Franco-German Defense Commission has been given the task of examining potential missions for the brigade that could make a tangible contribution to defense efforts. The working group is studying the idea of forming a unit of four or five regiments, stationed around the Rhine, that would be able to facilitate the movement of French forces on German soil in the event of a crisis and/or conflict.[76]

In the area of collaborative weapons projects, a final agreement in the coming months on the Franco-German helicopter is, of course, the key near-term development. A potential project that has received some emphasis in France is the development of a new air defense system to replace the *Hawk* network in the mid- to late 1990s. The new air defense system could be conceived to counter enemy aviation and air-launched missiles, as well as have a limited capability against tactical ballistic missiles. The fact that the system would counter a threat directed exclusively at European territory, as well as the very large cost of the project, are the two principal reasons this project has attracted interest in France as an important area for Franco-German collaboration.[77] Despite the limited ATBM capability the system could possess, the French do not regard it as the European equivalent of SDI since the focus would not be on anti-ballistic missile defense. Although Franco-German discussions have been held over collaboration on this 'enlarged' air defense system, nothing has surfaced yet.

The evolution of incentives and obstacles to cooperation

The incentives on the French side for continuing to intensify Franco-German defense ties are likely to remain strong. Since the French see the pressures in the US toward a denuclearization of European defense and an eventual disengagement at least partially from the continent as coming from all major political forces – Liberals and Conservatives, Republicans and Democrats – concern over US policy is likely to remain strong. In Germany, the Greens appear to be a durable aspect of the political spectrum, along with their leftward pull on the German defense debate. The German demographic problem and the perturbations it may create for German defense policy should also arouse French concern.

The French ambition of advancing the 'construction' of European defense is thus likely to remain strong for a variety of reasons. The goal of making Europe less dependent over the longer term on the United States has certainly been a fairly constant aspect of French policy over the past decades. Nor is the perception likely to change that Franco-German cooperation constitutes the 'locomotive' of European defense cooperation. Technological and financial realities should provide further incentives for France to attempt to enhance Franco-German and European defense cooperation. With the new demands placed on French resources in the 1980s and beyond, notably in the space area, and the increasingly poor prospects that emerged by the mid-1980s for French arms exports, it is clear that France will not be able to afford to develop and produce on its own a full range of weapons systems.

The evolution of French public opinion has apparently become an important 'enabling' factor for significant Franco-German defense initiatives. According to a 1987 Louis Harris poll, 63 per cent of French opinion supports the participation of French conventional forces in the defense of Germany (21 per cent against and 16 per cent no opinion), 51 per cent support the use of French nuclear forces for German defense (31 per cent against and 18 per cent no opinion), and 88 per cent favor the establishment of a common European defense, with 60 per cent of those wanting that defense entity to be independent of but cooperating with the United States.[78] French public opinion on these questions has perhaps been affected not only by the changing security environment, but also by the long-term impact of the exchanges in the numerous areas that have developed between the two countries during the preceding decades. By the early 1980s, more than 1300 'twinnings' of French and German towns had been established, more than five million children had participated in exchanges under the auspices of the Franco-German youth organization, and one quarter of French schoolchildren were studying German. As already seen, there are also important elements within all three of the mainstream French political parties in favor of taking additional steps to strengthen the Franco-German defense relationship. On the whole, French political elites as well as French public opinion appear to share the conviction that France and the FRG have a special relationship within Europe that is fundamental for the future destiny of both countries.

On the other hand, obstacles still remain in the way of moving Franco-German defense relations to a deeper level. These obstacles are four-fold in nature.

First, and perhaps the foremost, an essential condition for the progress of Franco-German defense cooperation is the maintaining by France of robust conventional forces, since it is the conventional area where Bonn feels France can make its most important contribution to West German security. The financial constraints on defense spending that will exist for the foreseeable future will make it difficult for France to find an easy equilibrium between its conventional and nuclear spending. Despite the relative amplitude of the 1987-91 military program law (a 40 per cent increase in the equipment budget), by 1995, for example, only one third of French armored divisions will be fitted with the new Leclerc tank.[79]

Secondly, the support in France for closer Franco-German relations in defense as well as other areas coexists with a still large and fairly widespread distrust of Germany, based on the 'simplistic and recurrent idea', to quote a recent *Le Monde* editorial, that German reunification is fundamentally all that the FRG is interested in.[80] As discussed in this chapter, the fear that the FRG cannot be counted on to remain firmly anchored in the West has been a significant factor inciting the French to greater defense solidarity. While the feeling has been growing in France that the two countries truly share common security interests, it is highly unlikely that this feeling alone could have inspired the French initiatives of the 1980s. On the one hand, a rapprochement that is based to a significant extent on distrust will have difficulty in achieving far-reaching objectives. There is also a strong tendency in

France to regard German proposals on the extension of France's deterrent or the taking of a front-line position as essentially designed to bring France back into the integrated NATO command. (These latter suspicions are not necessarily unfounded.)

A further French suspicion regarding cooperation with Germany is that Bonn will, in the final analysis, be too deferential or submissive toward US policy. Although the French have come to realize that presenting Germany with stark France versus the US choices is not a fruitful way in which to pursue collaboration with the FRG (which will inevitably choose Washington), France will be far less interested in tightening relations with the FRG if it appears to align itself automatically on US policy. The 1985 SDI episode illustrates the difficulties that can arise in the tripartite Paris-Bonn-Washington relationship.

Lastly, it is clear that the 'compensation' the French expect from Germany in return for French initiatives that enhance German security will not be easily achievable. Collaborative arms (and high-technology) projects are inherently difficult endeavors, requiring often laborious compromises between differing national requirements and industrial interests. Differences over nuclear deterrence and nuclear arms control could resurge, with Germany anxious to have negotiations begin on the reduction of battlefield weapons while France favors deferring such negotiations.

French interest in cooperation with Germany perhaps diminished somewhat during 1985, due to a more reassuring analysis of the strategic environment, the SDI imbroglio, and the perception that Bonn was again focused essentially on its American relationship and that further French concessions would simply be 'pocketed' without any Germany compensation.[81] This period of stagnation illustrates the pitfalls that await future progress. Furthermore, given the strong long-term French interest in building a more autonomous defense of Western Europe, far-reaching initiatives in Franco-German defense relations are probably to some extent hostage to broader European developments. While the role of the 'locomotive' is to be in front, it cannot be too far ahead of the others. In turn, the development of broader European defense cooperation depends in part on across-the-board progress in the 'construction' of Western Europe. In the words of Mitterrand: 'a common defense is only possible if a common policy is defined. It is thus necessary to improve still further the structures and foundations of European economic and political cooperation in order for military Europe to develop.'[82] While the progress during the 1980s of Franco-German defense ties has been significant, much remains to be done before a profoundly cooperative relationship, devoid of 'arrière-pensées', can emerge.

NOTES

1.   For an overview of this entire period, see Michael Harrison, *The Reluctant Ally: France and Atlantic Security* (Baltimore: Johns Hopkins University Press, 1981), pp. 6-111; and Edward A. Kolodziej, *French International Policy Under De Gaulle and Pompidou* (Ithaca: Cornell University Press, 1974), pp. 292-324.

2. Alfred Grosser, *Les Occidentaux* (Paris: Fayard, 1978), p. 43.

3. See, for example, General Jeannou Lacaze, 'Politique de défense et stratégie militaire de la France,' *Défense Nationale* (June 1983): 13-18.

4. Edward Kolodziej, 'French security policy: decisions and dilemmas,' *Armed Forces and Society* 8 (Winter 1982): 194-5; Yves Laulan, 'France and her army in the 1980s,' in Gregory Flynn (ed.), *The Internal Fabric of Western Security* (Totowa, NJ: Allanheld, Osmun & Co., 1981), p. 106.

5. See Robbin F. Laird, 'French nuclear forces in the 1980s and 1990s,' *Comparative Strategy* 4 (1984): 400-3.

6. Guy Mery, 'Une armée pour quoi faire et comment?,' *Défense Nationale* 32 (June 1976): 11-33.

7. See Pascal Boniface and François Heisbourg, *La Puce, les hommes et la bombe* (Paris: Hachette), pp. 239-40, for a positive assessment of Franco-German cooperation in the arms area during the 1960s; and Karl Kaiser and Pierre Lellouche (eds), *Le Couple franco-allemand et la défense de l'Europe* (Paris: Economica, 1987), pp. 353-4, for a list of major Franco-German cooperative weapons projects.

8. Telegram 2337, American Embassy, Paris, to the Secretary of State, 28 October 1965, *Carrollton Index of Recently Declassified Documents* (Arlington, VA: Carrollton Press, 1980), p. 77A.

9. For a sampling of this view, see Michel Tatu, 'Le problème américain,' *Défense Nationale* 38 (December 1982): 68; and Michel Aurillac, 'Une garantie nucléaire française pour l'Europe est-elle possible?,' *Politique Etrangère* 48 (Summer 1983): 373.

10. Charles Hernu, 'Face à la logique des blocs, une france indépendante et solidaire,' *Défense Nationale* 38 (December 1982): 12-13. A more recent official expression of the same view is in Général Jeannou Lacaze, 'Concept de défense et sécurité en Europe,' *Défense Nationale* 40 (July 1984): 22.

11. Jacques Amalric, 'Paris voudrait unifier les positions européennes face aux Etats-Unis,' *Le Monde*, 22 March 1985.

12. See Pierre Lellouche, 'La France, la SDI et la securité de l'Europe,' in Kaiser and Lellouche, *le Couple franco-allemand*, pp. 258-9.

13. Mitterrand argues along these lines in a book published shortly before the 1986 French presidential elections. See François Mitterrand, *Réflexions sur la politique extérieure de la France* (Paris: Fayard, 1986), pp. 50-66. Shortly thereafter, Andre Giraud, who became French Defense Minister, wrote a critique of Mitterrand's book in which he attacked the aggressive attitude the Mitterrand government exhibited toward the US on SDI, but fully agreed with Mitterrand's analysis that SDI would be a destabilizing factor in Europe. André Giraud, 'Oui sur les grandes orientations, non sur leur mise en oeuvre,' *Le Monde*, 12 February 1986.

14. During an early March 1987 ministerial meeting, Giraud, for example, reportedly termed it a 'nuclear Munich'.

15. The rise of neutralist-pacifist sentiments in the FRG was attributed in part to declining German confidence in the US nuclear guarantee. See, for example, Raymond Aron, 'En quête de la securité,' *Commentaire* (Winter 1982-3): 557.

16. See, for example, a parliamentary foreign policy debate of last June, in *Le Monde*, 18 June 1987.

17. The French reacted, of course, with dismay to the SPD agreement with the East German Communist Party on a Central European denuclearized zone. See, for example, ibid, 24 October 1986.

18. The speech is reprinted in *Défense Nationale*, June 1987.

19. Cited in *Le Monde*, 25 June 1987.

20. For a description of the Commission and its workings, see Boniface and Heisbourg, *La Puce*, pp. 241-3; and Isabelle Renouard, 'La coopération franco-allemande aujourd'hui,' in Kaiser and Lellouche, *Le Couple franco-allemand*, pp. 52-6.

21. See André Adrets [the pseudonym of a former French Defense Ministry official], 'Franco-German relations and the nuclear factor in a divided Europe,' in Robbin F. Laird (ed.) *French Security Policy* (Boulder and London: Westview Press, 1986), pp.107-8.

22. See Renouard, 'La coopération franco-allemande,' pp. 52-3.

23. See Lellouche, 'La France, la SDI,' pp. 264-70.

24. François Gorand, 'France-RFA, 1981–1986: une occasion manquée,' in Kaiser and Lellouche, pp. 209-12.

25. Lellouche, 'La France, la SDI, pp. 268-9.

26. Rapport à la Commission de la Défense Nationale et des Forces Armées sur le projet de loi de programme relatif à l'équipement militaire pour les années 1987–1991 (Paris: The National Assembly, 1987), pp. 102-3.

27. See the interview with Charles Hernu in *Le Monde*, 18 June 1983; and the statements of the Director of the General Studies Bureau of the French Joint Chiefs of Staff, also in *Le Monde*, 14 February 1984.

28. Interview with Hernu, *Le Monde*, 18 June 1983.

29. Charles Hernu, *Défendre la Paix* (Paris: J. C. Lattès, 1985), pp. 64-5; and General Jeannou Lacaze, 'Politique de défense et stratégie militaire de la France,' *Défense Nationale* 39 (June 1983): 13-18.

30. Text reprinted in *Le Monde*, 2–3 March 1986.

31. See Jacques de la Hersière, 'Les forces françaises en Allemagne,' *Défense Nationale* (April 1986): 165-7.

32. See *L'Express*, 25 September–October 1987.

33. For these two different emphases, see François Heisbourg, 'Coopération en matière d'armements: rien n'est jamais acquis . . .,' in Kaiser and Lellouche, p. 122; and Gorand, *France-RFA*, pp. 210-11.

34. *Le Monde*, 7 March 1987; and 18 July 1987.

35. Chirac has been somewhat prone to mercurial changes of tone and views.

36. Speech reprinted in *Défense Nationale* (November 1981).

37. André Fontaine, 'Entre la suite et le requiem,' *Le Monde*, 26 January 1983.

38. See General Franz-Joseph Schulze, 'La nécessité d'une réaction de défense immediate et commune,' in Kaiser and Lellouche, pp. 166-8.

39. *Le Monde*, 23–24 February 1986.

40. Ibid, 28 October 1983.

41. Karl Kaiser et al., *La Communauté européenne: déclin ou renouveau* (Paris: Institut Français des Relations Internationales, 1983), pp. 81-7.

42. *Le Monde*, 17 June 1987.

43. François Mitterrand, *Réflexions sur la politique extérieure de la France* (Paris: Fayard, 1986), pp. 92-3.

44. Rapport à la Commission, p. 103; *La Sécurité de l'Europe* (Paris: Parti Socialiste, 1985), p. 9; *Redresser la défense de la France* (Paris: UDF, 1985), pp. 66, 152.

45. Jacques Chirac, 'La politique de défense de la France,' *Défense Nationale* (November 1986): 13.

46. See his interview with *Le Monde*, 11 July 1987.

47. *L'Express*, 10 July 1987, p. 23.

48. Daniel Vernet, 'Paradoxes franco-allemands,' *Réflexions*, 25 June 1987.
49. See, for example, Mitterrand, *op. cit.*, pp. 95-7.
50. Robbin F. Laird, 'France's nuclear future,' in Laird (ed.) pp. 65-73.
51. Rapport à la Commission, pp. 104–5.
52. Adrets, *Franco-German Relations,* pp. 115–18; and Karl Kaiser and Pierre Lellouche, 'Le couple franco-allemand et la sécurité de l'Europe: synthèses et recommendations,' in Kaiser and Lellouche (eds) p.319.
53. *Le Monde*, 22 May 1987.
54. Boniface and Heisbourg, *La Puce*, pp. 268–9.
55. *Le Monde*, 18 February 1986.
56. Jacques Chirac, 'Construction de l'Europe et défense commune,' *Le Monde*, 28 February 1986.
57. Chirac, 'La politique de défense,' *op. cit.*, p. 12.
58. *Le Monde*, 15 October 1986.
59. Text in Charles Hernu, *Défendre la paix*, pp. 263-74.
60. *Le Monde*, 4–5 December 1983.
61. André Adrets, 'Franco-German relations,' pp.111–12.
62. Text reprinted in *Le Monde*, 19–20 January 1986.
63. Ibid., 4 April 1986.
64. Boniface and Heisbourg, *La Puce,* pp. 272–3.
65. Adrets, 'Franco-German relations,' pp.112–14.
66. Mitterrand, *Réflexions*, pp. 98-9.
67. Chirac, 'La politique de défense, p. 12; and Raymond Barre, 'De la sécurité en Europe,' *Défense Nationale* (June 1987): 26.
68. *Rapport à la Commission*, p. 17.
69. In 1983, the RPR accused the Socialist government of using the FAR to disguise a return to NATO integration. See *Contre-projet de loi de Programmation Militaire*, 1984–1988 (Paris: RPR, 1983); and *Le Monde*, 4–5 December 1983.
70. See the comments of Thierry de Montbrial, director of the French Institute of International Relations, at a hearing before the National Assembly Defense Commission, in *Rapport à la Commission*, p. 257.
71. Boniface and Heisbourg, *La Puce,* pp. 266-8.
72. A 1975 WEU study put the cost of relocating one brigade with its staff, four battalions, and support units, at a half billion deutschmarks. See General Franz-Joseph Schultze, 'La nécessité d'une réaction de défense,' pp.165-6.
73. Boniface and Heisbourg, *La Puce*, p. 267.
74. François de Rose, *La France et la défense de l'Europe* (Seuil: Paris, 1976), pp. 33-4.
75. *Le Monde,* 23 and 25 June 1987.
76. Ibid., 19–20 July 1987.
77. See François Heisbourg, 'Coopération en matière d'armements: rien n'est jamais acquis . . .,' and Kaiser and Lellouche, 'Le couple franco-allemand,' in Kaiser and Lellouche, pp. 126-7, 322-4.
78. *L'Express,* 24 April 1987.
79. Ibid., 17 July 1987.
80. *Le Monde*, 17 July 1987. Former French Foreign Minister Michel Jobert wrote, 'The reality is clear: Germany intends to go its own way in Mitteleuropa – that is, the way of a reunited German people.' Jobert was quoted in *The Washington Post*, 6 September 1987.
81. See François Gourand, *France-RFA*, pp. 209-12.
82. Quoted in *Le Monde*, 23 June 1987.

2 West German security policy and the Franco-German relationship

Barry Blechman and Cathleen Fisher

Geostrategic and historical factors have made the Federal Republic of Germany a non-nuclear state, a member of an alliance, and a state dependent on the nuclear deterrent of the United States to guarantee its security. This security position, moreover, has not changed significantly in four decades. Until recently, West German leaders, on the whole, appeared more or less content with this relationship of dependence – or, if not content, then at least resigned.

In the late 1970s and early 1980s, developments at the international level, particularly the actions of American leaders, provoked a fundamental reassessment of West German security needs and policies. The revival of West German interest in defense cooperation with France is part of that reassessment; it is related to elite fears that, in the long run, continued dependence on the United States may not be politically sustainable or militarily desirable.

In this chapter, we discuss West German perspectives on the broader strategic environment that provides the framework for Franco-German cooperation. We begin with a brief review of the FRG's security position – basic geostrategic, historical, and political factors that form both the point of departure and prism through which West German political leaders view bilateral cooperation with France. Second, we examine the changes at the international level and the domestic factors that prompted the first Helmut Schmidt and then Helmut Kohl to revive the security dialogue with France in three areas: (1) nuclear strategy and issues; (2) conventional defense; and (3) arms production. We then focus on four key individual German perspectives and conclude with a discussion of the factors on the German side that will broadly determine progress generally in Franco-German defense cooperation.

SECURITY POSITION OF THE FEDERAL REPUBLIC

Structural factors broadly define the FRG's security position and provide a context for understanding West German perspectives on Franco-German defense cooperation. Three elements of Bonn's security position are of principal importance in this regard: the Federal Republic's (1) membership in NATO; (2) non-nuclear status; and (3) division into two separate states astride the East–West European border. These geopolitical factors determine the range and scope of viable security policy alternatives and thus, indirectly, influence West German perspectives on the role of Franco-German defense cooperation. Partisan differences in the FRG over the means or ends of cooperation with France reflect, in essence, divergent views of the most appropriate response to the FRG's security predicament.

Membership in NATO

The Bundeswehr is conceived of as 'an army within an alliance.'[1] Barring any major changes in the current NATO structure, Franco-German defense cooperation must proceed from the fact that Bonn's military forces are fully integrated into the NATO command while those of France are not. West German military doctrine is Alliance doctrine. National planning must be carried out within the NATO framework and coordinated with Bonn's allies. Arms requirements are determined by Bonn's defined military tasks within the Alliance. Budgetary priority is accorded to those items which allow Bonn to fulfill its Alliance commitments and demonstrate 'sufficient' defense effort to warrant an American defense commitment.[2] In practical terms, the FRG's membership in NATO means that efforts to coordinate and harmonize defense resources and requirements with France must be reconciled with simultaneous efforts to do the same within the Alliance and, in particular, with the United States.

Non-nuclear status

The Federal Republic is a non-nuclear power and is likely to remain one. At the time of West German rearmament, the Federal Republic constraints were fixed in the Western European United Treaty, in which the FRG agreed that it would not produce atomic, biological or chemical weapons, and in the Non-Proliferation Treaty. Legal limitations are underscored by a broad political consensus at the elite and public level. Public opinion polls show no evidence of a desire to change the FRG's non-nuclear status.[3] On the contrary, the debates in the early 1980s over deployments of NATO intermediate-range nuclear forces (INF) revealed an abiding ambivalence regarding nuclear weapons and Western deterrence strategy in general. West Germans may chaff at the difficulties inherent in dependence on the nuclear deterrent power of the United States, but few see the acquisition of nuclear weapons as an acceptable or viable option. For the above reasons, issues of nuclear weapons and strategy, though critical to the West German–French defense dialogue, will remain politically sensitive and fraught with difficulties.

Division and 'front-line' status

The division of Germany into two separate states has given the West Germans a special interest in maintaining good relations with the East; at the same time, its position as the 'front-line' state most directly exposed to Soviet military threats generates a sense of unique vulnerability. In the first case, leaders in Bonn are forced to consider the potential impact of any policy initiative in the security realm of the Federal Republic's relations with the East. In the postwar period, West German leaders of all political parties claim that national interest and identity place the FRG firmly in the Western camp; but since the early 1970s and the advent of Bonn's successful *Ostpolitik*, all political parties have come to support a policy of dialogue and cooperation with the FRG's Eastern neighbors, in particular the German Democratic Republic. On the other hand, with regard to defense policy more specifically, lacking strategic depth, Bonn's leaders insist on NATO's strict adherence to forward defense. Moreover, painfully cognizant of the fact that any war fought in Central Europe necessarily would involve German territory and entail widespread destruction, they are equally insistent on the primacy of deterrence of any war, conventional, or nuclear.

NEW IMPETUS FOR FRANCO-GERMAN COOPERATION

As a rule, interest in greater defense cooperation with France has been very limited. The exception was a brief flurry of activity in the early 1960s, but this was attributable in large measure to Chancellor Konrad Adenauer, a noted francophile with a personal interest in forging better relations between the FRG and France. Adenauer's primary achievement in this area was the completion of the Franco-German treaty, which was intended to provide the basis for cooperation in security affairs and other areas. The Franco-German (Elysée) Treaty, signed on 22 January 1963, advanced three explicit goals for cooperation in security affairs. Specifically, the Treaty called for (1) 'shared concepts in strategy and tactics'; (2) a more intensive exchange of personnel, namely officers and instructors at the respective general staff training academies; and (3) greater efforts to coordinate the planning and financing of arms production.[4]

Yet it was twenty years before the security portion of the Elysée Treaty was activated. During the months following the signing of the treaty, Adenauer's plan for a Bonn–Paris axis gave way before the forces of Atlanticism in the Federal Republic. On 16 March 1963, the Bundestag voted unanimously to attach a preamble to the Elysée Treaty, which listed the major foreign policy goals of the Federal Republic as: close relations with the United States; cooperation with NATO; and the integration of Western Europe, including Britain. De Gaulle took strong offense at the new preamble, which he viewed as a violation of the spirit of the Treaty. Six months later, Ludwig Erhard replaced Adenauer as West Germany Chancellor. Relations between the two countries entered a period of prolonged tension, aggravated in large measure by France's withdrawal in 1967 from the NATO integrated command, which further complicated cooperation in security affairs. The Treaty's security clause was forgotten.

In short, despite the goals laid down in the Elysée Treaty, the Federal Republic and France remained divided by significant differences in military thinking. Cooperation in the area of arms production was the only (relatively) bright spot, and even here progress had come in fits and starts. Early successes (the HOT, MILAN, and *Roland* tactical missiles and the *Alpha* military trainer jet) had been followed by a series of marked failures, including a joint tank venture in the 1970s, which former Chancellor Helmut Schmidt had backed personally.[5]

Developments in the late 1970s and early 1980s, revived interest at the elite level in the possibility of Franco-German defense cooperation. A long series of German–American irritations provided the catalyst for Schmidt's overture to Paris.

President Carter's reversal in 1978 on the deployment of enhanced radiation weapons (ERW) in the Federal Republic, and the American boycott of the Olympic Games in 1980 had been major irritants in relations between Bonn and Washington. The situation was aggravated by the ongoing Polish crisis and the imposition of martial law in December 1981, and Soviet missile deployments.

These specific incidents, however, were merely symptomatic of an underlying and recurring problem in relations between the United States and the Federal Republic. Beyond the personality clashes between Helmut Schmidt and Jimmy Carter, there was growing mutual irritation at what each side perceived to be the shortcomings of the other's national decision-making and leadership style. The problem persists. American leaders often charge the West Germans with considerable naiveté in their dealings with the Soviet Union, and argue that détente should not be preserved at all costs. The West Germans, for their part, cite the never ending struggle between the American executive and legislative branches, which, they argue, results in erratic policy swings. Further, they are critical of the perceived heavy-handedness of American leadership, and the overly moralistic tone and unduly ideological nature of policy toward the Soviet Union. Coming from a country with a strong tradition of professional civil service, West German policy-makers criticize the American system for its failure to reward knowledge or expertise in forcing affairs. A recurring complaint is the American lack of *Gesamtkonzept* – a grand strategy – which, in the German view, results in continuous policy reversals, contradictions and discontinuities. From the West German perspective, continuing American hostility toward the Soviet Union, a perceived propensity on the part of US leadership to take unilateral decisions, and a generally deteriorating East–West climate may threaten to place severe constraints on Bonn's ability to sustain a dual policy of Western defense solidarity and détente with the East. Schmidt was expressing a view more broadly shared when he later reported a sense of growing frustration at being held hostage to the whims of erratic and unpredictable American leaders.

Nevertheless, in Schmidt's view, the blame did not entirely lie with the United States leadership. Schmidt believed that the Europeans, in failing to coordinate their foreign policies and actions more closely, were partly to blame for American unilateralism; European submissiveness only encouraged this tendency. The solution lay in a European counterweight to American influence within the Alliance, and the key to such an endeavor was in Paris.[6] Coordination of French and German foreign and security policy, in Schmidt's view, would give both countries an added weight and recognition that neither could achieve alone. Schmidt maintained that neither he nor the then French president Valéry Giscard d'Estaing questioned the continued importance of the Alliance but, as Schmidt wrote later, 'We did not want to allow our nations to be reduced to client states that would be dependent on ever-changing American moods and trends.'[7]

Schmidt's close relationship with Giscard was probably critical in the evolution of the West German leader's thinking. First as Finance Ministers, then heads of government, Schmidt and Giscard gradually intensified cooperation between the two countries developing over time a close working relationship and personal friendship. The first area marked for action had been economic policy, but substantive discussions on security policy followed.[8] By Schmidt's account, the two gradually came to a unity of views on the need to reconcile Franco-German differences in military thinking. In Schmidt's words, 'We had no illusions about the difficulties, at home and abroad, that would have to be overcome,' but they hoped that 'the depressing experience of two unpredictable American presidents' would help to persuade publics of the need for change.[9] Concrete measures were to be taken as soon as Schmidt and Giscard had secured re-election, in 1980 and 1981 respectively.

Schmidt was not deterred by Giscard's loss in the French national elections. Despite the change in leadership in May 1981, Schmidt remained convinced of the need to extend the scope of bilateral cooperation to the more sensitive areas of security and defense. At the close of the routine Franco-German political consultations on 24 and 25 February 1982, Schmidt and Mitterrand announced that 'in the spirit of the Elysée Treaty', the two governments would begin more intensive discussions on security issues.[10]

In October 1982, Schmidt's governing social-liberal coalition (SPD–FDP) collapsed, leaving the fate of the Franco-German security dialogue uncertain. The new Christian Democratic Chancellor, Helmut Kohl, however, quickly embraced Schmidt's initiative as his own. To emphasize the special importance to be accorded the FRG's relations with France, Kohl made his first visit to Paris on 6 October 1982, before he had even taken the official oath of office in Bonn.[11] Two weeks later at the fall Franco-German summit on 21–22 October, 1983, Chancellor Kohl and French President François Mitterrand announced at a joint press conference the decision to activate the Elysée Treaty's security clause formally.[12]

In part, Kohl may have been motivated by a genuine commitment to the idea of closer relations between France and the FRG. Kohl, it should be remembered, is a dedicated Atlanticist, but, born in the Rhineland and a Catholic, he also has a special affinity for France (not unlike his mentor Konrad Adenauer). Kohl also is known to be an impulsive and sometimes emotional leader, who acts at times without fully thinking through initiatives to their logical conclusions. Kohl's initial trip to France symbolized the new Chancellor's commitment to the Franco-German entente.

While Kohl's initial resolve to enhance Franco-German defense cooperation may have been based on a deep emotional commitment to the process of European integration and rapprochement with France, he also had more pragmatic reasons for following in the footsteps of his predecessor. Despite Kohl's lofty words on Franco-German friendship and European unity on that first and subsequent occasions, the new Chancellor was interested in securing French support in the short term for a difficult *West German* political agenda. The new coalition (Christian Democratic Union/Christian Social Union-Free Democratic Party) came to power committed to implementing the 1979 NATO dual-track INF decision; in the event that the United States and the Soviet Union failed to reach an arms control agreement in Geneva, the deployment of INF was scheduled to begin in late 1983 and the decision promised to be difficult to implement. Facing a large and vocal anti-nuclear movement at home, and sensing a broad domestic need for reassuring actions, Kohl may have followed through on the Schmidt initiative in the hope of securing what one commentator aptly termed 'protection on the flanks'.[13] In return for French support, first of the INF deployment in the FRG and, second, of West Germany's uninterrupted dialogue with the East, Kohl was prepared to back Mitterrand's position that French nuclear systems be excluded from arms control negotiations in Geneva. Visible expressions of solidarity between Paris and Bonn in support of the INF decision would demonstrate to a skeptical West German public the broad European support of the Alliance commitment.

If Kohl's short-term concern was to shore up support for NATO in a highly charged and emotional atmosphere, his longer-term goals remained somewhat obscure in the early months of his administration. Kohl's strident declarations on the unchanged primacy of German–American defense relations hinted at unwavering support for the status quo arrangement, rather than a conversion to a belief in a 'Gaullist' security alternative. Subsequently, aside from periodic bursts of activity, usually at the time of regular Franco-German consultations, the new enthusiasm for Franco-German cooperation gradually died down over the course of Kohl's first term as Chancellor.

Developments in late 1986 and spring 1987 provoked a spate of new proposals for Franco-German defense cooperation. The radical arms control proposals nearly agreed to by President Reagan at the November 1986 US–Soviet summit in Reykjavik shocked the West German government deeply. In the eyes of the CDU/CSU, the sense of trust between the two Conservative governments had been betrayed. Above all, there was a sense that West German interests had not been adequately considered nor Bonn's leaders sufficiently consulted. As if to add insult to injury, in the spring of 1987 the Americans made clear their desire to accept Soviet leader Michail Gorbachev's 'double-zero' proposal to remove all intermediate-range nuclear forces with a range greater than 500 km from Europe. Though the party rank-and-file and the majority of CDU/CSU parliamentarians favored the proposal, a number of prominent party figures did not. Volker Ruehe, the party's moderate foreign policy spokesman in the Bundestag, in the past had been a steady supporter of arms control, but in the ensuing debate he came out as a vocal opponent to the Soviet offer, even making a solo trip to Washington to try to convince American policy-makers of the folly of accepting the Soviet proposal. Ruehe predictably was joined in his opposition by the Conservatives Alfred Dregger and Franz Josef Strauss.

With some reservations, the government eventually acquiesced to the US position, but the episode, coming in the wake of Reykjavik, left some CDU members bitter and disappointed with the US leadership. In June 1987, a series of new proposals for Franco-German defense cooperation surfaced. Conservative *Fraktion* leader Alfred Dregger proposed in a meeting of the CDU Executive in June 1987 the creation of a Franco-German 'security union'. For Dregger, the INF dispute was the final proof that the Americans could not be relied upon. Discontent within the party may have spurred Kohl to propose the formation of a Franco-German combat brigade under French leadership. In a speech before French socialists at the Sorbonne, former Chancellor Helmut Schmidt, apparently sensing the atmosphere ripe, repeated his proposal for a fully integrated conventional force.[14]

The revival of interest in Franco-German defense cooperation in 1982–83, and again in 1987, was linked inextricably to external developments, in particular the actions of US leaders. The broader political climate at home and abroad had altered West German perceptions of American reliability. At issue were the future adequacy of existing arrangements to deter a foreign enemy *and* reassure the West German population. Fundamental elements of Bonn's security position had not changed between 1962 and 1982, but there was growing frustration in Bonn over American actions and a perceptible shift in the policy conclusions drawn by West German political leaders. The decision to explore the possibility of closer cooperation with France grew out of the security debates of the 1980s, in which existing security arrangements were scrutinized and widely varying alternatives proposed.

WEST GERMAN OBJECTIVES

The Franco-German security dialogue serves two separate policy agendas. The first encompasses genuine security goals, the second political goals of both foreign and domestic policy. In general terms, Bonn seeks to bind France to the defense of West Germany (in effect, a functional reintegration of France into the NATO integrated command); to improve Western European defense capabilities; or, at a minimum, to put in place an infrastructure for bilateral consultation and planning. From these three broad objectives, it is possible to identify more specific goals with regard to nuclear strategy and issues, conventional defenses, and arms cooperation. The second, 'hidden' agenda aims to secure greater leverage for Bonn *vis-à-vis* the United States and, on the domestic front, to relieve growing frustration and dissatisfaction with American actions and leadership. The objectives of each policy agenda are discussed in greater detail below.

Broad security objectives
The overarching aim of Franco-German cooperation is to bind France to the defense of the Federal Republic, particularly in the area of conventional planning. Since France's withdrawal from the NATO integrated command in 1966, French troops have remained in the FRG under a separate agreement with the Bonn government, but Paris has guarded jealously its autonomy in nuclear and conventional defense planning. All West German political parties (with the exception of the Greens) more or less accept France's independence in this regard and disavow publicly any desire to bring Paris back into the NATO integrated command structure, but they are increasingly adamant on the need for Paris to clarify the role which French forces, nuclear and conventional, would play in the event of an attack on the central front. Recent evidence of this sentiment is found in the domestic debate surrounding the Soviet 'double-zero' offer to remove all intermediate nuclear forces with a range of 500–5000 km from Europe. Alfred Dregger, chairman of the CDU/CSU Bundestag *Fraktion*, criticized President Mitterrand's pledge to 'consult' the West German government before the use of French 'pre-strategic' weapons as woefully inadequate, and called instead for a formal accord to govern their use.[15] In short, Bonn seeks visible reassurance, in specific and practical measures, that Paris sees its security as indivisible from that of the FRG, and is willing to plan and act accordingly.

Second, most West Germans perceive Franco-German cooperation as part of a broader effort to improve European cooperation on defense. West German leaders hope that cooperation in the conventional field will contribute to the harmonization of European defense policies and the more efficient use of scarce resources. Arms cooperation, joint research ventures in high technology, or European initiatives in space technology are intended to maintain a sufficient technological base to remain competitive in a variety of defense and civilian industries. Most West Germans agree that France and Germany must reconcile their differences on defense if Western Europe is to achieve greater autonomy in security affairs to counter the preponderant weight of the United States within the Alliance, let alone create a distinct West European defense identity.

At the very least, cooperation is designed to create an infrastructure and procedures for bilateral consultations on strategy, military procurement, and industrial and technological collaboration. To this end, the Kohl government already has concluded a number of agreements with Paris to regularize and institutionalize the bilateral defense dialogue. The two countries agreed in October 1982 to create a steering committee, composed of high-ranking ministerial officials, to oversee all discussions of bilateral cooperation. Three working groups were formed to deal with strategy, military cooperation and arms procurement, respectively. In January 1986, they further agreed that representatives of the two nations' Foreign Ministries would meet monthly and would include officers from the respective arms control divisions. In a similar vein, Kohl and Mitterrand laid down general guidelines for greater operational cooperation between the French and German armed forces, specifically, plans for joint maneuvers and joint officer training. In 1985, 1986 and 1987, Franco-German maneuvers of increasing size and scope were held in successive autumns. While these measures are modest in scope, they nevertheless demonstrate a desire to improve and routinize the procedures for a bilateral security dialogue, regardless of Bonn's longer-term goals.[16]

Nuclear strategy and issues

From the outset, most West German political leaders have been very clear about what Franco-German cooperation in the nuclear field is *not* intended to accomplish: namely, a French substitute for the American nuclear deterrent. Most West Germans take the view that as long as the Federal Republic remains dependent on the threatened use of nuclear weapons for its defense, the FRG has no alternative but to rely on the American nuclear deterrent. Despite some signs of changes in French thinking, political and defense elites generally share the skeptical view of France's commitment to West German defense. The West German public has little reason to believe France to be a more credible guarantor of its security than the United States, or one more reticent to use nuclear weapons targeted on West German soil. Consequently, neither the current government in Bonn nor the opposition have demanded a formal pledge from Paris to extend the 'deterrent effect: of the *force de frappe* to West German national territory'.[17] Furthermore, Bonn has sought deliberately to avoid creating the impression in Washington of a Franco-American trade-off. In 1963, the Bundestag refused to ratify the Elysée Treaty without first adding a preamble which reaffirmed Bonn's commitment to a defense within NATO, and the integration of West German armed forces in the Alliance.[18] This has become a pattern in Franco-German cooperation. Following the announcement of the treaty's reactivation in October 1982, for example, Kohl reaffirmed the FRG's continued allegiance to security cooperation with the United States, saying that there could be no policy of 'either' Franco–German 'or' German–American defense cooperation for the FRG.[19] Subsequently, each symbolic step in Franco-German relations has been accompanied by official West German proclamations of the central importance of the German–American defense connection.

Official statements similarly reject any aspirations toward German national control over French nuclear weapons. Even though the reactivation of the Elysée Treaty prompted speculation that Bonn now had nuclear aspirations, these are not borne out by governmental or CDU/CSU statements.[20] A majority of West German leaders would seem to support the view expressed by Defense Minister Manfred Woerner that security cooperation with France has nothing to do with forming a Franco-German 'nuclear axis'.[21]

The opposition, for its part, does not seek any form of nuclear collaboration whatsoever. The Social Democratic Party, with its current emphasis on the reduced reliance on nuclear weapons for German defense, and broad East–West European cooperation, has little interest in a bilateral nuclear force or a German finger on the French (or US) nuclear trigger.

With regard to French tactical nuclear weapons, West German aims are more specific, if similarly restrained. At a minimum, most West Germans desire more detailed information and clarification on plans for the use of French short-range systems which, by definition, would be employed over West (and East) German territory. With regard to French strategic forces, the principle of French independence is generally accepted, but when it comes to the potential use of French tactical forces (*Hades* and *Pluton* missiles) West German leaders insist on Bonn's right at least to be consulted beforehand. From the West German perspective, consultations on strategy and tactics are intended to determine, specifically, where, when and under what circumstances French tactical nuclear weapons would be used in the defense of the FRG. Such information would provide the basis for operational coordination of West German and NATO plans with French defense planning. In this connection, West Germans welcomed the French pledge in February 1986 to 'consult' Bonn before using tactical nuclear weapons on West German soil. Woerner hailed French Defense Minister Hernu's reference to defense of the FRG as a French 'vital interest' as a sign that French leaders no longer view the FRG simply as a French glacis.[22]

Last, most West Germans favor better coordination of French and German positions on arms control, in particular negotiations on the reduction of conventional forces in Europe. Most would like to see a greater willingness on the part of the French to participate in the arms control process.

Conventional

The primary West German objectives in the conventional field are to enhance Western conventional capabilities and thereby reduce reliance on the early first use of nuclear weapons. To this end, Bonn seeks a clear commitment of French conventional forces to the forward defense of the FRG. The focal point of much discussion has been the French *force d'action rapide* (FAR). Bonn's aim is to obtain a commitment from France and work out detailed plans to bring in French troops more rapidly and further forward in the event of hostilities in Central Europe.[23] The CDU/CSU-FDP government has sought agreement on practical measures to incorporate French forces in West German defense planning, training and logistics. These include plans to hold more joint Franco-German maneuvers with the participation of the French FAR, exchanges of senior officers and military personnel, and joint officer training. In general, the Social Democrats have supported governmental initiatives in the conventional field.

Armaments cooperation

Arms cooperation with France is intended to serve a variety of military, economic and political objectives. To begin, bilateral co-production arrangements must be seen as part of a broader West German effort to link the conventional efforts of the two nations in a more effective manner. The synchronization of French and German defense procurement plans and financing is intended to promote inter-operability and standardization of respective national weapons systems. Second, in times of growing budgetary stringencies, most West German leaders view Franco–German arms cooperation as a means of ensuring more efficient use of defense resources. For most, if not all European countries, sole production of any major defense item entails a substantial and politically controversial financial burden on overstrained state resources. The current West German government, in which Finance Minister Gerhard Stoltenberg has kept a tight hand on budgetary strings, is no exception. The aim is to identify areas of joint need, to eliminate duplicate research, development and production efforts, and to exploit economies of scale.

West German leaders stress the economic and political side-benefits of bilateral (Franco-German) or multilateral (European) arms cooperation as well. Co-production is perceived as one means of maintaining the viability of national defense industries, ensuring their continued competitiveness in the world export market, and increasing the overall European share of weapons purchases within NATO. Additionally, Franco-German arms cooperation, like collaboration space and technology research, may be seen as part of a broader effort to increasingly 'Europeanize' West German defense and lend the FRG and Europe more influence *vis-à-vis* the United States.

Other political objectives

Under the Kohl government, the Franco-German security dialogue has been used as a tool to manage relations with the United States. New initiatives in the area of Franco-German defense cooperation, such as Schmidt's original overture to Paris or, more recently, Kohl's proposal in June 1987 to create a Franco-German combat brigade, followed closely on the heels of German–American frictions. Largely symbolic as they may be, such gestures may function as visible reminders to American policy-makers of West German dissatisfaction with US policies; they also may be intended to provide Bonn with a source of leverage *vis-à-vis* the United States in a more general sense.

Governmental support for Franco-German initiatives has been targeted at a domestic audience as well. In the eyes of Conservative members of the CDU/CSU, the American response to Soviet proposals at the Reykjavik summit, and Washington's rapid acceptance of the 'double-zero' proposal have become symbols of American unreliability and disregard for West German security interests. In at least one instance, criticism of American policies from the party's right wing was capped by a call to 'reorient' Bonn's security policy toward greater cooperation with France.[24] Franco-German initiatives, such as Kohl's proposal to create a Franco–German combat brigade or ongoing negotiations to create a joint military council may be partially intended to silence anti-American voices within the Chancellor's own party.

In an even broader sense, the Franco-German dialogue functions as a safety-valve to relieve domestic frustration with American policies. If the public perceives that the United States has treated Bonn 'unfairly', the result may be a backlash of anti-Americanism. Greater defense cooperation with France is one way of demonstrating to the West German public that Bonn can and will act independently of the United States. The latter, it is hoped, will defuse anti-American feeling and shore up domestic support for the FRG's membership in NATO and own national defense efforts.

SPECIAL PERSPECTIVES

Beyond the general consensus described above, West German perspectives on Franco-German defense cooperation vary considerably across the political spectrum. As political parties differ on the best policy to enhance West German security, naturally they assign different long-term goals and varying degrees of priority to Franco-German defense cooperation. Moreover, depending on the political party, one area or another of cooperation may be targeted for greater efforts, for example, conventional defense efforts in the case of the SPD, arms control in the case of the FDP. In short, special perspectives on Franco-German defense cooperation fall in line with partisan positions on security policy broadly defined. The views of a political party's leaders or defense experts tend to reflect related positions on nuclear weapons and strategy, the German-American security relationship, and the role of a European defense identity either within the current NATO framework or under some alternative security arrangement.

Four special perspectives on Franco-German defense cooperation are examined below: (1) Christian Democratic Party; (2) Hans-Dietrich Genscher (Free Democratic Party); (3) Social Democratic Party; and (4) former Chancellor Helmut Schmidt.

CDU/CSU

Most members of the CDU/CSU view Franco-German defense cooperation as an insurance against dependence on the US and the failure of present security arrangements. Cooperation is another means of giving Western Europe more influence, politically and economically, vis-à-vis the United States, but, generally speaking, expectations of significant military benefit are low. Consequently, aside from largely symbolic gestures and praise for the idea of the Franco-German partnership, defense cooperation with France traditionally has been given rather low priority within the party. In fact, the party rank-and-file or members of the parliamentary *Fraktion* have shown little interest in the Franco-German defense relationship. Except for a very few vocal members of the party's small group of defense experts, few initiatives for security cooperation with France have originated in party circles.[25]

This relative lack of enthusiasm is rooted in the parties' traditional emphasis on the German–American relationship and the maintenance of an adequate and credible deterrent. The historical triumph in the 1960s of the party's 'Atlanticists' over the 'Gaullists' has resulted in a deep-rooted bias in favor of cooperation with Washington over Paris. The debate, then as now, was over the degree to which the FRG can and should depend on the United States' nuclear guarantee for its ultimate security. The 'Atlanticists' argue that there is no alternative in a bipolar world to the United States as the final guarantor of West German security. In this view, Franco-German or European efforts may be allowed to supplement the German–American axis, but never to threaten or supplant the vital defense link between the FRG and the United States. For the Christian Democrats, it is an iron law: the US–West German defense link must not be endangered in any way.

This view, though recently more greatly contested, still prevails in CDU/CSU security policy, and helps to explain the party's relatively low expectations and minimal interest in pursuing truly *substantive* defense cooperation with France. The majority of party members support the principle of greater cooperation with Paris but, beyond that, have only modest aims. The emphasis is on small steps: procedures to ensure West German consultation on the use of French tactical nuclear weapons; more detailed plans for the incorporation of the French FAR in the defense of Germany; steady progress on joint arms production measures, either bilaterally, or in concert with other European allies. Above all, any initiatives for Franco-German cooperation, at least at the declaratory level, must not be seen as a challenge to current security structures. France is to be integrated into defense planning for NATO and the FRG without altering the nature of existing arrangements.

Kohl's objectives are more unclear. On one level, Kohl may indeed embrace the notion of Franco-German cooperation, but at least until now, he has often failed to follow up symbolic gestures or statements of solidarity with substantive action. Kohl has made a concerted effort to avoid being forced into a situation (or the appearance of one) in which a choice between Paris and Washington would be necessary. In the view of one analyst, Kohl has not fully worked out how far he would be prepared to go in defense cooperation with France. Instead, he has attempted to satisfy both allies at once. At the routine Franco-German consultations, held every spring and autumn in Bonn and Paris alternately, almost every announcement on Franco-German defense cooperation has been paired with a reference to the continued importance of the American defense connection. Moreover, he dismissed suggestions in June 1987 from within his own party, that France and West Germany strive to create a bilateral or trilateral 'security union' under the French nuclear umbrella. Reiterating the formula first espoused in January 1983, Kohl repeated that there is no policy of 'either/or' for the Federal Republic; defense cooperation with France can never replace the American nuclear guarantee.[26]

In the conventional field, the CDU/CSU has supported modest governmental measures to improve the integration of West German and French forces. These have included steps to increase the number of joint maneuvers and training, and the exchange of officers.

In an unusual departure, Chancellor Kohl in June 1987 made a more ambitious proposal to create a German–French combat brigade. The proposal followed a period of intense controversy between the coalition parties and in the CDU/CSU over acceptance or rejection of the Soviet 'double-zero' proposal. Kohl was not specific about the precise design for the brigade and critics were quick to point out the organization, linguistic and other difficulties. The proposal's primary value, however, lay in its symbolism; it was at the same time a signal to the French of Kohl's continued interest in defense cooperation and to the Americans of the government's lingering frustration with the handling of the INF episode.

On technological cooperation, the CDU/CSU has tended to favor the United States over France. The party majority doubts whether cooperation with France will bring worthwhile returns. They consider collaboration with the United States a more cost-effective use of scarce funds. Faced with the choice of participation in the American Strategic Defense Initiative (SDI) or the French-proposed European Research Initiative (Eureka), Chancellor Kohl and Defense Minister Manfred Woerner displayed a clear preference for cooperation with the United States. Bavarian leader Franz Josef Strauss, similarly, supported a West German role in SDI, and cautioned against dividing scarce resources between the two projects. The concern was well founded. Finance Minister Gerhard Stoltenberg was strongly opposed to governmental subsidies to support participation in the Eureka research program.[27]

Only a handful of CDU/CSU defense experts assign greater priority to Franco-German defense cooperation. This group, led by *Fraktion* leader Alfred Dregger, draws on the party's Gaullist tradition and, thus, is more apt to voice doubts about the durability and reliability of the American defense commitment. Dregger has been one of the strongest proponents within the party of an European defense community, built around a Franco-German axis, as an alternative to the current defense structure of NATO. Following the controversy in spring 1987 over Bonn's response to the Soviet INF proposals, Dregger argued that the FRG should 'reorient' its security policy toward the achievement of a Franco-German 'security union'. In Dregger's view, American pressure on Bonn and Washington's blatant disregard for West German security interests was indicative of a longer-term trend toward disengagement from Europe. The policy implications are clear: France must be persuaded to extend its nuclear umbrella to West German territory, and NATO restructured. In this vein, Dregger supports the notion of a French rather than an American Supreme Allied Commander in Europe (SACEUR). The Alliance would continue to exist as a political union, but its military function and organization would be changed fundamentally.[28]

Nuclear issues typically play a prominent role in Dregger's thinking on Franco-German defense cooperation. Dregger, along with CSU leader Franz Josef Strauss, has been highly critical of French independence in nuclear strategy and targeting and has made more strident demands than others within the party with regard to French nuclear forces. 'Consultation' on the use of French tactical weapons is said to be inadequate, because they are directed at targets in 'Germany', a term which includes implicitly both the Federal Republic and the German Democratic Republic. In Dregger's words, France's refusal to commit its nuclear weapons to the defense of the FRG and Europe makes a mockery of Franco-German cooperation or European solidarity: 'Talk of German–French friendship lacks credibility when it does not include vital questions of defense.'[29]

Two points must be kept in mind with regard to Dregger's goals and his influence within the party. First, the group which supports these more ambitious demands and goals is a tiny minority within the party. As stated above, the number of party members with knowledge of and expertise of defense matters is small; and even within this group, Dregger represents a clear minority. At present, Dregger's views hold little sway either with other defense experts, with current party leaders, the *Fraktion*, or with the party rank-and-file. Without mentioning Dregger by name, Kohl immediately rejected the notion that France could ever replace the United States defense connection.[30] In all likelihood, Dregger's ambitious plans for Franco-German defense cooperation are aimed at stirring debate within the party.

Free Democratic Party (FDP)/Hans-Dietrich Genscher

The position of the Free Democratic Party with regard to the objectives for Franco-German cooperation is best represented as the views of the party's premier foreign policy spokesman, and West German Foreign Minister, Hans-Dietrich Genscher. The promotion of Franco-German cooperation across a broad spectrum of security issues has become a clear foreign policy priority for Genscher. In the long term, Genscher views Franco-German defense relations as the key to a separate, European security identity, and greater European influence within Europe and in the global arena. In Genscher's words, a Franco-German 'security community' (*Sicherheitsgemeinschaft*) is to serve as the catalyst (*Kristallisationspunkt*) for European identity.[31]

Consistent with Genscher's more general emphasis on security issues, arms control has played a prominent role in Genscher's initiatives for greater security cooperation with France. Like other West German leaders, Genscher has not challenged French independence with regard to nuclear strategy and decision-making, nor has he insisted on including French nuclear forces in strategic arms control negotiations in Geneva. Genscher's recent efforts have been directed at ensuring French participation in European talks on convention arms control.[32] He supported French initiatives to create a new forum for such negotiations within the CSCE framework and independent from intra-alliance negotiations. Other initiatives bearing Genscher's stamp include measures to facilitate the coordination of the two countries' arms control positions through the exchange of Foreign Office personnel assigned to respective arms control desks. In a highly symbolic gesture, Genscher appeared with his French counterpart before the opening session of the ninth round of the CDE conference in Stockholm.[33]

Genscher has been a forceful proponent of collaborative research efforts in space and technology. The Foreign Minister was an early supporter of West German participation in Eureka. Similarly, Genscher has emphasized the importance of FRG participation in French plans to build the *Ariane V* rocket and the space shuttle, *Hermes*, and has made a concerted effort to soothe French irritation over the government's refusals to commit formally to cooperative space ventures.[34] Franco-German cooperation in space and technology research, in Genscher's view, is vital if Europe is to remain competitive in important areas of technology. Without this, Europe can never attain greater autonomy and independence *vis-à-vis* the United States. The Foreign Minister's support for cooperation projects is consistent with his desire to develop a separate and independent European security identity within the Atlantic Alliance.[35]

Social Democratic Party

The Social Democrats have displayed little enthusiasm or even interest in Franco-German defense cooperation. In part, this is due to the party's preoccupation with unresolved internal divisions and the problem of leadership succession. Successive electoral losses at the national level in 1983 and again in 1987 have contributed to a general sense of disarray within the party and indecision as to the party's future course. The party is divided between a left-wing faction, now in the majority, and a more conservative group with solid support in the trade unions. This division is mirrored at the leadership level as well. Willy Brandt, the longstanding chairman of the Social Democrats, stepped down in June 1987. The new chairman is Hans-Jochen Vogel, a moderate and head of the SPD *Fraktion*; his deputies are Johannes Rau, the 1987 Chancellor candidate, whose support is concentrated in the trade unions, and Oskar Lafontaine, premier of the Saar and favorite of the party's left wing.

The party's relatively low level of interest in Franco-German defense cooperation is related as well to recent changes in the party's security policy. In the early 1980s, the SPD was rent by dissension over the party's support of the NATO dual-track decision. In response to widespread pressure from within the party, the SPD formed a commission to review the party's policy on West German security. The resulting document, approved in April 1986, put forth the major tenets of a policy of 'common security' or 'security partnership'. The SPD called for a broad range of cooperative initiatives with the Soviet Union and Eastern Europe. The party proposed the creation of a nuclear weapon-free corridor in Central Europe, and drastic reductions (and the eventual elimination) of all intermediate-range nuclear weapons, including French and British systems, in Europe. In the conventional field, the party advocates revisions in NATO strategy and a restructuring of its forces to create a 'defensive deterrent capability'. The Bundeswehr would be restructured into smaller, skeletonized units with greater reliance on territorial units of trained reservists.[36]

The Social Democrats' program for security fails to address Franco-German defense cooperation directly; moreover, many of the party's policies clearly conflict with French security notions. The divergence of views is particularly acute with regard to issues of nuclear weapons and strategy. Like other parties, the SPD has criticized French targeting policy and refusal to participate in arms control initiatives. The party generally is critical of the idea of an extended French nuclear deterrent for the FRG. In the view of party defense specialist Hermann Scheer, though admittedly unlikely, 'extended sanctuary' would entail an 'unacceptable price' for the FRG. The SPD is critical of France's positions on arms control as well. At a time when the SPD would like to see a reduced reliance on nuclear weapons in general and the elimination of tactical nuclear weapons from Europe, France is engaged in a build-up and modernization of its nuclear forces. On the whole, the party appears deeply skeptical about Franco-German cooperation in the nuclear field.[37] While the SPD would welcome clarification and information on French targeting policy, the SPD's overall de-emphasis on nuclear weapons puts the Social Democrats at odds with French priorities.

The Social Democrats have been more willing to consider conventional defense cooperation with France, which is more easily reconcilable with the party's security policy. The SPD would welcome a French commitment of its forces to defense at the inter-German border. Conventional cooperation, in the party's view, must be translated into practical measures to include French armed forces, including reservists, in plans for the defense of Central Europe. The party's 'joint European initiative', introduced in the Bundestag in March 1987, calls for greater cooperation with France in the conventional field. But the party has insisted on the principle of non-singularity; Franco-German defense cooperation must be supplemented by closer collaboration with Britain and the Federal Republic's other European allies.[38]

The Social Democrats have endorsed joint ventures in research and technology. The party was adamantly opposed to West German participation in the SDI, and urged the government to embrace the French initiative for a European research program in non-military high-technology products (Eureka). In March 1987, the party called on the government to reconsider its rejection of an earlier French proposal to build a reconnaissance satellite, meant to reduce dependence on the United States for intelligence information. The Social Democrats' support for the latter project is couched in terms of the need to establish a basis for 'equality of status' in the Alliance, but may be related as well to the desire to create a separate intelligence capability to support an independent European arms control policy.[39]

Helmut Schmidt

The initiator of the Franco-German security dialogue, former Chancellor Helmut Schmidt, today occupies a rather anomolous position. Within the Social Democratic Party, Schmidt's views hold little sway; his stature is so diminished that the party at periodic party conferences routinely fails to acknowledge the accomplishments of its former Chancellor.[40] Consequently, Schmidt's statements on bilateral cooperation with France seem targeted at a broader audience: political elites in the Federal Republic and abroad. As co-publisher of the West German economic and political weekly, *Die Zeit*, Schmidt has a readily available platform from which to espouse his views on a variety of political and economic topics.

In a series of significant statements, Schmidt took up the topic of Franco-German cooperation in some detail.[41] Schmidt has a fondness for 'grand strategies' and Franco-German defense cooperation is no exception. In Schmidt's view, overdependence on the United States is unsustainable. 'Europe' must become a reality. In

Schmidt's vision, France is the only appropriate choice to lead Europe, for it alone possesses the requisite diplomatic and political influence, and military might. The Federal Republic, still constrained by a turbulent German history, cannot embrace this role; Great Britain, jealous of its 'special relationship' with the United States and still ambivalent with regard to Europe, will not; Italy and the smaller European nations are unsuitable as well.

Schmidt has become one of the strongest advocates of defense cooperation with France. Building on his original ideas, Schmidt has developed an ambitious proposal for a Franco-German conventional army under French command. Such a bilateral force, Schmidt argues, would be sufficient to deter any Soviet conventional military threat, and would reduce NATO reliance on the use of nuclear weapons. Though cognizant of the additional financial burden that such restructuring would require, Schmidt believes it is a price that West Germans must be willing to pay. The Western Alliance would not be fully disbanded; the European pillar would require a link to the forces of the United States and Canada. Schmidt has suggested that France extend its nuclear guarantee to the Federal Republic. In exchange, the FRG, with its vast economic resources, should be prepared to help finance French nuclear forces.

Schmidt advocates extensive technological cooperation with France as well. In a series of letters sent in spring 1985 to all political party chairmen (Helmut Kohl, Martin Bangemann and Willy Brandt) and parliamentary *Fraktion* leaders (Alfred Dregger, Wolfgang Mischnick and Hans-Jochen Vogel), Schmidt warned against participation in SDI, which would deplete funds available for joint projects with France. He advised closer cooperation with Paris, even to the extent of making extensive financial commitments.[42] .

CONSTRAINTS

From the West German perspective, future Franco-German defense cooperation will be constrained by external and internal political economical and military factors.

International
The single most powerful constraint on Bonn will continue to be the need to ensure that greater defense integration with France does not weaken the US defense link. Doubts about the long-term reliability of the US guarantee provoked the search for alternatives in the first place. To do nothing may be dangerous, if Bonn's worst fears are realized. Yet, if Bonn pushes defense cooperation with France too far, there is a concern that it may actually encourage those forces in the US that favor the withdrawal of American troops from Europe. Until now, Kohl has been careful to stress that cooperation with France is not and will never be a substitute for the United States' nuclear guarantee. Anxious to avoid making the impression that the FRG was ready to dispense with the American defense link, for example, Kohl was quick to refute Dregger's notion of a French replacement for the American nuclear umbrella.

Avoiding choice can be difficult, however. With regard to SDI and Eureka, Bonn tried to please both France and the United States. Gorbachev issued enthusiastic statements in support of the French technology initiative, Kohl postponed a final decision on participation in either program as long as possible, and Stoltenberg insisted that Bonn simply did not have the financial resources to make good on both commitments. The French were reported to be very irritated with Kohl.[43] A similar dilemma arose with regard to European space cooperation. Despite French pressure at regular meetings between Kohl and Mitterrand, Bonn refused to commit itself to participation in the preparatory phase of the French space shuttle *Hermes*. The FRG had already accepted a leading role in trans-atlantic collaborative efforts for the US space station, *Columbus*. Bonn has now agreed to limited participation in the French project, but government members are already voicing concerns about the huge outlay of funds. (The Bundestag will have to approve additional funds for the projects, estimated at DM 255 million.) Research Minister Heinz Riesenhuber is concerned that space projects will take up the lion's share of the ministry's budget, while Finance Minister Stoltenberg is considering the potential financial risks of participation in all projects.[44] On a related issue, though the Bonn government eventually may reconsider a proposal to build an advanced reconnaissance satellite, financing constraints would almost certainly ensure the project's renewed rejection.

A second major constraint concerns nuclear issues, which are centrally important to Franco-German cooperation but politically troublesome. Changes in current nuclear arrangements are unacceptable to the majority of West German political leaders. As seen by the reaction to Dregger's comments, it is still virtually a political taboo to speak of a French nuclear deterrent for the FRG, let alone Franco-German co-determination.

The extreme sensitivity that surrounds nuclear issues constitutes an effective barrier to progress in this area. The question of Germany and nuclear weapons remains Pandora's box which most West Europeans, above all the West Germans, are reluctant to open. West German political elites are cautious for a number of reasons. In the first place, Bonn would be loathe to take any steps in Franco-German defense cooperation that might seriously endanger the continuation of its dialogue with the Soviet Union and the GDR. Second, most political leaders have generally low expectations of France's willingness to compromise in this area. Last, they may sense that the West German public, already decidedly ambivalent on nuclear weapons, would not necessarily feel less at risk under a French nuclear umbrella than an American one.[45] In short, the tendency in the Federal Republic is toward increasing conventionalization of defense. Growing anti-nuclear sentiment in the FRG puts Bonn clearly at odds with France and, to the degree that Paris continues to stress reliance on nuclear forces, will constrain Franco-German defense cooperation.

Domestic factors
Domestic factors, primarily political and economic, will influence Bonn's commitment to bilateral defense cooperation. These include the nature of the governing coalition in Bonn, limits on financial resources, public opinion and leadership changes.

The pace of developments under the CDU/CSU will be affected by the evolution of the Atlanticist/Gaullist debate within the party. The difference of views between Kohl and Dregger is indicative of deeper divisions within the party over the long-term reliability of the American defense connection. Up to now, the Atlanticists have dominated the party's thinking on West German security. Dregger and other like-minded members of the CDU may hope to reorient the party's thinking toward a Franco-German alternative. But the commitment to Atlanticism is deeply rooted in the party, and is supported by a broad public consensus on membership in NATO.

Given current trends in the SPD's defense policies, any further progress in Franco-German defense cooperation would be virtually impossible if the SPD entered the government. The future of Franco-German defense cooperation would be more uncertain in the event of an SPD-led government. The party's security policies leave little room for extensive Franco-German cooperation, and the party has been insistent on the need for broader Western European initiatives. Moreover, the SPD's energies are likely to be directed toward arms control and a 'second phase of détente' with the East, two areas which would bring the party into direct conflict with France's position. In short, if the SPD continues along its present track, as must be anticipated, its foreign policy would emphasize East–West rather than West–West initiatives.

Fiscal constraints will slow or block any Franco-German initiatives which require substantial outlays of funds. Helmut Schmidt may talk of the need for West Germany to make extensive financial commitmnts to bilateral conventional defense efforts or collaborative arms and technology projects, but he stands alone in doing so. The current government is firmly committed to a policy of fiscal conservatism, which will require $4 billion cuts over four years in current defense spending plans, much less permit increases to support French programs. The Social Democrats advocate a freeze, and then gradual reduction, in defense expenditures. Of course, if a political decision is made that the long-term benefits justify short-term losses, collaborative projects may be approved, but financial constraints will make such decisions controversial and possibly politically risky for the government.

Even assuming that elites could be won over to the importance of intensifying Franco-German cooperation, public support would still have to be won. As stated earlier, debate over the objectives and constraints on collaboration with France has been limited largely to political elites. As yet there are few indications of support for radical departures in the direction of defense alliance with France. Though faith in American leadership has waned, public trust in NATO remains high. Public enthusiasm in the Federal Republic for the European ideal has waned, with few indications of early revival. Further, though West Germans are distrustful of American leadership, there is no reason to believe that they would be even more trusting of French leadership, as evidenced in the statements of party leaders and commentaries on Franco-German relations. The remarks in June 1987 of former French Foreign Minister Laurent Fabius and other French politicians that Paris should extend its nuclear umbrella to the FRG were reported, but were the subject of only limited and cautious commentary. Talk of extended sanctuary is welcomed as a sign that France no longer views the FRG as its western glacis, but arouses few hopes in the FRG that France might be willing to make significant concessions to its independence and autonomy in the security field. In short, the public displays little tendency to abandon current arrangements in pursuit of an uncertain alternative which entailed any greater dependence on France rather than on the United States.

FACTORS FAVORING CHANGE

For the foreseeable future all discussions of Franco-German defense cooperation proceed from the fact that the FRG has no alternative to continued reliance on the American nuclear guarantee. The security position of the Federal Republic defined the opportunities for, and limits of, defense cooperation with France. The choices made in the early postwar years remain binding: membership in NATO; nonnuclear status; dependence on the United States.

Nevertheless, a number of factors favor broader changes in the long run. These factors are a generational change of leadership in the Federal Republic and a renewed sense of national assertiveness both on the left and the right.

The generation of leaders slated to assume top positions in each major political party is bound to have a different view on the priority of Atlanticism. As one analyst pointed out, the commitment of these leaders to cooperation with the United States and with NATO must be based on a calculation of interests; it cannot be an emotional commitment. As a consequence, these younger leaders are more willing to speak out in defense of what they view as German national interests. This sentiment finds expression on both ends of the political spectrum, on the left, in the statements of leaders such as Oskar Lafontaine or defense specialist Karsten Voigt; on the right, in Volker Ruehe's campaign against the 'double-zero' option, or Alfred Dregger's advocacy of a 'reorientation' in security thinking. Though the long-term aims of critics on the right and left are widely disparate, nevertheless, they can be mutually reinforcing. The result is likely to be pressure on any party or government to be a strong defender or proponent of 'German national interest', however defined.

The pressure for greater national assertiveness will be bolstered by a more general sense of disillusionment with American leaders or, among some groups, anti-Americanism. In this view, the United States, unable to keep its own house in order, as witnessed by persistent trade and budget deficits, is not up to the task of Alliance, let alone global, management. There is less willingness in Bonn to follow Washington's lead, greater resentment at pressure to do so. Indeed, probably a growing number of West Germans would agree with Helmut Schmidt, who wrote of the motivation underlying early Franco-German initiatives: 'We did not want to allow our nations to be reduced to client states that would be dependent on everchanging American moods and trends.'[46]

Generational changes in public disillusionment with the United States may fuel the search more generally for a 'European alternative'; Franco-German cooperation will be an integral part of this effort. As former governmental spokesman, now political commentator for the respected weekly *Die Zeit*, Kurt Becker, wrote: 'Despite all the well-meaning and far-reaching rhetorical departures, the topic of "European security policy" essentially turns out to be a question of the Franco-German dialogue.' In a concurring view, Konrad Seitz, former head of policy planning in the Foreign Office, commented: 'For two decades, there has been talk of constructing a European pillar in the alliance. To finally begin with this task, to lay the foundation for it – in the final analysis this should be the foremost goal of Franco-German security cooperation.'[47] Most West German political and defense elites agree that a European defense alternative must be built around a Franco-German axis, above all in the conventional field.

The quality of American leadership will have a decisive impact on West German desire for greater defense cooperation with France. The renewal of activity and interest in Security cooperation with France in early 1982 and again in 1987 was preceded by a period of tensions in German–American relations. Schmidt was exasperated with what he viewed as American unpredictability and unreliability. The rush of initiatives in June and September 1987 was partially related to a bitter sense of disappointment in the CDU/CSU over the rapid American acceptance of the Soviet INF proposal. The quality of American leadership has a great deal to do with perceptions of the soundness of the US–West German defense link. When the latter seems in question, West German leaders will start looking for alternatives as a form of insurance. At a minimum, they will pursue dialogue with France to express displeasure with the United States or in pursuit of leverage *vis-à-vis* Washington.

In sum, changes at the international level and in the Federal Republic have made the relationship of dependence on the United States more constraining and commensurately more frustrating from the West German perspective. With changes in the Soviet-American strategic balance and 'unpredictable' American leadership have come doubts on the reliability of the US nuclear guarantee. The growing economic power of the FRG in the 1980s and its greater political role in Europe, East and West, in Bonn's view, may be ill-suited to existing military arrangements. The West German public, above all younger West Germans, have begun to re-examine the terms of those early postwar agreements and become more insistent on the need for West German leaders to be more assertive. In one sense, Franco-German cooperation is an attempt to make dependence on the United States more palatable domestically or sustainable politically at the elite and public level over the long term.

West German interest in Franco-German defense cooperation has been inherently political. Initiatives in the nuclear or conventional field or with regard to arms cooperation, while also designed to serve ostensible security goals, have a great deal to do as well with political reassurance and insurance against US failure or unpredictability.

If the motivation is political, the primary constraints on Franco-German defense cooperation are practical realities: Bonn's security position, economic constraints, military requirements. Kohl presumably is genuinely committed to the idea of greater bilateral cooperation with France, but ideas may run foul of real constraints. There are considerable difficulties to be worked out whether the subject is nuclear targeting, integration of and planning for conventional forces or military requirements for major weapons systems. Substantial political will will be necessary to overcome these obstacles.

NOTES

1. Federal Minister of Defense, *White Book 1985* (Bonn: 1985).
2. Catherine McArdle Kelleher, 'The defense policy of the Federal Republic of Germany,' in *The Defense Policies of Nations*, edited by Douglas J. Murray and Paul R. Viotti (Baltimore, MD: Johns Hopkins University Press, 1982): 276-9.
3. David Capitanchik and Richard C. Eichenberg, *Defence and Public Opinion* (London: Routledge and Kegan Paul, 1983); Gregory Flynn and Hans Rattinger (eds), *The Public and Atlantic Defense* (Totowa, NJ: Rowman and Allanheld, 1985).
4. 'Der deutsch-franzoesische Vertag vom 22. Januar 1963,' *Europa-Archiv* 18 (25 February 1963): D83-6.
5. David Marsh, 'The strains are beginning to tell,' *Financial Times,* 28 February 1986, p. 18.
6. Helmut Schmidt, 'Die Nachbarn im Alltag,' *Die Zeit,* 15 May 1987, pp. 14-15.
7. Ibid.
8. According to Schmidt, he and Giscard had discussed defense issues in several private conversations. Schmidt attempted to make clear three points: (1) Though undesirable, overdependence on the US was inevitable because the French refused to participate in a common defense organization; (2) Schmidt was convinced that French and German troops and reserves, taken together, would be nearly sufficient to deter any Soviet conventional attack on Europe; and (3) NATO's reliance on the early first use of nuclear weapons could only result in a subsequent loss of German will to resist. See Helmut Schmidt, 'Der General und seine Erben,' *Die Zeit,* 8 May 1987, p. 9.
9. Schmidt, 'Der General.'
10. 'Gemeinsame Erklaerung des Praesidents der Franzoesischen Republik, François Mitterrand, und des Bundeskanzlers der Bundersrepublik Deutschland, Helmut Schmidt, anlaesslich der 39. deutsch-franzoesische Konsultatioinen, in Paris, am 24. und 25. Februar 1982,' *Europa-Archiv,* 37, no. 7 (1982): D193-4.
11. 'Staunen in Paris–ein Helmut schneller als der andere,' *Frankfurter Allgemeine Zeitung* (herafter *FAZ*), 6 October, 1982, p. 3.
12. 'Bonn und Paris suchen eine gemeinsame Sicherheitspolitik,' *FAZ,* 23 October, 1983, pp. 1–2.
13. Ernst Weisenfeld, 'Flankenschutz aus Paris,' *Die Zeit,* 29 October, 1982, p. 11.
14. James M. Markham, 'Paris and Bonn to start to think of a special alliance,' *New York Times,* 24 June 1987, p. 3; Robert J. McCartney, 'Kohl proposes Joint German-French combat unit' *Washington Post,* 20 June 1987, p. 20; 'Dregger: Die Bundesrepublik soll sich unter Frankreichs Nuklearschirm stellen,' *FAZ,* 19 June 1987, p. 2; 'Kohl distanziert sich von Sicherheitspolitik,' *FAZ,* 20 June 1987, pp. 1-2.
15. *FAZ,* 5 June 1987.
16. *Foreign Broadcast Information Service* (Western Europe), 25 October 1982, J3-4; 'Gemeinsame Erklaerungen des Bundeskanzlers der Bundesrepublik Deutschland, Helmut Kohl, und des franzoesischen Staatspraesidenten, François Mitterrand, in Paris am 28. Februar 1986 nach zweitaegigen bilateral Konsultationen,' *Europa-Archiv,* 41, no. 9 (1986), D235-7; 'Kohl und Mitterrand beschliessen engere militaerisch Zusammenarbeit,' *FAZ,* 1 March 1986, pp.1-2.
17. This is not to say that many West Germans would not welcome an 'informal' extension of the French deterrent. See, for example, the comments by Konrad Seitz, head of Policy Planning in the Foreign Office, 'Deutsch-franzoesische sicherheitspolitische Zusammenarbeit,' *Europa-Archiv,* 37, no. 22 (1982): 661.

18. Nicole Gnesotto, 'Der sicherheitspolitische Dialog 1954 bis 1986,' in *Deutsch-franzoesische Sicherheitspolitik: Auf dem Wege zur Gemeinsamkeit?*, eds Karl Kaiser and Pierre Lellouche (Bonn: Europa Union Verlag, 1986), pp. 11-12.

19. 'Bonn und Paris suchen eine gemeinsame Sicherheitspolitik,' *FAZ*, 23 October 1982, pp. 1-2.

20. The reactivation of the Elysée Treaty at the October 1982 Franco-German summit led to some speculation that Bonn might seek participation in French nuclear strategy. The official reaction in Bonn was reportedly very restrained. Woerner was quick to dispel rumors of supposed nuclear ambitions. See 'Frankreichs Staatspraesident Mitterrand in Bonn,' *FAZ*, 23 October 1982, p. 1. Woerner's deputy, MoD state secretary Lothar Ruehl, was also clear on this point. Ruehl listed the three constraints on Franco-German cooperation, originally articulated by French President François Mitterrand: there would be no transfer of nuclear technology to the FRG, no German participation in French nuclear policy; and no financial contribution from the FRG to support French nuclear forces. 'Defense Secretary Ruehl interviewed by *Le Matin*,' FBIS (Western Europe), 1 February 1983, J9-11.

21. 'German–French summit begins,' *FBIS* (Western Europe), 21 October 1982, J3-4.

22. Hernu, 'Paris shares "security interests" with FRG,' *FBIS* (Western Europe), 2 June 1985, K1-2.

23. Seitz, 660.

24. Dregger, 'Die Bundesrepublik soll sich unter Frankreichs Nuklearschirm stellen,' *FAZ*, 19 June 1987, p. 2.

25. In part, this reflects a tendency within the party and parliamentary *Fraktion to* leave defense issues primarily to the CDU/CSU's defense experts, including Volker Ruehe and Willy Wimmer.

26. 'Kohl distanziert sich von Gedanken ueber eine Neuorientierung der deutschen Sicherheitspolitik,' *FAZ*, 20 June 1987, pp. 1-2; Kohl, 'Reykjavik ein Erfolg deutscher Politik,' *FAZ*, 24 June 1987, pp. 1-2.

27. 'Kohl will keine finanziellen Zusagen geben,' *FAZ*, 21 October 1985; 'Strauss kritisiert Eureka-Initiative,' *FAZ*, 30 November 1985; 'Parteienstreit im Bundestag: Was darf Eureka den Staat kosten,' *FAZ*, 4 November 1985, p. 2.

28. Alfred Dregger, 'Paris muss Farbe bekennen,' *Die Zeit*, 23 March 1984, p. 4; further remarks quoted in 'Sturmische Debatte in den unionsfraktion ueber die doppelte Null-Loesung,' *FAZ*, 3 June 1987, pp. 1-2.

29. 'Strauss verlangt Aufklaerung ueber Frankreichs Atomwaffenziele,' *FAZ*, 9 April 1984, p. 1; 'Bonn seeks wider influence on French nuclear targeting,' *Washington Post*, 20 April 1984, p. 1; Alfred Dregger, 'Paris muss Farbe bekennen'; Dregger, 'Die Bundesrepublik soll sich unter Frankreichs Nuklearschirm stellen.'

30. 'Kohl distanziert sich'; 'Kohl: Reykjavik ein Erfolg.'

31. 'Genscher views bilateral relations with France,' *FBIS* (Western Europe), 23 May 1986, pp. J1-2; 'Einigen sich Washington und Paris?,' *FAZ*, 9 June 1987, p. 5.

32. 'Bonn und Paris wollen 1986 zum Jahr der deutsch-franzoesischen Beziehungen machen,' *FAZ*, 8 January 1986, p. 1.

33. Hans-Dietrich Genscher, 'Sicherheit hat nicht nur eine militaerische Dimension,' *Sueddeutsche Zeitung*, 4 November 1986.

34. Despite initial signs of support by Kohl, not infrequently, a formal commitment from Bonn or financing have not been forthcoming. On a few occasions, Genscher made an obvious effort to counter French disappointment and irritation with repeated delays in Bonn. See, for example, 'Der Kanzler hat allen Grund zur Gaensehaut,' *Der Spiegel*, 13 May 1985, pp. 19-21; 'Kohl ruiniert sein Ansehen,' *Der Spiegel*, 27 May 1985, pp. 19-

21; 'Kohl, Mitterrand discuss "Star Wars," Eureka,' *FBIS* (Western Europe), 29 May 1985, J1-2.

35. For statements typical of Genscher's views on technological cooperation, see, 'Genscher views bilateral relations with France,' *FBIS* (Western Europe), 23 May 1986, pp. J1-2.

36. Social Democratic Party, 'Peace and security policy of the Social Democratic Party of Germany,' April 1986.

37. Scheer, in fact, rejects entirely the notion of a European defense based on Franco-German cooperation as 'doomed to failure'; and suggests, instead, collaboration with Britain. See Hermann Scheer, 'Der Zerfall waere programmiert,' *Der Spiegel*, 39, 18 February 1985, pp. 112-13.

38. Horst Ehmke, 'After Reykjavik: proposal for a joint European initiative,' Trilateral Memorandum no. 6, March 1987.

39. Scheer, Ehmke.

40. To note but the most recent example, Willy Brandt's farewell speech before a special party congress, cited the SPD's many accomplishments but omitted any specific references to Schmidt's contributions.

41. Helmut Schmidt, 'Die Nachbarn'; 'Der General'; 'Europa muss sich selbst behaupten,' *Die Zeit*, July 1987.

42. 'Der fruehere Bundeskanzler Schmidt warnt vor deutsch SDI-Beteiligung,' *FAZ*, 30 May 1985, p. 2.

43. 'Bonn: Das Konstanzer Treffen bestaetigt die Zusammenarbeit,' *FAZ*, 30 June 1985, p. 1; '*Le Monde* views Mitterrand-Kohl meeting outcome,' *FBIS* (Western Europe), 4 June 1985, K1; 'Lange Themenliste fuer den 46. deutsch-franzoesischen Gipfel,' *FAZ*, 7 November 1985, p. 1.

44. 'Fuer die Vorbereitung von Columbus, Ariane-5 und Hermes muss der Bundeshaushalt 255 Millionen Mark zusaetzlich bereitstellen,' *FAZ*, 20 June 1987, p. 6.

45. This reservation has been expressed in a number of commentaries, representing various viewpoints along the political spectrum. Critics in the SPD reject the argument that 'extended sanctuary' would enhance the FRG's security through an added 'element of uncertainty'. The author asks: 'But who would be the first in line in this division of nuclear risk?' See Gerhard Hirschfeld, 'Die Karte im Raketen-Aermel,' *Vorwaerts*, 4 August 1983. In a similar vein, in a critical report of French nuclear policy in the West German weekly, *Spiegel*, the author commented on the possibility of a French nuclear deterrent for the FRG: 'As if the Germans would even desire this type of deterrent, over which they have as little control as the American deterrent.' See 'Grosses Land,' *Der Spiegel*, 29 November 1982, p. 164.

46. 'Die Nachbarn im Alltag.'

47. Kurt Becker, 'Wo endet die Abschreckung?', *Die Zeit*, 24 February 1984, p. 5; Konrad Seitz, 'Deutsch-franzoesische sicherheitspolitische Zusammenarbeit.'

3 Franco-German cooperation in conventional force planning
Cathleen Fisher

Five years after activation of the Franco-German (Elysée) Treaty, bilateral conventional force planning remains limited to more frequent and regular use of established consultative channels, more extensive contingency planning, and bilateral military exercises of more ambitious size and scope. Incrementalism and caution have been the hallmarks of Franco-German cooperation in conventional defense.

Future initiatives are likely to be equally modest in scope. More ambitious schemes for cooperation exist, including former Chancellor Helmut Schmidt's proposal to create a 30-division Franco-German conventional force, but the two countries are unlikely to move beyond further incremental steps in consultation, planning and joint maneuvers. The only initiative that may prove an exception to this judgement is the proposal made in June 1987 by Chancellor Helmut Kohl to create a Franco-German combat brigade. But even if activated, this unit would have mostly symbolic value and, at any rate, would not lead to more radical restructuring efforts.

The slow pace of progress in bilateral conventional force planning is due to the considerable financial, military and, above all, political constraints on both countries. Tight defense budgets will prevent any bilateral measures in conventional defense that require significantly higher outlays. Cooperation between France and the Federal Republic is complicated as well by the two countries' different positions with regard to NATO. Most important, progress in bilateral conventional force planning depends ultimately on the degree of political commitment in Paris and Bonn and the evolution of the public defense consensus.

In this section, is examined the scope and nature of Franco-German cooperation in conventional force planning. We begin with an overview of the infrastructure and procedures for bilateral consultations on conventional defense issues and then describe the primary topics of bilateral discussions: (1) political consultations on arms control; (2) the role of French conventional forces in defense planning for Central Europe; (3) operations of the French *Force d'Action Rapide* (FAR); and (4) joint maneuvers.[1] A brief description of likely future initiatives follows. We conclude with a discussion of the factors likely to constrain future Franco-German cooperation in conventional force planning.

PLANNING INFRASTRUCTURE AND PROCEDURES

Efforts beginning in 1982 to improve bilateral conventional force planning resulted in the creation of a planning infrastructure. This required both the revitalization of existing mechanisms and the formation of a new coordinating agency. Both older institutions and procedural innovations are described below.

Existing mechanisms of consultation and exchange

The Franco-German Friendship Treaty of 1963 (the Elysée Treaty) contained two measures to facilitate cooperation in conventional force planning. Consultations between the defense and army ministers were to be held at least every three months, and between the chiefs of the general staffs, every two months. The Elysée Treaty stated that the purpose of these bilateral consultations was to develop 'shared concepts' of strategy and tactics. Second, the treaty called for a more intensive exchange of military personnel, in particular of instructors and officers at the general staff training academies. The treaty mentioned the possibility as well of exchanging entire units of the French and West German armed forces. The French and West German governments were to take appropriate steps to provide language training for relevant personnel.[2]

The treaty provisions, however, were only partially fulfilled. By the early 1970s, meetings between the French and German Defense Ministers and chiefs of staff generally were limited to two a year, instead of the planned bi- or tri-monthly consultations provided for in the treaty.[3] Rather than arriving at 'shared concepts' of strategy and tactics, France and West Germany moved further apart. After France's withdrawal from the NATO integrated command in 1966, France insisted on retaining independence in national defense planning and decision-making. The French government would undertake no specific advance commitment as to the time, location and circumstances of its participation in the defense of Central Europe. French forces remained in the Federal Republic near the Franco-German border, but the special bilateral agreement governing their presence in the FRG reserved to the French President the right to withdraw these troops at any time.

Since 1966 special liaison officers or delegations have been responsible formally for communications between the French armed forces and the Bundeswehr and other Allied troops. The French Second Corps, stationed in the FRG at Baden-Baden near the Franco-German border, has liaison officers with the German Second Corps (headquartered in Ulm), the German Territorial Southern Command (Heidelberg), and military district commands IV, V and VI. The Federal Republic, in turn, is represented by the German Commissioner to the Supreme Commander of the French Forces in Germany (*Deutscher Beauftragte beim Oberbefehlshaver der franzoesischen Streitkraefte in Deutschland* – DBFFA). The latter is an authorized deputy of the federal government and serves as the official contact between the French supreme commander and all official agencies of the West German government.[4]

The officer exchanges foreseen in the Elysée Treaty have occurred on a regular, if limited basis. The Federal Armed Services Command and General Staff College in Hamburg and the French Center for Advanced Military Studies (Centre des Hautes Etudes Militaires) in Paris provide training and extension training of field grade officers. In the Federal Republic, after approximately six years of line or staff duty, regular officers (captain rank) complete a basic course of training. After successful completion of the qualifying examination, field grade officers then pursue a two-year course of instruction in preparation for duty as general or admiral staff officers. At this point, Franco-German exchanges are possible. Selected West German field grade officers may spend the first year at the Hamburg academy and the second in Paris, receiving full credit for the two-year course as if completed in Hamburg.[5] French officers normally must complete the full two-year course of study in Paris before one year of supplemental training at the Hamburg academy.

Other exchanges included the temporary assignment of West German troops to French command and vice versa. In 1982, for example, 361 West German troops (including 238 enlisted personnel) were assigned to the French armed forces in the FRG and 1395 (855 enlisted personnel) to French troops outside the Federal Republic. In return, 670 French troops (230 enlisted personnel) were attached to units of the Bundeswehr. Moreover, 33 French and West German units or partial units were involved in exchanges within the FRG, and four units or partial units in exchanges abroad.[6]

Procedural innovations – 1982–87

Reactivation of the Elysée Treaty's security clause in October 1982 gave new life to the consultative process. At the Franco-German summit in October 1982, West German Chancellor Helmut Kohl and French President François Mitterrand agreed to two measures related to conventional defense issues: (1) the Foreign and Defense Ministers would henceforth meet twice a year to discuss security issues of concern to the FRG and France; and (2) the formation of a Franco-German commission on security and defense. The first measure, however, publicity notwithstanding, was hardly a departure, as meetings between the Foreign and Defense Ministers had averaged two a year well before 1982.

Still on the political level, ministerial consultations have been held on a regular and well-publicized basis. Since October 1982, the West German and French Defense Ministers have met at least twice a year, at the regular spring and autumn Franco-German summits in Paris and Bonn. West German Defense Minister Manfred Woerner met first with Minister Charles Hernu and then with his successor André Giraud on other occasions as well, for example, on the occasion of joint maneuvers in June 1985 or Woerner's recent trip to Paris in July 1987.

Meetings between the chiefs of the French and German general staffs have been less frequent, or at least less well publicized. The first record of official consultations between West German Inspector General Wolfgang Altenburg and General Jean-Michel Saulnier is December 1985.

The Franco-German Commission on Security and Defense has the task of overseeing discussions on cooperation and preparing for the ministerial consultations. Composed of 'high-level' ministerial officials, and a limited number of military, political and administrative leaders, the commission is subdivided further into three working groups responsible for political and strategic questions, military cooperation and arms cooperation. West German parliamentary state secretary Lothar Ruehl and François Heisbourg, international security adviser to the French Defense Minister from 1981 to 1984, were appointed as the commission's first co-chairmen. The commission met for the first time on 7 December 1983 and two or three times a year in 1984–87.

It is difficult to determine, however, what, if anything, the new body has accomplished. The proceedings of the commission's meetings are not generally a matter of public record, which, given the sensitive political nature of the issues, is hardly surprising. In 1986, Heisbourg commented on the work of the commission: 'The extent to which it has touched on basic strategic issues should not be overestimated at this stage . . . .. The difference of status *vis-à-vis* NATO integration and the fear of upsetting, in the case of France, a much appreciated defense consensus has made progress inevitably slow.'[7]

The latest initiative with regard to consultative procedures involves negotiations between Bonn and Paris to create a formal joint security council. Discussions between the two countries have been underway for several months, but President Mitterrand chose the occasion of joint maneuvers in September 1987 to make an official announcement on the council proposal.[8] According to Mitterrand's statement, the purpose of the council would be 'to coordinate decisions and harmonize analyses in the areas of security, defense, research, armaments and the organization and development of joint units.' The council would be composed of senior ministers and military officers. It is not clear what would differentiate the security council from the existing Commission on Security and Defense. The Council, which would be a more formal structure with greater visibility and prestige, may be intended to supplant the Commission.[9]

Since the activation of the Elysée Treaty, steps also have been taken to provide additional joint-training opportunities for senior officers to supplement the existing exchange program. Generals Altenburg and Saulnier first discussed the possibility of joint training for German and French general staff officers in December 1985. A subsequent meeting of their representatives in January 1986 addressed the same issue. These efforts culminated in an initiative, announced at the regular Franco-German summit in March 1986, to create a limited program of integrated training for French and German officers. The first phase of the plan calls for joint courses to be held in the FRG and France on an alternating basis.[10] The first such seminar of approximately 24 German and French officers was held in July 1987 at the French military academy in Paris. A similar course was held in 1988 at the German General Staff College in Hamburg. If continued on a regular basis, officers would attend courses on an alternating basis in Hamburg and Paris and would receive instruction in the native language of the respective academy.[11]

Continued implementation of the plan, however, will depend on the extent of political and military support in Bonn and Paris. Then French Defense Minister André Giraud in a public statement before the German and French seminar participants hailed the trial seminar as the foundation of a 'new European defense institute', but it is not clear what this implies in the way of real governmental support. The German Ministry of Defense is said to support the initiative because it provides welcome justification for long-standing plans to create a national war college. At present, aside from functional and special training courses at the Hamburg academy, the FRG lacks an institution or program of training for officers above the rank of Lt-Colonel/Colonel.

While the steps taken thus far are modest in scope, they may yet contribute to more substantive progress in bilateral conventional defense planning. These initial, mostly procedural, efforts have created an institutional basis for a sustained, rather than spasmodic, discussion of conventional force planning. Moreover, this infrastructure is largely autonomous of NATO consultative and decision-making bodies. The number of opportunities for frequent and regular consultations has multiplied. Furthermore, the infrastructure provides link-up points between high-level political and military leaders and extends to lower levels in the hierarchy as well, through joint officer's training and exchanges and liaison delegations.

SUBJECTS OF CONSULTATIONS

Consultations at the ministerial and general staff levels have addressed a limited number of topics directly related to conventional force planning. The main foci of discussion are: (1) the role of the French conventional forces in the defense of Central Europe; and (2) operations of the French *Force d'Action Rapide* (FAR). Of secondary importance and dealt with here only briefly are the consultations between the respective Foreign Ministers on conventional arms control. The result has been more extensive contingency planning and a number of joint maneuvers unprecedented in size and scope.

Political consultations on arms control

Political consultations on conventional arms control issues have become frequent and visible. Private bilateral consultations have been punctuated by highly symbolic joint appearances of the French and West German Foreign Ministers before multilateral negotiation fora, the first in January 1986 in Stockholm before the final session of the Conference on Disarmament in Europe, the second in November 1986 before the opening session of the CSCE follow-on conference in Vienna. The influence in this regard of West German Foreign Minister Hans-Dietrich Genscher should not be underestimated. Genscher has been a strong supporter of French efforts to house negotiations on conventional forces in the CSCE framework. Further, at the Franco-German summit of February 1986, the two Foreign Ministers agreed to a greater exchange of Foreign Office personnel, to begin in 1986, and to include representatives from the two ministries' planning staffs and CSCE desks.[12]

French conventional forces

Consultations on conventional force planning proceed within the parameters of current defense arrangements in Europe. Since its withdrawal in 1966 from the NATO military command, France has insisted on the non-automaticity of its response to an attack in Central Europe. The time, nature and circumstances of French participation in Western defense are the prerogatives of the French President. Within Franco-German bilateral channels there has never been any question of France rejoining NATO military command, nor of an express commitment to participate in the forward defense of West Germany. Thus, Franco-German consultations on the role of French forces in Allied defense are best characterized as efforts to improve and expand contingency planning without actually securing, or even creating the appearance of, an explicit, specific commitment of French forces to a particular mission or the defense of a defined geographical area.

The French Forces in Germany (FFA) nevertheless constitute an important security link between France and the Federal Republic. The FAA, under the command of the French first Army, consists of the Second French Corps, headquartered in Baden-Baden, which comprises three armored divisions (Trier, Freiburg and Landau), command and support units. French forces deployed in Germany total 50,000.[13]

An obvious point of German concern in these bilateral discussions has been to maintain the size and combat capability of these forces. The reorganization of French conventional forces in the early 1980s and the creation of the FAR in 1983 provoked concern in the FRG that the number of French troops stationed in the Federal Republic would be reduced. In 1983, reports appearing in the German press forecast a reduction of 10–14,000 French troops; others rumored that the fifth armored division, stationed in Landau, would be fully dissolved.[14] French President Mitterrand and former Defense Minister Charles Hernu countered quickly with public denials and called attention to an ongoing weapons modernization program.[15]

In general, details of consultations on conventional forces are not readily available, but there is little indication that French and German political or military leaders have radical departures in mind. There is no evidence that the FRG has sought or will seek a commitment by Paris to automatic participation in defensive operations in the FRG. Further there is no question of redeploying French troops along the inter-German border nor of a functional reintegration of French forces into NATO, nor of any other measures which would threaten France's independence of decision and action. Rather, the aim would appear to be to enhance the credibility of French involvement by improving combat capabilities and inter-operability and by making intervention more plausible. To this end, discussions focus on extended and routinized contingency planning, and on joint maneuvers, which may pinpoint and solve operational problems as well as add versimilitude to plans for joint operations in the event of war.

Force d'Action Rapide

The FAR has played a central role in bilateral efforts to enhance the credibility of French involvement in the conventional defense of Central Europe. The FAR has the potential to play an enhanced military and political/symbolic role in West German defense. As Heisbourg points out, the FAR 'by its very nature, has theater-wide potential', and, from the French perspective 'was largely born of the recognition that forward defense could be implemented in a politically acceptable way through the use of highly mobile transport, communication and combat equipment.'[16] The FAR is composed of five divisions, of which three would come into consideration for operations in the FRG: the 4th Airmobile Division, the 6th Light Armored Division and the 9th Naval Infantry Division.[17] By late 1985, discussions to include the FAR in contingency plans for Central Europe were well advanced.

French analysts have proposed a number of conceivable roles for the FAR in case of conflict in Central Europe: (1) the fourth (airmobile) and sixth (light armored) divisions could be used in limited operations on the Central theater flanks or in Berlin; (2) the FAR could be employed as a first-echelon counter-attack force, to relieve West German or Allied units and prepare for intervention by the French Second Corps; or (3) the FAR could be used outside the French First Army area at considerable distance from its prepositioned bases.[18]

Each role has different implications for future Franco-German conventional planning. If attached to the first Army command, the 4th and 6th divisions would be split between the First and Second Corps; in peacetime, all or part of the forces could be deployed in the Federal Republic. The symbolism of such a deployment should not be underestimated. If, however, the FAR remained outside First Army command (the current situation), extensive preparation and planning with West German or Allied forces would be required to ensure that adequate logistical and combat support for the FAR were provided.

Some progress has been made toward including the FAR in bilateral contingency planning. At the November 1985 Franco-German summit, Kohl and Mitterrand in a joint statement announced that 'more intensive studies' would be made on the use of the FAR in West German defense and that joint maneuvers would be held. At the Franco-German summit in February 1986, West German and French leaders announced plans to hold bilateral maneuvers at the staff level in 1986 and a full-scale exercise in 1987, which would include units of the FAR.[19]

There are considerable stumbling-blocks, however, to further progress in this area. Logistics continue to be a national responsibility, though this is a common problem between other NATO allies. To solve logistical and support problems, West German press reports hinted that French agreement to the inclusion of the FAR in bilateral planning might be obtained if a bilateral 'Wartime Host-Nation Support' Agreement, similar to that between the United States and the FRG, could be negotiated.[20] Also unclear at that time was the question of whether France would be willing to have these divisions included in NATO defense planning.

Joint maneuvers

So far the most visible sign of progress in the area of bilateral conventional force planning has been a series of Franco-German maneuvers held in successive autumns, in 1985, 1986 and 1987.

In June 1985, 4600 French and West German troops were involved in a series of maneuvers near the town of Nuensingen in southern Germany. Press reports described the joint exercise as the 'longest, most intensive and largest' Franco-German bilateral maneuver ever held.

The joint maneuver *Frankischer Schild*, held in autumn 1986, involved not only substantially greater numbers, but a departure in command procedures. Approximately 150,000 French and West German troops participated in the exercise. Though French officials later denied it, during the *Frankischer Schild* maneuvers French troops were briefly assigned to West German command.

A third joint exercise in September 1987 is further evidence of some progress in bilateral planning. The Bold Sparrow *(Kecher Spatz)* maneuver took place near the southern German city of Ulm. For the first time, the FAR participated in joint exercises of French and German troops; units designated to take part in the exercise included elements of the FAR's command and support units, the 4th airmobile division (DAM) (deployed in Nancy), the 6th light armored division (Nimes), the 9th naval infantry division (St Malo), and a mixed infantry group composed of troops from the FAR's paratroop (Toulouse) and alpine divisions (Grenoble).

The location of the maneuvers is significant as well; no previous Franco-German military exercise has been held so far to the east. This is said to signify French agreement to move its defense perimeter eastward from a line between 80 and 120 km east of the River Rhine to one in the vicinity of Ulm, located approximately 100 km from the Franco-German border. Moreover, the 1987 maneuvers involved large numbers of troops, including approximately 20,000 French troops. Altogether 80,000 men, 3000 track vehicles, and 400 helicopters participated in the exercise. Cooperative efforts included transport of French infantry units with French and German Transall aircraft. The maneuvers also called for experimentation with integrated Franco-German command structures. The French commander of the FAR, was placed under the 'operational control' of the German corps commander. Conversely, a German brigade was assigned to the French FAR.[21]

Minimal cooperation took place in the area of logistical support, however. The Bundeswehr did provide limited supplies of vehicle and aircraft fuel, and several hundred HOT and MILAN anti-tank missiles were made available for French use. In all other areas logistical support remained a national responsibility. Because of differences between French and German equipment and weapons, the FAR and French First Army had to provide the munitions, some fuel, and the spare parts used by their units.

Bold Sparrow highlighted the military and political difficulties presented by bilateral cooperation in conventional defense. The exercises were hampered by the unfamiliarity of French forces with NATO command procedures, language difficulties, and problems with logistical support. French political sensitivities prevented French ground forces from using NATO command and control arrangements, although operations in the air followed NATO procedures and were controlled by NATO command centers. French leaders generally resisted actions that would link the maneuver with the NATO command. At the insistence of the French, an invitation to General John Galvin, Supreme Allied Commander Europe, and West German General Wolfgang Altenburg, Chairman of the NATO Military Committee, had to be withdrawn.[22]

Despite the greater size and scope of joint Franco-German maneuvers, certain factors are unchanged. The exercise did not necessitate French participation in forward defense; at the outset of hostilities in 1987, for example, the exercise scenario calls for defense by German troops alone. The FAR intervenes in support of West German troops fighting off an enemy attack launched through a neutral country in the area between Stuttgart and the Schwabisch Alb; thus, in this scenario the FAR serves as the first echelon French counter-attack, to be followed by other units from the French First Army, including the Second Corps, already stationed in the FRG. Nor do the maneuvers suggest a reintegration of France in NATO command. French leaders, for example, rejected holding the maneuver near the West German-Czechoslovakian border, which might have been interpreted as French integration into NATO's forward defense strategy. Further, as noted above, French and German leaders were careful to avoid the appearance of a link to the command structure of NATO.[23]

FUTURE INITIATIVES

As in the past, future progress in bilateral conventional force planning will be slow, undramatic and incremental. Political consultations between governmental heads, the Ministers of Defense, and military representatives are likely to become even more frequent. Likewise, joint military maneuvers can be expected to increase in number and scope, in order to test for operational difficulties in contingency plans. Multilateral initiatives to revitalize the Western European Union may lead to greater discussion among the European members, but few substantive results.

More ambitious proposals have been made, but are unlikely to be realized. Former West German Chancellor Helmut Schmidt has suggested a radical alternative to the current modest program of cooperation. In a speech before the Bundestag in June 1984, and on repeated subsequent occasions, Schmidt proposed the creation of a 30-division integrated Franco-German conventional army under French supreme command. As at present, the decision to use nuclear weapons would be reserved to the French President. In Schmidt's view, the new structure would soon attract other European members: Belgium, the Netherlands, Luxembourg and Italy, eventually even Britain.[24] The FRG would assume most of the financial burden for fielding such a large bilateral conventional force while Paris would divert its funds to the maintenance and modernization of French nuclear forces. A new 'integrated West European Defense System' would serve as the umbrella organization for the Franco-German force; the latter would be closely allied to the US and Canada but ultimately would supplant the Atlantic alliance. Although Schmidt provides few details on how the transition to an 'integrated European defense system' would be made, his proposal suggests a certain sequence of events: (1) the creation of a Franco-German integrated conventional force, to include joint operational planning, and a French commitment to the general defense of Western Europe; (2)

extension of the defense system to include Belgium, the Netherlands, Luxembourg, Italy and, eventually, Great Britain; and (3) formal creation of a new European defense union. At some unspecified point in this process, Schmidt contends, 'sizeable, but only partial' US troop withdrawals could be carried out.[25]

A much more modest proposal, put forth by West German Chancellor Helmut Kohl, has better prospects for success. In June 1987, Kohl suggested the creation of a 3000-man Franco–German 'combat brigade'. The suggestion was characteristically vague and contained few details other than the statement that it would be a useful 'experiment' to see whether operational and doctrinal difficulties could be worked out at this lowest possible level before proceeding with more ambitious restructuring schemes.

The proposal can only be understood in light of the struggles within the CDU/CSU which preceded it. In the spring of 1987, the governing coalition in Bonn was rent by dissension over the government's response to the Soviet offer to remove all intermediate range nuclear forces (INF) from Europe with a range between 500 and 5000 km – the 'double zero' option. The coalition's eventual acceptance of the Soviet proposal left many members of the CDU/CSU's right wing extremely bitter and dissatisfied, blaming the US for placing the government in an untenable position. In the wake of the INF controversy, parliamentary *Fraktion* leader Alfred Dregger declared that Bonn should 'reorient' its security policy toward greater cooperation with France and demanded an extension of the French nuclear deterrent to West German territory. Partly to appease his right wing, Kohl launched his initiative to create a Franco-German integrated military unit.

The official French public response was positive but cautious. French President François Mitterrand, Prime Minister Jacques Chirac, and Defense Minister André Giraud each expressed support for the proposal, but hastened to point out that Paris had no intention of rejoining the NATO integrated command, a position reiterated by Giraud in a meeting with former West German Economics Minister Otto Graf Lambsdorff (FDP).[26]

Despite the formidable obstacles, the two countries created a Franco-German unit. A working group was formed in July 1987 to produce a detailed plan for implementation, and former West German Inspector General Hans-Henning Sandrart and French army chief Maurice Schmitt were instructed to begin negotiations on the unit's formation. The new unit is to be headed first by a French officer and, later (according to Woerner), by a German officer, on a rotating basis, and will fall outside NATO's integrated military command. West German troops assigned to the brigade are drawn from units of the national Territorial Army. The nuclear issue must be resolved as well. Giraud said that France was willing to act on the proposal but hinted at the difficulties of assigning an operational role to the 'brigade': 'The question is how this unit will be used, because we cannot imagine putting French soldiers in a position where they would not be covered by some level of nuclear deterrence.'[27] The unit's possible military function is still cloudy. In an interview, Woerner emphasized that the brigade would have to have more than just symbolic worth as a 'parade showpiece'.

FACTORS LIMITING COOPERATION

Financial, military and political factors will constrain further bilateral cooperation in conventional force planning. Together, these factors favor small, incremental steps and a focus on pragmatic, low-visibility cooperation.

Financial

The competition for defense resources is the least important factor limiting Franco-German cooperation in conventional force planning. A greater conventionalization of defense efforts in general or the fielding of a Franco-German army as envisioned by Helmut Schmidt would require massive outlays of public funds. This is impossible under current circumstances and is likely to remain so. In the Federal Republic, the West German MoD will have to cut its budget by DM 1.8 million annually from 1987–91. In France, an ongoing program of nuclear modernization is effectively limiting the scope of conventional force modernization, both of the French First Army and the FAR.[28] In sum, budgetary constraints alone preclude any major restructuring of conventional forces or a costly Franco-German conventional alternative.

Military

Two military factors are relevant to bilateral conventional force planning: (1) the different positions of France and the Federal Republic *vis-à-vis* NATO; and (2) resulting doctrinal differences between the two countries.

To state an obvious but fundamental point: the Federal Republic is a member of the NATO integrated military command, and France is not. Force planning in the FRG must take into account first and foremost Alliance goals and requirements. In contrast, France retains essential independence in force planning. National freedom of action is retained through the refusal to make concrete commitments in advance of a battle contingency. Thus, bilateral cooperation in conventional force planning can be used to improve the inter-operability of forces and equipment; but obvious problems arise because of the two countries' disparate positions and consequent differences in doctrine, tactics and equipment.

Political

Two separate, but related, political factors will affect the pace of progress in Franco-German cooperation in the conventional field: (1) the degree of political commitment in Paris and Bonn; and (2) the evolution of the defense consensus in both the FRG and France.

Substantial and sincere political commitment will be necessary to overcome the major military obstacles described above. In short, progress will depend on the extent of political will in Paris and Bonn. A cynical view would suggest that political leadership in Bonn and Paris have separate national agendas that have little to do with the substantive military benefits of cooperation or shared Franco-German security concerns. In this view, France may see limited 'gestures of solidarity' as measures that cost little but reassure the uneasy West Germans and solidify the

FRG's ties to NATO. The FRG, for its part, may want to use the specter of greater Franco-German cooperation as a lever against the United States, a reminder of alternatives, such as in the recent combat brigade episode.

For West German leaders, however, use of the Franco-Geman lever carries certain risks. Franco-German initiatives must not be allowed to alienate leaders in Washington nor undermine the American defense connection. Thus, announcements of new cooperative proposals are accompanied by pledges of commitment to NATO and statements which underscore the continued need for an American presence in the Federal Republic. There is a decided hesitancy in Bonn to exchange proven structures for European or Franco-German alternatives of uncertain value. This view was expressed clearly by West German Defense Minister Woerner: 'We cannot compensate for the concrete guarantees of today with the hope of tomorrow . . .. Whoever declares himself in favor of this [restructuring], runs the risk of damaging the existing arrangements and forcing a split between America and Europe.'[29]

A second related point concerns changes in the defense consensus in the FRG and France. French leaders will be prevented from offering too much too quickly by a general public consensus on the desirability of maintaining a position of independence and non-automaticity of action. Paris simply cannot give an advance commitment, nor limit its defense options. In Bonn, though French cooperation may be welcomed, many leaders remain skeptical of the change in French attitudes. There is a tendency to wait and see whether gestures of solidarity are simply a passing phenomenon or indications of a fundamental change in French military thinking. As one analyst points out, 'West Germany is well aware of the need for discretion, given the risk that asking France for more commitments or giving the FAR too much public prominence could cause France to recoil.'[30] In Paris as in Bonn, the low visibility of cooperative efforts testifies to a recognition that progress must come slowly.

In sum, as the past record shows, progress is apt to be slow and incremental, and will occur far removed from the public eye. High-level political and military consultations will increase in number and regularity, but will yield few substantive results. Steady, undramatic progress will be made in bilateral contingency planning to improve the inter-operability of French and West German forces and to make French intervention in a conflict in Central Europe, particularly by the FAR, more plausible, if not more certain. Joint maneuvers will provide the most tangible military benefits by pointing out operational difficulties in bilateral force planning and operations. But military and political factors, inextricably linked, will slow and limit the nature and pace of cooperation in conventional force planning.

NOTES

1. An additional topic of discussion, cooperation in conventional armaments production, is examined in greater detail elsewhere in the book.
2. 'Der deutsch-franzoesische Vertag vom 22. Januar 1963,' *Europa-Archiv*, 18 (25 February 1963): D83-6.

3. Peter Schmidt, 'Neuere Sicherheits- und Verteidigunspolitische Entwicklungen in Frankreich,' *Ebenhausen: Stiftung Wissenschaft und Politik*, March 1987, pp. 120-3.
4. Wolfgang, Flume, 'Frankreichs Soldaten in Deutschland,' *Wehrtechnik* no. 4 (April 1980), p. 56.
5. The Franco-German exchange is an exception. Officers who later receive additional training, for example, in the United States are required to complete two years in Hamburg. Additional training is a supplement but not a substitute for one year of coursework at the General Staff College.
6. 'Bericht des Koordinators fuer die deutsch-franzoesische Zusammenarbeit. Stand 30 September 1983, Abschnitt Sicherheitspolitik,' in Carl Otto Lenz and Helga Wex, 'Die deutsch-franzoesische Zusammenarbeit, Stand: 30. September 1983,' Federal Republic of Germany, Presse- und Informationsamt, *Reihe: Berichte und Dokumentationen* (Bonn, 1984), pp. 29-38; quoted in *Deutsch-franzoesische Sicherheitspolitik: auf dem Wege zur Gemeinsamkeit?*, eds Karl Kaiser and Pierre Lellouche (Bonn: Europa Union Velag, 1986), pp. 320-4.
7. François L. Heisbourg, 'Conventional defense: Europe's constraints and opportunities,' in *The Conventional Defense of Europe*, eds. Andrew J. Pierre (New York: Council on Foreign Relations, 1986), p. 101.
8. According to one report, Mitterrand's announcement came as a surprise to some West German officials, who had planned an announcement on the council to coincide with the occasion of the fiftieth Franco-German summit, scheduled for November 1987 in Karlsruhe. See 'Daumen senken,' *Der Spiegel,* 28 September 1987, p. 136.
9. 'Paris and Bonn negotiating a joint military council,' *New York Times*, 16 September 1987, p. 7.
10. 'Gemeinsame Erklaerungen des Bundeskanzlers der Bundesrepublik Deutschland, Helmut Kohl, und des franzoesischen Staatspraesidents, François Mitterrand, in Paris am 28. Februar 1986 nach zweitaegigen bilateralen Konsultationen,' *Europa-Archiv* 41 (10 May 1986): D235-6.
11. Based on an interview with DoD officials. 'Das Europa der Sicherheit ist auf dem Weg,' *Frankfurter Allgemeine Zeitung* (hereafter referred to as *FAZ*), 9 July 1987, p. 5.
12. 'Bonn und Paris wollen 1986 zum "Jahr der deutsch-franzoesischen Beziehungen" machen,' *FAZ*, 8 January 1986, p. 1; 'Deutsch-franzoesischen Zusammenwirken bekraeftigt,' *FAZ*, 29 January 1986, pp. 1-2; 'Fuer internationale Nuklear-Konvention,' *FAZ*, 25 May 1986, p. 2; 'Gemeinsame Erklaerung,' D236-7; 'Bonn und Paris vereinbaren engere militaerische und sicherheitspolitische Zusammenarbeit,' *FAZ*, 29 October 1986, pp. 1-2.
13. *The Military Balance 1986-87* (London: International Institute for Strategic Studies, 1986), p. 66.
14. *Foreign Broadcast Information Service (FBIS)* (Western Europe), 9 June 1983, K6.
15. James M. Markham, 'Bonn and Paris to seek a common military Project,' *New York Times,* 23 October 1983, p. 2; 'France to reduce troops stationed in FRG,' *FBIS* (Western Europe), 29 March 1983, J1; '100 more tanks to divisions stationed in FRG,' *FBIS*, 19 March 1983, K2.
16. Heisbourg, p. 104.
17. The other two units are the 11th Paratroop Division and the 27th Alpine Division. These five divisions plus command and support units bring the FAR's total strength to 45,000. See David S. Yost, *France and Conventional Defense in Central Europe* (Boulder, Colorado: 1985), p. 30; *The Military Balance 1986-87*, p. 64.
18. General François Valentin, 'Deutsch-franzoesische Zusammenarbeit in Europa-Mitte,' in *Deutsch-franzoesisch Sicherheitspolitik,* pp. 147-8.

19. 'Kohl und Mitterrand beschliessen engere militaerische Zusammenarbeit,' 1 March 1986, p. 1; 'Kohl und Mitterrand vorsichtig und zurueckhaltend: Zwie Entscheidungen beim Bonner Gipfel,' *FAZ*, 9 November 1985, p. 1.

20. The WHNS agreement stipulates that West Germany will provide military support and services to United States' armed forces in the FRG within ten days of the start of crisis or war. See, Federal Minister of Defense, White Paper 1985, Bonn, 1985; 'Lange Themenliste fuer den 46 deutsch-franzoesischen Gipfel,' *FAZ*, 7 November 1987, pp. 1-2.

21. 'Keine Vorneverteidigung, wohl aber sehr weit vorne und sehr schnell,' *FAZ*, 13 July 1987, p. 5.

22. 'FAR from perfect,' *The Economist*, 2 September 1987; 'Daumen senken.'

23. Detlef Puhl, 'French and Germans hold combined maneuvers,' *German Tribune*, 13 September 1987, pp. 4, 15.

24. Schmidt adds the ironic note in the latter case, 'but only after it is proven a success'. See 'Schmidt would disband NATO, establish a Franco-German Force,' *Wall Street Journal*, 16 June 1987, p. 26.

25. 'Schmidt would disband NATO'; 'Speech of Helmut Schmidt on the occasion of the awarding of the Adolphe Bentinck Prize on 24 February 1987,' Paris; 'In Paris wird ueber eine Ausweitung der "Nukleargarantie" auf die Bundesrepublik gesprochen,' *FAZ*, 19 June 1987, pp. 1-2.

26. 'Kritik an doppelter Null-Loesung,' *FAZ*, 2 July 1987, p. 6.

27. 'Franco-German defense,' *Aviation Week and Space Technology*, 13 July 1987, p. 21. See also reports of similar comments made in a radio interview with Giraud. Quoted in 'Woerner: In der sicherheitspolitischen Debatte wiede Boden unter die Fuesse bekommen,' *FAZ*, 30 June 1987, p. 3.

28. Yost, pp. 87-8.

29. Woerner, 'In der sicherheitspolitischen Debatte.'

30. Yost, *op. cit.*, p. 98.

4 Franco-German armaments cooperation
Cathleen Fisher

Reactivation of the Franco-German Friendship Treaty of 1963 (the Elysée Treaty) has had little effect on the pace or scope of bilateral cooperation in either armaments development and production or technological research. Between 1963 and 1982, progress was slow but fairly steady. Paris and Bonn created an effective infrastructure to administer Franco-German armaments programs and to identify projects suited to bilateral efforts. Significant project successes were achieved. Since 1982, divergences in French and German military needs and financial constraints have slowed or blocked cooperative ventures.

Political will, a meshing of military needs, and a cost-effective program for development and production are all necessary for joint arms production efforts to succeed. If one or more of these conditions is lacking, trade-offs are necessary. For example, a strong commitment at the political level to a joint project may sometimes override both military and financial constraints, forcing compromise on weapon specifications or delivery timetables, or resulting in more costly systems.

Since 1982, the number of distinctives to cooperation has grown. Financial constraints, particularly, are tending to override political incentives for cooperation. Alternatives to Franco-German cooperation appear to be more cost-effective. Existing systems, manufactured domestically or in third countries, are sometimes available; or when a cooperative European solution is desired, multilateral projects with several other countries which have more similar military needs may diminish the attractiveness of solely bilateral efforts between the Federal Republic and France. In short, though joint armaments projects provide visible symbols of the new Franco-German commitment to defense cooperation, they appear to be more and more dificult to attain.

This chapter examines the nature and scope of armaments and technological cooperation between France and the Federal Republic of Germany. We begin with a chronological overview of Franco-German collaboration, with special attention to organizational models and the infrastructure of cooperation. We then describe specific weapon projects, dividing them into two groups, first the success stories and then the failures; and evaluate the contribution of political, financial and military factors to project outcomes. We conclude with a discussion of the factors that will make Franco-German arms cooperation more difficult in the future, in particular, the decisive consideration of weapons costs.

SURVEY OF FRANCO-GERMAN COOPERATION

Armaments cooperation between France and the Federal Republic is not a recent development. In this one area at least, the promises of the Elysée Treaty have been partially fulfilled. Franco-German cooperation in armaments and technological projects began in the early postwar period and can be divided roughly into three phases. From 1955 to 1965, the FRG and France worked together on a limited basis, though on very unequal terms, and succeeded in laying the organization foundation for later joint ventures. During the second phase of cooperation, 1965–82, cooperation between the two countries flourished, and resulted in numerous project successes and the institutionalization of the cooperation process. The post-1982 period, in contrast to other areas of military cooperation, has been marked by successive failures in bilateral cooperation, while even the showcase project of Franco-German cooperation – the PAH-2 combat helicopter – has been beset by repeated delays and near failures.

Over the years, three organizational solutions have been devised and applied to the development and production of different systems. We provide below a brief description of the evolution of Franco-German armaments cooperation, and follow with a discussion of the organizational and institutional aspects of Franco-German collaboration in weapons production.[1]

1955–62: early cooperation in arms production

The earliest form of cooperation has been aptly described as one of victor to vanquished. Armaments missions, attached to the French forces in Germany in 1945 were responsible for the seizure of war material. In addition, German engineers were brought back to France and, together with French technicians, worked to produce the first wire-guided anti-tank weapons, DEFA airborne cannon, and the first rockets of the French space program.

The years 1955 to 1957 reshaped cooperation on a more equal basis. Following West German rearmament in 1954, French armaments agencies were converted into a single procurement office located at the Federal Office for Military Technology and Procurement (BWB) in Koblenz. In 1957 the two nations created the Franco-German Institute of Saint-Louis to facilitate cooperation in scientific and technological research and development. Its early activities included exploration of theoretical and experimental physics, aerodynamics, ballistics, and the design and development of prototypes for institute-sponsored experiments.[2]

A number of joint systems were produced in these early years. Between 1955 and 1957, Paris and Bonn concluded agreements for the licensed production of *Noratlas* and *Fouga Magister* aircraft. In an effort to rebuild the West German aircraft industry, the Ministry of Defense in autumn 1955 began to consider four different designs for licensed aircraft production: the Piaggo P-149 (Italy), Dornier Do-27 (FRG), Nord-Aviation Noratlas (France), and Potez Air Fouga Magister (France). In the end, French designs were chosen for 43 per cent of the planned production. The participating firms on the West German side were Flugzeugbau Nord GmbH (a consortium of Hamburger Flugzeugbau and Weserflugzeugbau) and

Siebelwerke ATG, which were responsible for the licensed production of the French transport Nord 2501 Nor Atlas. Under the agreement, 186 aircraft were built between 1957 and 1961. These early cooperative projects not only facilitated the recovery of the West German aircraft industry, but also paved the way for a follow-on project – a new European military transport aircraft, the 'Transall'.[3]

The 'Transall' program expanded significantly the scope of bilateral cooperation in aerospace. The project had its roots in separate national efforts in the late 1950s to develop a European transport aircraft comparable to the American C-130. The program eventually was to involve three main contractors and numerous subcontractors. Experience gathered at the industrial and political level supplied the foundation for later cooperation in the Airbus civilian aerospace venture. (The 'Transall' program is discussed in greater detail below.)[4]

1962–82: Franco-German successes

During the 1960s and 1970s, Franco-German armaments cooperation flourished. Projects which came to fruition during this period include the 'Transall' transport aircraft; the *Alpha Jet* trainer; the *Roland* air defense and HOT and MILAN anti-tank weapons; RASIT and RATAC battlefield radars, and the West German Kormoran naval missile. In late 1979, the two countries agreed to develop a new anti-tank helicopter; this was followed a year later by an accord to jointly produce the second generation *Roland II* air defense system. (Each of these weapon programs is described in greater detail below.) Extensive cooperation between the two countries on these projects also resulted in the expansion and institutionalization of the bilateral infrastructure. In 1968 the 'Mission Technique de l'Armementen RFA' (armaments mission of the French Forces Germany) was created to support cooperative projects. The West German counterpart is the defense research attaché at the FRG embassy in Paris. The implementation of the MILAN, HOT and *Roland* missile programs involved the creation of two program offices, the Bureau of French-German Programs [Bureau de Programmes Franco-Allemand (BPFA)] in Rueil Malmaison, and a parallel office in Ottobrunn (DFPB).[5]

1982–present

In contrast to other areas of military cooperation, the reactivation of the Elysée Treaty's defense clause has had little impact on the pace or scope of Franco-German armaments cooperation. At best, the new political impetus for greater bilateral cooperation has only ensured that the great showpiece project, the PAH-2 helicopter, has been kept alive despite major military and financial obstacles.

In the early 1980s, the West German and French armaments directors, Karl-Helmut Schnell and Emile Blance ordered a 'comprehensive view' of current and potential bilateral projects. The program review included a list of approximately 50 projects divided into three subgroups. The first category included projects for which a military demand has already been specified and on which there is military, technical and economic agreement. Listed in this first category were third generation anti-tank missiles; the PAH-2 anti-tank helicopter; the fighter-90; ANS anti-ship missiles; ABC defensive equipment; folding roadway equipment; rapid mine clearing devices; 120 mm DE munitions; remote air-to-surface weapons; midget aircraft; and an intermediate-range air-defense system. The second category included projects for which no military requirement had been specified but which should be studied at an early date for potential collaboration. Second category weapons included sub-assemblies for new battle tank programs; a light fighter and long-range naval reconnaissance aircraft; IFF tracking system NIS; and electronics systems. A third category listed weapon programs with the potential for long-term cooperation, such as research on a caseless automatic gun and a successor to the Transall.[6]

Despite this ambitious inventory-taking, Franco-German arms cooperation in the 1980s is characterized by a few modest successes, primarily follow-on generations of earlier cooperative projects such as the HOT and *Roland* guided missiles systems, and a number of major failures, namely, a joint combat tank (1982); the multilateral European fighter aircraft (1985); and a reconnaissance satellite (1986). Agreement on technological and space program (Eureka, *Ariane 5* and *Hermes*) also has come slowly and has been hampered by financing difficulties. New institutions for cooperation have been created, a subgroup of the Franco-German Commission on Security and Defense; and a working group housed in the German Society for Foreign Policy (DGAP); which brings together members from science, government and industry. But these groups appear to have contributed little to greater progress in bilateral armaments cooperation.

Organizational models of cooperation
Over the course of 30 years of armaments cooperation, the FRG and France have devised three organization solutions (with some variation) to manage and implement bilateral projects. These are: (1) the 'integrated solution'; (2) the 'pilot nation solution'; and (3) the 'cooperation solution'.[7] The primary features of each model are described below along with each solution's relative advantages and disadvantages.

The integrated solution is designed to guarantee that each nation has equal influence over the development and production of a weapon system. In this model, the two nations create a binational program office which manages and oversees the implementation of the weapon program. The principal supplier under the integrated solution is generally a joint company, such as Euromissile. While the integrated solution ensures that each country has approximately equal influence, this model may also be more cumbersome and costly: it requires more personnel than the other organizational models and a special implementing office. The MILAN and HOT anti-tank missile program (after 1969) number among the projects which utilized the integrated solution.[8]

Under the pilot national solution, one partner assumes the primary administrative task of project implementation. The 'implementing agency' is an executive national authority, such as the West German Federal Office for Military Technology and Procurement (BWB) or the French Direction Technique des Constructions Aeronautiques (DTCA). The prime contractor generally comes from the pilot nation as well, the subcontractor from the partner nation. In practice, project leadership has been assigned on an alternating basis. France assumed the leadership for production of the *Alpha Jet,* MILAN, HOT and *Roland I* missile projects; the FRG, in turn for *Roland II* and the PAH-2 anti-tank helicopter. The advantages of the pilot nation program are tighter management and lower personnel costs; but in order for such a solution to function successfully, development goals must be carefully defined in order to ensure that the non-pilot nation's needs are adequately met.[9]

The cooperation solution involves a more loosely organized structure and reserves a greater implementing role to executive national authorities. A bi-national steering committee, composed of representatives of the French and German defense ministries, oversees the work of the national authorities, which are equally responsible for managing the development of sub-assemblies or different versions of the weapon system. The major advantage of the cooperation solution is the added degree of flexibility it introduces at the national level; for instance, if a need for technical changes arise, it can be more quickly incorporated into design and production efforts. However, the decision-making process is more complicated and ultimately more costly. Under the cooperation solution, development costs are generally higher, delays may occur, and work may be duplicated. The cooperation solution was adopted to produce the Transall aircraft and is being applied in the ANS program as well.[10]

In practice, a weapons program may incorporate various features of each stylized solution as the program evolves. The three guided-missile programs (HOT, MILAN and *Roland*) began as pilot nation ventures, but later developed into models of integrated cooperation. Binational steering committees (one comprehensive and three program committees) oversee the work of the implementing agents, initially the binational program offices in Rueil Malmaison and Ottobrunn, later the French program office alone. The institutes' directors (German and French) have national responsibilities as well. The prime contractor for the missile programs is a Franco-German consortium – Euromissile – a creation of MBB and Aerospatiale.

Other implementing agencies
In addition to project-specific offices and agents, there are a number of standing bodies which support and facilitate bilateral armaments cooperation. These include the Mission Technique de l'Armementen RFA, and the West German defense research attaché in Paris. In addition, there are two newer fora relevant to longer-term planning of potential Franco-German projects: the Franco-German Commission on Security and Defense, and, indirectly, the Independent European Programme Group.

The *Mission Technique* fulfills a general support function for Franco-German cooperative projects. In 1984 the mission consisted of a staff of 33 under the direction of the French military attaché in Bonn and the Division of International Relations in the French Ministry of Defense. The head of the mission is assisted by four deputies from the branches of the armed forces.[11]

The West German counterpart is the defense research attaché posted to the FRG's embassy in Paris. Attached to the staff of the military attaché but directly responsible to the ambassador, the defense research attaché is the West German government's representative on all armaments issues. He also collects information on, and analyses of, French arms and arms export industries. The defense research attaché is assisted by a small staff.[12]

The Franco-German Commission on Security and Defense is broadly responsible for armaments cooperation. The commission, which is composed of ten to twelve senior civil servants, military officers and political figures, meets three to four times annually. Three working groups, one of which deals directly with armaments cooperation, carry out the preparations for the commission's meetings. The commission provides a forum of discussion on Franco-German defense cooperation more generally and oversees the implementation of any decisions taken by the two governments. Its impact on the scope or pace of armaments cooperation may be negligible. The commission's meetings are in addition to regular discussion on armaments to the routine Franco-German general staff meetings.[13]

Last, a private discussion group, under the auspices of the West German Society for Foreign Policy (DGAP), has brought together 40–50 French and German leaders from science, government and industry for the past three years. The defense representatives included West German MoD parliamentary state secretary Lothar Ruehl, and the head of the planning staff, Hans Ruehle. West German industrial members included representatives from MBB and Dornier.[14]

The Independent European Program Group (IEPG) within the North Atlantic Council framework appears to have contributed little to Franco-German armaments cooperation. The IEPG was created in 1976 to promote greater European cooperation in the development and production of defense equipment. The goals of the IEPG are to reduce costs through the elimination of duplicate efforts and exploitation of economies of scale; to maintain European technological and industrial competitiveness; and to contribute to greater efficiency in the Alliance. At the first meeting of European Defense Ministers under IEPG auspices, the member countries resolved to make greater use of the IEPG. In an effort to improve links to defense industries, the group recognized the European Defense Industrial group (EDIG) as an official adviser to the IEPG on European armaments industries. Despite these measures, however, collaborative European and Franco-German projects have tended to evolve outside the IEPG framework through industrial or governmental channels.[15]

PROJECT OVERVIEW

In the project review we examine more closely specific Franco-German collaborative efforts (see Table 1). The projects are grouped into two categories. We begin with a discussion of successful ventures, and then turn to a series of failed attempts at joint development and production. For each project, a general description of the weapon program and its evolution is provided, and an evaluation of the factors decisive to its success or failure. We conclude this section with a detailed look at the PAH-2 anti-tank helicopter project and Franco-German cooperation in technology and space. The repeated delays and difficulties encountered in these initiatives are likely to plague all future efforts at armaments cooperation.

Table 1   Franco-German Armaments Programs

Program	Description	Organization Model	Type of Agreement	Partner Firms	Exports
Noratlas	Aircraft	—	Industry	Flugzeugbau Nord Siebelwerke ATG	
Fouga Magister Transall	Aircraft Military Transport Aircraft	— Cooperation	Industry Industry/ Government	Flugzeug-Union Sued Nord-Aviation Arbeitsgemeinschaft Transporter	X
Alpha Jet	Military Trainer Jet	Pilot Nation	Government	Dassault-Breguet Dornier	X
MILAN	Tactical Missile	Pilot Nation/ Integrated	Government	Euromissile (Boelkow/Nord-Aviation)	X
HOT	Tactical Missile	Pilot Nation/ Integrated	Government	Euromissile (Boelkow/Nord-Aviation)	X
Roland	Tactical Missile	Pilot Nation/ Integrated	Government	Euromissile (Boelkow/Nord-Aviation)	X
Komoran	Naval Missile	—	Industry	Boelkow-Entwicklungen Nord-Aviation CSF TRT SPE Bodenseewerke-Geraetetechnik	X
ANS	Anti-ship Missile	Cooperation	Industry/ Government	Aerospatiale/MBB	
PAH-2/HAP/HAC	Helicopter	Pilot Nation	Government	Eurocopter MTU/Turbomeca	

Successes

Transall

The Transall program had its origin in separate industry efforts in France and the Federal Republic to develop and produce a military aircraft similar to the American C-130. By April 1958, four designs were under consideration: the Nord-Aviation C-40; Hurel-Dubois/Sud-Aviation SA-HD 120; Hamburger Flugzeugbau and Weserflug AT-180 and AT-150. Design specifications issued by a trilateral (French, German, Italian) commission eliminated all but the Nord-Aviation and Weserflug designs. On 28 January 1959, representatives of Nord-Aviation and Arbeitsgemeinschaft Transporter (a conglomerate of Weserflug and Hamburger Flugzeugbau) signed an agreement to begin joint development of the Transall ('Transporter Allianz'). This was followed in December 1959 by a governmental agreement to begin work on three prototypes and two partial airframes.[16]

The organizational model which evolved resembled the cooperation solution. The two governments, which split the development costs evenly, created a binational 'Transall' working group to act as industry contact and final implementing authority. Industry representatives of Weserflug and Nord-Aviation represented West German and French interests respectively. Technicians and engineers from both countries worked together on the final design of the Transall. Each major contractor assumed one third of the production tasks: Nord-Aviation supplied the wings and nacelle; Vereinigte Flugtechnische Werke (VFW), the main fuselage; and Hamburger Flugzeugbau (HFB), the nose and tail assemblies. Other French, German and British firms participated as subcontractors. Between August 1967 and October 1971, 178 Transall aircraft were produced, with 50 delivered to France, 110 to the FRG, and 9 to South Africa.[17]

The program was successful enough to spawn a subsequent agreement between the participating firms to develop a second generation Transall. The accord assigned 50 per cent of the production share to Aerospatiale (which had merged with Nord-Aviation), 27 per cent to VFW-Fokker, and 23 per cent to MBB contractor Hamburger Flugzeugbau. Production of the new version began in December 1981 and ran through August 1985. Of the 35 units produced, six were exported to Indonesia, and the remainder delivered to France.[18]

A number of factors contributed to the success of the Transall program. France and the Federal Republic shared a common military need. Leaders of the two countries were able to agree on specifications, as seen in the work of the trilateral commission, which, after consultation with the respective national air forces, issued a design handbook stipulating the military requirements which would have to be met by the new aircraft. The system proved exportable as well. Last, there was a strong technological and industrial incentive for the Federal Republic, which was interested in further rebuilding and developing a national aerospace industry.

MILAN, HOT and Roland missile systems

One of the earliest and most successful examples of Franco-German cooperation was the production and development of the MILAN and HOT anti-tank and *Roland* air defense guided missile systems. As with the Transall program, the original contracts were between industry representatives (Boelkow and Nord-Aviation), followed by governmental negotiations and agreement. By mid-1962, industrial representatives had already worked out an agreement on the joint development of guided missile technology, which specified the terms of joint technical and industrial support, and production, and provisions for sub-contractors. In February 1963, shortly after the completion of the Elysée Treaty, Bonn and Paris agreed to develop jointly two anti-tank guided missiles.[19]

The early evolution of the *Roland* program followed a somewhat different pattern. In 1960–61, the West German Ministry of Defense ordered a study on the technical feasibility of defense against low-flying aircraft. On the basis of this and other analyses completed in France and the FRG, the two governments in 1964 reached an agreement to develop the *Roland* air defense missile. Contracts were awarded to Nord-Aviation and Boelkow-Entwicklungen KG.[20]

All three guided missile programs initially employed the pilot nation solution, but later evolved into integrated models. The executive and implementing authority was the French-based Bureau of French-German Programs (BPFA). The Bureau's West German counterpart in Ottobrunn became responsible for the second generation (all-weather version), *Roland II* (for which West Germany assumed the role of pilot nation). The BPFA, originally empowered to oversee technological issues and project implementations, later took on other responsibilities as well, including actual series production, procurement and price negotiations. In 1972, the primary French and West German contractors formed a consortium company, Euromissile, which became the principal supplier for all three missile programs.[21]

An extended production run and sizeable export orders have made the three projects lucrative for West German and French industry and less costly to both governments. By December 1984, 182,958 MILAN had been ordered, with 171,322 delivered to 32 countries; 58,436 HOT had been ordered, and 46,752 delivered to 14 countries; and 20,181 *Roland* had been ordered, and 14,506 delivered to eight countries. The three Franco-German guided missile programs accounted in 1985 for a large portion of contracted work done by Aerospatiale and MBB, partners in Euromissile.[22] Export orders extended the length of production runs, reduced unit costs, and led to the partial or complete recovery of development costs. German industry reports indicate that export sales of the three weapons systems increased the volume of orders by approximately 50 per cent over that generated by national demand alone. Longer production runs are said to have reduced the unit cost by 10–20 per cent. All three generated follow-on systems (MILAN and HOT with night vision sights; *Roland II* with an extended range and more powerful warhead).

The success of the guided missile programs is due to a fortuitous combination of factors. In general, MILAN, HOT and *Roland* succeeded because the systems were designed with similar military requirements in mind, and were exportable and affordable. There were no disagreements over military specifications of the magnitude typical of later collaborative projects. Moreover, the projects were implemented efficiently; the consolidation of implementing authority in one body streamlined management. The result was the avoidance of extensive development or production delays and cost overruns.

Alpha Jet

The *Alpha Jet* program encountered problems at an early date that were to become typical of later cooperative ventures. In the late 1960s, Paris and Bonn had launched separate national studies on a new trainer jet, and in 1969 the governments decided to combine their efforts. Design of the aircraft was complicated, however, by diverging military requirements. France wanted a trainer for an air combat role, the FRG for close air support. A final accord on development of the *Alpha Jet* was reached in February 1972, with the decision to produce two versions of the aircraft.[23]

The *Alpha Jet* was produced under a pilot nation program, with France taking on the leadership role; the aircraft were jointly manufactured by Dornier and Dassault. The *Direction Technique des Construction Aeronautiques* (DTCA) directed the project and represented the interests of both nations' air forces. A bi-national management committee, composed of members of the DTCA and the West German Federal Office for Military Technology and Procurement, was responsible for project oversight. A bi-national integrated team of industry experts worked at the final aircraft design. Marketing and export were handled through France. Export contracts again allowed extended production runs. In addition to the 175 aircraft delivered to the FRG, and 176 to France, 33 were exported to Belgium, 24 to Morocco, 7 to the Ivory Coast, 24 to Nigeria, 5 to Togo, 6 to Qatar, 6 to Cameroon, and 43 to Egypt.

As in the case of the guided missile system, there were no major delays nor large cost over-runs. The primary obstacle to co-production was divergent military requirements. The FRG had specified a need for a dual-purpose aircraft able to fulfill training and light combat roles. In contrast, France was interested only in developing a trainer aircraft. To resolve this difference, two versions of the aircraft were built. Thus, Dassault, as primary contractor, was responsible for the fuselage, forward and mid-sections, and the final assembly of the desired French version and units slotted for French export. Dornier, the largest subcontractor, was responsible for the wings and tail unit and the final assembly of the second version, as well as units for German export.[24]

Kormoran

The *Kormoran* naval missile was a West German program, but was developed through cooperation with France. In the early 1960s, parallel programs were underway in the Federal Republic (contracted to Boelkow-Entwicklungen KG) and France (Nord-Aviation and CSF). The Federal Office of Military Technology and Procurement in 1967 awarded the contract to Boelkow to develop the *Kormoran/ F-104G*. Among the subcontractors were several French firms, including Nord-Aviation, CSF and TRT. A 1983 contract to develop a second generation system similarly featured MBB (Boelkow's successor) as primary contractor and Thomson CSF, TRT, and Aerospatiale as subcontractors.[25]

ANS anti-ship missile

Franco-German collaboration on the ANS (*Anti-Navires Supersonique)* ramjet anti-ship missile had its origin in a multilateral (US, France, United Kingdom, Netherlands and Norway) project for a second-generation, anti-surface ship missile (ASSM). The initiative failed, but in June 1981 Aerospatiale and MBB decided to proceed with a joint project to develop and produce the ANS missile.[26]

The two countries employed a loosely cooperative solution. A bilateral steering committee oversees the project while Aerospatiale acts as project director. A permanent bilateral project team is located at Aerospatiale's headquarters. Each participating firm is developing different jet propulsion systems until a final decision on project design is taken.[27]

Failed projects

The earlier successes of the 1960s and 1970s encouraged leaders in Bonn to seek more ambitious collaborative projects in the 1980s. But different military requirements, increasing financial difficulties, and the availability of seemingly more cost-effective alternatives resulted in a number of failed initiatives.

Joint tank project

In February 1980, the French and West German Defense Ministers signed a declaration of intention to produce a combat tank for the 1990s. The new combat tank was intended to meet a military need in the FRG for a successor to the *Leopard I*, in France to the AMX-30.[28] The participating companies were Krauss-Maffei, a Munich-based firm which had built the FRG's *Leopard I* and *II*; Mak Maschinen-bau (based in Kiel); and the French state concern, GIAT. Plans called for the formation of a bilateral consortium.

The project failed, both for military and financial reasons. In the Federal Republic, there was great pressure to develop a successor the the *Leopard II*, while the French favored development of a completely new battle tank which would be as light and compact as possible. In response to pressure from the Bundestag to cut costs of defense equipment procurement, West German representatives suggested that the two countries build a new two-man turret which could be mounted on the *Leopard II* chassis. The design alternative was supported by a number of industry and military figures, who favored further work on the existing West German system. In December 1980, the French agreed in principle to the turret proposal, but the two sides could not agree whether this would be designed to fit the *Leopard II* or the new tank favored by France, which would require a smaller turret. In March 1981, as part of the cost cutting program, West German Defense Minister Hans Apel ordered the cancellation of a number of major military equipment programs, among them the planned Franco-German battle tank.[29] Then Chancellor Helmut Schmidt attempted to revive the program, but the initiative was opposed by all parties in the Bundestag. Coming in the wake of the successful but expensive multilateral *Tornado* project, parliamentarians were loathe to approve another costly project, despite Schmidt's personal commitment. In spring 1982, the project was finally buried.[30]

European fighter aircraft

The original five-nation initiative (UK, France, FRG, Italy and Spain) to build a combat fighter failed due to divergent military requirements and a dispute over the project's leadership. The UK, the FRG and Italy wanted an aircraft designed for air-to-air combat to replace the obsolete F-4s and *Jaguars*. Thus, military requirements called for a single-seat, twin-engine, agile fighter. According to initial plans, the first prototype flights were to take place in 1990–91 with an initial delivery date of 1995. In contrast, France, with the project's exportability in mind, wanted a lighter aircraft, capable of fulfilling a ground attack role. In December 1983 the Chiefs of Staff of the five countries' air forces were able to arrive at a framework agreement, the 'Outline Staff Target for a Future European Fighter Aircraft'. A subsequent agreement between the Defense Ministers contained a compromise on the aircraft's weight and engine size, which, it was hoped, would allow the system to meet the partners' different military needs.[31]

Domestic pressures in Great Britain and France led to a major dispute over project leadership, however. Dassault of France pressed the government to insist on the leadership role or abandon the project altogether. Britain, citing employment considerations, made its own case for project leadership. The FRG, apparently not wanting to side with either, equivocated; in summer 1985, in an apparent last-ditch effort to secure French participation, Woerner proposed a compromise formula. But France rejected the proposal and the FRG, UK and Italy proceeded with plans to build a heavy air-to-air combat fighter without French participation.[32]

In November 1985, in an obviously symbolic gesture to Franco-German solidarity (and possibly also in the hope of persuading the FRG government to agree to French space or satellite proposals), Mitterrand offered a 'symbolic participation' in the EFA. In a vaguely-worded pledge, the French President said that Paris would assume 5–10 per cent of the project's costs. The report has not yet been followed with any further public details on the substantive nature of France's 'symbolic participation' in the multilateral fighter project.[33]

Reconnaissance satellite
The proposal to build an all-weather reconnaissance satellite originated in Paris and reflected French military and financial needs. French proponents of the project argued the need for an independent source of intelligence to free France from reliance on US reconnaissance sources. German participation was needed because of the considerable development cost involved. Joint development of the reconnaissance satellite was to build on previous work done under the French Samro program, which had reached an advanced definition phase when defense spending constraints forced cutbacks in the program in 1982. The new reconnaissance satellite was to have used an adapted imaging system and telemetry links from the French Spot and European Agency's ERS-1 civilian observation satellite.[34]

Despite an initial expression of support from West German Chancellor Kohl in 1983, other West German actors were not so enthusiastic. Objections were made on technical/military and financial grounds. West German MoD officials rejected the first French proposals, citing the plan's insufficient technical capabilities (no all-weather capability), and called for further study of the project. Furthermore, they argued, there was no adequate military justification for the FRG's participation in the project, particularly at a cost of DM 10–15 billion over 8–10 years. Throughout 1984 and 1985 West German political and military leaders continued to stall, refusing to commit to participation in the project's financing. At the October 1984 Franco-German summit, one West German defense ministry official was quoted as saying, 'If the French are in a hurry, there is no possibility of an agreement. ... We must organize our own analysis within the government and define our priorities. We need a little time for that.'[35] In November 1985, despite repeated French pressure at the highest level, Bonn rejected the proposal. The estimated cost was considered unacceptable; the military need insufficient.[36]

PAH-2/HAP/HAC-3G helicopter

The evolution of the PAH-2 anti-tank helicoper project highlights the difficulties likely to hamper Franco-German armaments cooperation when few of the necessary preconditions for bilateral production are met. From the outset, disagreements, repeated delays and near failure have marred the project. These difficulties are rooted in different military requirements and, most important of all, an overriding concern with containing development and production costs.

In the late 1970s, following a number of Franco-German successes, the FRG sought a partner to develop the new combat helicopter.[37] The Federal Republic was designated as the pilot nation for the program, something Bonn had insisted upon after French leadership of the *Alpha Jet* project. The implementing agency was the Federal Office for Military Technology and Procurement (BWB), the prime contractor, MBB, the subcontractor, Aerospatiale.

From the beginning, France and the FRG had different military roles in mind for the new system. In 1975–76, West German MoD state secretary Mann specified the FRG's need for a craft capable of flying 2.5 hours with a 20-minute reserve. Procurement was scheduled to begin in 1986. In contrast, France had decided on a lighter craft, suitable for ground support and air-cover missions.

The real sticking point was the helicopter's targeting system. The FRG favored the purchase of an existing system, the American-produced Target Acquisition Designation System/Pilot's Night Vision System (TADS/PNVS), which, military officials argued, would enhance standardization between American and West German forces. The French were adamant on the need for a new, European-developed targeting system based on infrared technology (infrared charged coupled devices: IR-CCDs); without this system, France argued, its armaments industries could not remain competitive on world export markets of the 1990s.[38]

This disagreement over the helicopter's targeting system had military and financial repercussions. In the first place, each targeting acquisition system required a different seating configuration, which might mean greater development costs, especially if two prototypes were developed but only one produced. Second, and a crucial point from the German perspective, the development of a completely new night vision sight would increase substantially the cost of the PAH-2 as well as the risk of failure or unexpected delays.[39]

Between October 1979, the date of the initial Memorandum of Understanding between the FRG and France, and late 1983, the respective armaments directors, industrial and military leaders struggled to come to some agreement on the design of a basic airframe that could be equipped with different equipment packages to produce two versions of the system: an anti-tank helicopter for the FRG and air-to-air and anti-tank versions for France. Aerospatiale and MBB conducted feasibility studies but an intergovernmental accord could not be reached. At the regular spring Franco-German summit in 1983, Woerner and Hernu reported 'good progress' on the project but no concrete results.[40]

Between autumn 1983 and summer 1987 there were repeated false starts. In November 1983, Woerner and Hernu signed an agreement declaring their governments' intention to initiate the development phase for the helicopter project. An agreement on military specifications was not reached, however, until May 1984, when it was decided that three versions of the helicopter would be produced from one basic airframe: (1) 75 HAP support and air cover helicopters for France, with delivery to begin in 1992; (2) 212 PAH-2 anti-tank helicopters for West Germany, equipped first with HOT anti-tank missiles and later with the multilaterally developed third-generation anti-tank missiles (PARS 3) and outfitted with the American TADS/PNVS system (delivery date 1993); and (3) 140 HAC anti-tank helicopters for France, equipped with third generation AC-3G anti-tank missiles and outfitted with a European developed night vision sight (delivery in 1996). The accord further stipulated that development work be divided equally between the FRG and France. Four prototypes would be built, featuring the set configuration appropriate to the respective targeting system. Test flights were scheduled to begin in 1988. To settle the cost question each government agreed to set a development cost ceiling; if costs exceeded this set limit, 'other means of financing' would be sought, possibly through an invitation to other countries to join the project.[41]

Two years later, a final decision on the PAH-2 was still outstanding. The original contract on the project's definition phase had expired on 31 December 1985; work continued on the project in industry, but without any further influx of governmental funding. The obstacles to any final agreement once again were a dispute over the targeting system and the overall cost of the project. In July 1986, Bonn finally approved 'in principle' the parallel development of a new night targeting system, but a new MOU was not completed at that time. As the year wore on and the time of scheduled national elections drew near (January 1987), the Bonn government was reluctant to give final approval to a costly new weapon system.

Financial considerations played a prominent role in the negotiations. Woerner, reportedly anxious to avoid a repeat of the battle tank episode, was careful to inform the Bundestag on the projected costs and financing plans for the system.[42] Concern grew as cost projections continued to rise. Original governmental estimates had put the total at $1.1 billion. By 1986 industry reports projected a cost over-run of approximately 20 per cent; government studies put the figure at 80 per cent. France was said to be willing to reduce military capabilities in order to save costs, but the West German MoD balked at the trade-off. Cost increases were attributed to a variety of causes: (1) original government and industry figures had underestimated the system's cost; (2) logistical requirements had expanded since the original MOU of October 1979; (3) inflation figures had been higher than expected; and (4) repeated delays had increased the cost of administration.[43]

The unexpected delays had introduced a greater note of urgency into the negotiations. The FRG still wanted first delivery of the PAH-2 no later than 1995; in contrast, France was willing to wait a few years more. By October 1986 the project was already two years behind schedule. The original in-service date had been 1992; by autumn 1986, this had been pushed back to 1995–96.[44]

The French and West German governments ordered two new feasibility studies, the first on a combined alternative to the PAH-2, the second on the targeting acquisition system. The new study planned a combined version of the West German and French systems, but while the original cost target of $1.1 billion was met, the savings were achieved at the price of reduced military capabilities, which provoked strong objections from the West German military.

The final agreement contains several aspects. The PAH-2 will be built by MBB and Aerospatiale under the management of the Eurocopter consortium, the engines by Turbomeca and Motoren- und Turbinen-Union (MTU). Other countries may also be invited to participate. Current acquisition plans still call for a phased delivery of three versions of the system. As foreseen in the May 1984 agreement, France will receive the first HAP at the end of 1997; West Germany the first PAH-2 in 1998; and France the HAC in 1999. All three versions will be based on a single airframe design. The later 1999 anti-tank version will feature the European developed mast-mounted target sight system. The parallel development of the new targeting system was reported to have been a non-negotiable item from the French perspective.[45]

The essentially new feature of the agreement concerns costing provisions, which remain crucial to the project's successful completion. Under the Woerner/Giraud July 1987 agreement, both governments will set a program target cost objective and an absolute price ceiling, then the overrun will be jointly financed by government and industry. If costs exceed the government ceiling, then industry must assume responsibility for the overrun.[46]

Cost will be considerable. Development costs (not including the night vision sight) for the FRG, originally estimated at DM 900 million are now expected to reach DM 2.19 billion. As of July 1987, no terms had been specified on the regulation of cost for the new night vision sight; these must be worked out in a separate memorandum of understanding. The total cost of the PAH-2 (development plus additional equipment and procurement) could exceed DM 10 billion. No provision has been made yet in the Bundeswehr budget plan.[47] The French contribution is of the same magnitude. Not including armaments expenditures, Paris is expected to expend 6.47 billion francs for development; 2.01 billion francs for industrialization; and 21.67 billion for acquisition of 140 HAC and 75 HAP systems.[48]

The July agreement met with vocal opposition in the FRG. The Social Democratic Party (SPD) demanded that the government 'bury' the project, and instead purchase a comparable model already on the market. The opposition party criticized, in particular, the government's accession to French demands for the development of a new night vision sight.[49]

Military technology-related ventures

Franco-German cooperation in technology and space research has encountered the same obstacles as joint armaments projects. Generally, France has been the country to propose a joint project, either in a bilateral or multilateral framework. The West German response in the case of Eureka and cooperative space ventures has been the same: cautious and slow consideration while divisions within the cabinet are worked out, followed by an agreement to limited participation in the project. In both cases considered below, financing difficulties have played a crucial role in Bonn's deliberations.

Eureka – European technological cooperation

In 1985, Paris proposed the creation of a European Research Cooperation Agency (Eureka) and invited other European countries, the FRG included, to join in the initiative. Coming on the heels of the American Strategic Defense Initiative (SDI), Bonn's immediate reaction was to postpone a decision on both projects. Among the cabinet members, Foreign Minister Hans-Dietrich Genscher was the most vocal and enthusiastic supporter of the French proposal. The American SDI, in Genscher's view, presented a clear challenge to the technological competitiveness and future of European industries. In May 1985, Genscher expressed his views in strong words: 'The Americans are going through Europe with lamp and checkbook and are looking for the best intellects.' To stem the brain drain, Europe would have to pool its resources.[50] The West German Research Minister, Heinz Riesenhuber, was the least enthusiastic. Concerned that participation in both programs might overburden the research ministry's budgetary resources, Riesenhuber supported Finance Minister Stoltenberg's view that funds for Eureka projects should come primarily from private sources and only secondarily from public coffers. Kohl, in typical fashion, expressed cautious support for technological cooperation, and then created a commission of experts from industry, administration and science to study the proposal.[51]

At the second Eureka conference in Hanover in November 1985, Bonn and Paris, along with other participating European governments, approved ten project areas, but while a funding commitment was subsequently announced in Paris, the West German government refused to make any concrete financial pledge.[52] Genscher suggested a West German promotional volume of DM 300 million to match a French offer of 1 billion francs, but the commitment was not forthcoming. In November 1985, Kohl announced that Bonn would leave an unnamed category open in the research ministry's budget. Riesenhuber responded that his ministry could not be solely responsible for the cost of promoting Eureka, a position that was to be repeated in similar discussions of cooperative Franco-German space ventures.[53]

Franco-German cooperation in space

West German response to French initiatives in the area of space exploration and research follow a similar pattern. Since 1984, three programs have been under consideration by the member nations of the European Space Agency. The first is a

European contribution to the US space station *Columbus*. The FRG will assume the leadership role and contribute 37.5 per cent of the costs (DM 2.8 of 7.4 billion). The second project, the *Ariane 5* space launcher, features France as project manager, with the FRG contributing 22.5 per cent of the estimated *Ariane* budget of DM 7.5 million. The third project is a French proposal to construct a re-usable space shuttle, the *Hermes*. Prior to the ESA meeting on 31 January 1985, the Bonn cabinet approved financing for *Columbus* and the *Ariane* launcher, but it rejected a role in *Hermes*, arguing that the project was not 'technically mature', and contending that it would place too great a burden on the West German budget. The ESA likewise designated *Columbus* and *Ariane* as top-priority missions.[54]

Hermes has been the major point of contention in Franco-German discussions. As had occurred on other occasions, France launched the proposal, and then waited for a financial commitment from Bonn. The Kohl government at repeated Franco-German summits refused to offer any definitive pledge to participate in the space shuttle project. The cabinet was clearly divided. Genscher favored participation on political and technological grounds. Riesenhuber favored a West German role but wanted additional funds for the Research Ministry's budget in order to do so. Stoltenberg was obviously reluctant to grant an estimated additional DM 1 billion over three years. The West German MoD reportedly demanded more time to 'define our priorities'. In December 1985, Kohl suggested that France postpone the project's planning phase in the hope that a European financing system could be devised; at any rate, Bonn would not make a final decision until 1987, while the West German government made it clear that *Columbus* and *Ariane* remained Bonn's top financial priorities.[55]

Though Bonn did finally agree to a preliminary financial contribution to *Hermes*, the future of collaborative space projects remains uncertain, because of the huge costs involved. In October 1986, Kohl pledged 30 per cent participation in the preparatory phase to develop the French shuttle (DM 32 million).[56] The question of final participation was left open till mid-1987. The outcome of the Franco-German consultations on the shuttle may be influenced by the outcome of negotiations between Bonn and Washington over the terms of participation in *Columbus*. The Europeans want guarantees on access, participation in experiments and technology transfer.[57]

The cost of the three projects will be considerable. The FRG is scheduled to pay over DM 1 billion in 1988, DM 1.3 in 1989 and over DM 1.6 billion in 1995. Moreover, as with previous armaments or technological ventures, many fear that the current estimates are too low and that the cost of the programs could reach at least DM 3 billion annually by 2000. The budget committee of the Bundestag, which must approve funds for all three programs, is considering an additional funding request for DM 255 million for *Columbus, Ariane 5* and *Hermes*. Funds previously designated for each project in 1987–88 are insufficient. Shifts within the research and technology budget will free some DM 169 million in 1987 and DM 86 million in 1988, but this will be insufficient to cover cost increases in all programs.[58]

THE FUTURE OF ARMAMENTS COOPERATION

The history of Franco-German arms cooperation suggests that certain conditions must be met in order for a joint venture to succeed. In general, West German and French political and military leaders at the national level are more apt to favor a bilateral solution if: (1) the two countries have similar military requirements and scheduling needs; and (2) the project is financially sound. Additional economic, technological and political incentives make joint Franco-German projects more attractive to national leaders and may lead to a greater willingness to compromise, for example, on military specifications, timetables, or cost targets and ceilings. The requirements and incentives for cooperation are described below.

Military requirements

The more similar the military need of the two armed forces the greater the chance that a cost-effective plan for weapons development and production can be worked out. Unless delivery schedules and military missions of a proposed weapons system are similar, agreement on specifications is harder to reach. The development of two or more versions of a single system is one solution, but this may also increase costs or cause delays. In essence, this means that planning for bilateral projects must be integrated into national planning, so that possible areas for cooperation can be identified in sufficient time to complete the often lengthy process of bilateral cooperation.

Financial considerations

Franco-German initiatives are more likely to succeed if the project entails a reasonably effective use of defense resources. If a bilateral project is significantly more expensive than a national system, a multilateral alternative or an existing system, then political support for the project will be harder to secure. This has been particularly true in the West German case, where both the defense and budget committees of the Bundestag must approve major expenditures for new weapon systems of research projects. Projects that 'pay their own way' such as the MILAN, HOT and *Roland* missiles are the example to emulate; the jointly built (United Kingdom, FRG, Italy) *Tornado,* which involved huge cost over-runs, the nightmare to be avoided.

Political will

Political will is a necessary condition of success. Despite significant military and financial obstacles, the PAH-2 helicopter has not yet been terminated because it has become a test case of renewed commitment to Franco-German defense cooperation. Yet, political will is not of itself enough. Considerations of cost, particularly when Bonn has been asked to pay, may mean the demise of a project, even when the commitment of high-level political officials is well established. Former West German Chancellor Helmut Schmidt's personal commitment to the joint production of a new battle tank for the 1990s was not enough to overcome the objections of parliamentarians to the project's hefty price tag.

Economic incentives

Increased export opportunities are a strong economic inducement for French and West German industrial and political leaders. For France, the ultimate exportability of a new system is an important criterion of weapon design. On the West German side, co-production schemes offer German industry a way of circumventing restrictive West German export laws. At present, the FRG has more restrictive arms export policies than France; West German arms may be exported to other NATO countries and to selected other non-communist countries, but sales outside this sphere are limited. Sales to developing countries or countries in volatile regions are expressly prohibited.[59] Further, political sensitivities may make arms exports to some regions, above all the Middle East, difficult if not impossible.

These restrictions can be bypassed through bilateral arrangements. Joint Franco-German consortia, such as Euromissile (Messerschmitt-Boelkow-Bloehm and Aerospatiale), are headquartered in Paris or, as in the case of Eurocopter (the West German based consortium responsible for production of the PAH-2/HAP/HAC combat helicopter), have a marketing office located in France. In either case, West German firms benefit from arms sales which would have been impossible through national marketing efforts. To cite two examples, MBB supplied Euromissile with missile systems which were later sold to Syria. In the case of the multinationally developed and produced *Tornado* aircraft, sales to Saudi Arabia were arranged through London. West German companies, which had a 42.5 per cent production share of the aircraft, reaped the benefits.[60] And the gains to West German industry may be considerable. In the case of Euromissile, export orders accounted for a 50 per cent increase over the volume of French and German orders alone.[61]

The export incentive for the FRG, however, may be diminishing. The Kohl government has been under pressure from the right wing of the Christian Democratic Union/Christian Social Union (CDU/CSU) to loosen export restrictions. Franz-Josef Strauss, the late Bavarian leader of the CSU, was a strong proponent of liberalizing actions. (Not incidentally, both MBB and Siemens are headquartered in Bavaria.) If restrictions were relaxed, the FRG would be free to compete against France for heretofore prohibited sales. The incentive to use Franco-German ventures in order to circumvent West German laws would diminish.

The prospect of lower development and production costs also can be an important economic incentive for both France and the FRG. The development and production of major new weapon systems has become increasingly more difficult for one nation to finance alone. Bilateral and multilateral efforts are desirable to the extent that duplicate development efforts can be eliminated and precious budgetary resources saved. Joint production of MILAN, HOT and *Roland* reportedly reduced costs by 10–20 per cent through longer production-runs and lower fixed management costs. Moreover, development costs were partly recovered through export sales.[62]

Technological and industrial incentives

Bilateral cooperation may also be attractive because of the civilian technological spinoffs. Technological competitiveness is a concern shared by both France and West German political leaders. For France, nationally or bilaterally developed systems help to maintain independence of American know-how or systems, and may enhance competitiveness on world markets. For this reason, France insisted on the development of a new European targeting acquisition system for the PAH-2 helicopter.[63] Foreign Minister Hans-Dietrich Genscher strongly supports Franco-German collaborative efforts in space and technology, referring on repeated occasions to the need for Europeans to pool their resources in order to meet the challenge posed by American efforts in both areas.

Political incentives
The political symbolic value of joint Franco-German efforts should not be dismissed lightly. Collaborative weapon projects are a testament of political commitment to Franco-German cooperation. The PAH-2 combat helicopter is a case in point. As negotiations over the definition and development of a new combat helicopter dragged on, French leaders at successive bilateral summits argued that the project was a test case of West German commitment to the Franco-German security dialogue.[64] Though the project faced considerable military and financial obstacles, considerable political commitment ensured the project's eventual implementation.

In sum, Franco-German collaborative efforts may only succeed if the benefits and incentives outweigh the costs. Certain conditions, some more critical than others, must be met. Sufficient political will on both sides, similar or compatible military requirements, and affordability are critical to a project's success. The exportability of a system, or the promise of technological spinoffs, may enhance the project's attractiveness; when this is the case, the program is more apt to enjoy political support in the executive and legislative branches.

Moreover, consensus must be forged at the national level between multiple and often competing players with disparate interests. The stakes of national ministries of defense, armaments directors, military leaders of the armed forces, and industrial chiefs must be reconciled before intergovernmental accord can be reached in often protracted and complicated negotiations. A weak executive, such as in the West German case under Kohl, may hinder progress as surely as disputes between Paris and Bonn. The negotiations between 1976 and 1987 to conclude an intergovernmental agreement on the production of the PAH-2 were significantly complicated by disagreement among national players, particularly within the FRG.

Over time, as projects have grown more complex, more specialized to specific military missions, and above all more costly, Bonn and Paris have found it increasingly more difficult to meet the prerequisites for success. The tale of the PAH-2 – the repeated rounds of negotiations, protracted delays, and many near-failures – highlights the difficulties of reconciling often conflicting military, political and financial interests. Incentives such as potential economic or technological gains, or the desire to conclude politically symbolic ventures, can increase the attractiveness of a cooperative venture but alone are insufficient to ensure a project's success.

Cost considerations may tip the future balance in favor of alternatives to bilateralism. As illustrated by the history of the European fighter aircraft, if a bilateral agreement cannot be reached on military requirements and financing plans, then the search may begin for alternatives. In the future, Franco-German collaborative projects will face more competition from multilateral proposals. If the interest is in reducing unit cost by spreading the financial burden of development and eliminating duplicate efforts, then projects between countries with more similar military needs may prove more attractive than bilateral ventures.

Finally, Franco-German cooperation in weapons production and technological research will be linked to developments in other areas of defense cooperation. When West German leaders balk at footing the bill for collabortive projects, it may be due not only to fiscal conservatism, but to a deep-rooted skepticism regarding French commitment to Franco-German security cooperation. West German political leaders may ask themselves why they should agree to French proposals of doubtful military or technological value, simply in the service of a symbolic political dialogue on security issues. In this sense, the future of Franco-German armaments cooperation may also be tied to compromise or progress in other areas of cooperation – without substantial gains, for example, on nuclear or conventional defense issues, West German leaders may be reluctant to loosen Bonn's purse strings to finance Franco-German collaborative projects.

NOTES

1. For a more detailed account, see Appendix A, which provides a chronology of important events and agreements in the evolution of Franco-German defense cooperation.
2. Lars Benecke, Ulrich Krafft and Friedrich Meyer zu Natrup, 'Franco-West German technological cooperation,' *Survival* (May/June 1986), p. 234.
3. Gustav Bittner, 'Eine positive Bilanz,' in *Deutsch-franzoesische Sicherheitspolitik: Auf dem Wege zur Gemeinsamkeit?* eds Karl Kaiser and Pierre Lellouche (Bonn: Europa-Union Verlag, 1986), p. 114.
4. Ibid., pp. 114-16.
5. Wolfgang Flume, 'Ruestungskooperation mit Frankriech,' *Wehrtechnik,* vol. 16, no. 2 (February 1984), p. 26; Benecke et al., pp. 235-6.
6. Flume, pp. 24-5.
7. Ibid., pp. 29-30; and Benecke et al., pp. 235-6.
8. Ibid.
9. Ibid.
10. Ibid.
11. 'Deutsche-franzoesische Zusammenarbeit,' *Wehrtechnik,* vol. 16, no. 2 (February 1984), p. 15.
12. Ibid.
13. François Heisbourg, 'Fuer einen neuen Anfang,' in *Deutsch-franzoesische Sicherheitspolitik,* p. 130.
14. Flume, *op. cit.*, p. 24.
15. 'The Independent European Programme Group (IEPG): The Way Ahead,' *NATO Review* 32 (August 1984), pp. 17-21; 'IEPG resolution on European collaboration in the field of defense equipment,' *NATO Review* 32 (June 1984), p. 33.

16. Bittner, *op. cit.*, pp. 114-15.
17. Ibid., p.115.
18. Ibid., pp. 115-16.
19. Ibid., pp. 121-2.
20. Ibid., p. 123.
21. Flume, p. 33; Benecke et al., pp. 235-6.
22. Flume reports that MILAN, HOT and *Roland* accounted for a volume of 7 billion francs for the tactical missile division of Aerospatiale; and 80 per cent of the volume of the corresponding division at MBB. See Flume, p. 33; Benecke et al., pp. 235-6.
23. Bittner, p. 118.
24. Benecke et al., p. 236; Bittner, pp. 118-19.
25. Bittner, pp. 124-5.
26. Ibid., p. 125.
27. Ibid.
28. 'Franco-German tank likely to be given go-ahead,' *Financial Times*, 24 January 1980, p. 2.
29. Other cancellations included the advanced tactical fighter for the 1990s and an order for 200 Euromissile *Roland II* missile systems for the West German air force and navy. See 'Germany cancels *Roland* missile order,' *Aviation Week and Space Technology*, 23 March 1981, p. 24.
30. 'Bonn's Interesse am "politischen Gleichklang" mit Paris,' *FAZ*, 24 February 1982, p.5.
31. 'European ministers sign pact to study new fighter program,' *Aviation Week and Space Technology*, 9 July 1984, p. 23; Michael Donne, 'Why three into one will go,' *Financial Times*, 3 August 1985, p. 6.
32. Ibid.
33. 'Kohl, Mitterrand meet for consultation,' Foreign Broadcast Information Service *(FBIS)* (Western Europe), 8 November 1985, J1-2; John Tagliabue, 'Paris and Bonn set accord on projects,' *The New York Times*, 9 November 1985, p. 41; 'Kohl und Mitterrand vorsichtig und zurueckhaltend. Zwie Entscheidungen beim Bonner Gipfel,' *FAZ*, 9 November 1985, pp. 1-2; 'Deutsch-franzoesische Konsultationen,' *FAZ*, 27 February 1986, p. 2.
34. 'French-German study recon satellite plan,' *Aviation Week and Space Technology*, 4 June 1984, p. 23.
35. 'Mitterrand-Kohl summit yields few results,' *FBIS* (Western Europe), 14 November 1984, K2; 'Bonn und Paris bekraeftigen den Willen zu technologischer Zusammenarbeit,' *FAZ*, 28 June 1985, p. 2; 'Genscher, Woerner meet French counterparts,' *FBIS* (Western Europe), 7 June 1985, J1; 'Lange Themenliste fuer den 46 deutsch-franzoesischen Gipfel,' *FAZ*, 7 November 1985, pp. 1-2.
36. 'Kohl und Mitterrand vorsichtig und zurueckhaltend.'
37. 'PAH-2 deutsch-franzoesische Kooperation oder?'
38. Ibid.
39. 'Germany agrees to development of European avionics for PAH-2/HAP,' *Aviation Week and Space Technology*, 28 July 1986, pp. 21-2.
40. 'Joint helicopter development,' *FBIS* (Western Europe), 20 May 1983, K3-4; 'FRG Chancellor arrives for summit talks,' *FBIS* (Western Europe), 17 May 1983, K1-2.
41. 'PAH-2/HAP/HAC-3G,' *Wehrtechnik*, vol. 17, no. 1 (January 1985), p. 21.
42. Ibid.
43. 'Germany agrees to development'; 'PAH-2/HAP decision postponed until fall,' *Aviation Week and Space Technology*, 23 June 1986, p. 29.

44. 'Germans, French to study substitute for PAH-2 helicopter,' *Aviation Week and Space Technology*, 20 October 1986, pp. 38-9; 'Conflicting requirements stymie German/ French PAH-2 project,' *Aviation Week and Space Technology*, 19 January 1987, pp. 80-1.

45. France, Germany authorize combat helicopter development,' *Aviation Week and Space Technology*, 27 July 1987, pp. 20-2; 'Gemeinsame Entwicklung eines deutsch-franzoe-sische Hubschraubers,' *FAZ*, 17 July 1987, pp. 1-2.

46. 'France, Germany authorize.'

47. 'Gemeinsame Entwicklung.'

48. 'France, Germany authorize.'

49. 'SPD: Hubschrauber beerdigen,' *FAZ*, 21 July 1987, p. 2.

50. 'Genscher zeigt sich in Paris ermutigt,' *FAZ*, 24 May 1985, p. 6.

51. 'Kohl, Mitterrand discuss "Star Wars", Eureka,' *FBIS* (Western Europe), 29 May 1985, J1-2; 'Bonn: Das Konstanzer Treffen bestaetigt die Zusammenarbeit,' *FAZ*, 30 May 1985, pp. 1-2; 'Parteienstreit im Bundestag: Was darf Eureka den Staat kosten?,' FAZ, 9 November 1985, p. 1.

52. Most of the projects are oriented toward market or industrial needs. They include: (1) the development of a European standard microcomputer for education and household use; (2) a compact vector calculator; (3) production of amorphus silicon; (4) robots for textile production; (5) development and production of filter membranes; (6) a 'Euro-laser'; (7) a European system for tracing environmental changes in the atmosphere; (8) a European research network; (9) the development of diagnostic techniques based on monoclonal antibodies; and (10) a flexible fabrication system on the basis of optical electronics. See Lutz Stavenhagen, 'Tendenzen und Akzente technologischer Kooperation,' Dokument, vol. 42, no. 4 (August 1986); 289-9; *Bulletin des Presse- und Informationsamts dr Bundesregierung*, no. 123 (9 November 1985); 1076; quoted in Peter Schmidt, 'Neuere Sicherheits- und Verteidigungspolitische Entwicklungen in Frankreich,' *Ebenhausen: Stiftung Wissenschaft und Politik*, March 1987, p. 54, note 92.

53. 'Kohl will keine finanziellen Zusagen geben,' *FAZ*, 30 November 1985.

54. Benecke et al., p. 241; Stavenhagen, pp. 297-8; 'Policy discussions split German space community, '*Aviation Week and Space Technology*, 17 July 1986, pp. 16-17.

55. 'Mitterrand-Kohl summit yields few results'; 'Kohl und Mitterrand vorsichtig und zurueckhaltend'; 'Deutsch-franzoesische Konsultationen,' *FAZ*, 27 February 1986, p. 2.

56. 'Deutsche und Franzosen feiern in Frankfurt die Freundschaft zweier Voelker,' *FAZ*, 28 October 1986, pp. 1-2.

57. 'Deutsch-franzoesische Konsultationen in Paris,' *FAZ*, 3 February 1987, p. 2; 'Policy discussions'.

58. The respective cost increases are as follows:

Project	Expended (to 3/1987)	Additional Funds Required
Ariane 5	DM 142 million	DM 59 million (by 7/1987)
		DM 91 million (by 12/1987)
Columbus	DM 77 million	DM 57 million
Hermes	DM 28 million	DM 48 million

See 'Fuer die Vorbereitung von Columbus, Ariane-5 und Hermes muss der Bundeshaushalt 255 Millionen Mark zusaezlich bereitstellen,' *FAZ*, 20 June 1987, p. 6.

59. John Tagliabue, 'Marketing West German arms,' *The New York Times*, 29 March 1987.
60. Tagliabue.
61. Flume, p. 26.
62. Ibid.
63. 'PAH-2 Deutsch-franzoesische Kooperation, oder?,' *Wehrtechnik*, no. 4 (April 1981), pp. 74-5.
64. 'Agreement in sight for joint construction of helicopter,' *FBIS* (Western Europe), 20 May 1983, K3-4.

5 The accomplishments of bilateral security cooperation – a West German view

Jorg Baldouf

INTRODUCTION

France's role in the defense of Western Europe has attracted much increased attention in the FRG during the past five years. This is reflected not only in the much more frequent visits of political leaders and officials of the two countries but also in public discussions on France's role in the defense of West Germany in military journals and official speeches. The interest also finds its expression at the level of military planning, as recent joint exercises of French and German forces in southern Germany underline.

In the first two decades after the signing of the Elysée Treaty between France and Germany, the provisions regarding military cooperation were not implemented. Except for talks at the general staff level and some limited cooperation regarding minor German logistics and training bases in France, there was no movement toward developing joint strategic concepts as called for in the treaty. Germany's decision to adopt flexible response in the 1960s – despite much reservation and sympathy for the French position – and the French decision to leave the NATO integrated military structure in 1966 and pursue an independent strategy increased the differences in strategic outlook between these two countries.

Steady Soviet advances in the strategic, nuclear theater and conventional areas refocused German interest in France. Doubts about the degree of US commitment to Western Europe in terms of troop presence and extended nuclear deterrence, as well as domestic fiscal and political constraints, pointed to France as the major existing reservoir of increased conventional strength.

It is therefore not surprising that the two countries intensified contacts at the beginning of the 1980s during an intense debate over the implementation of the 1979 double-track decision and the implications of that decision for European security. The motivations for these renewed attempts at improved military cooperation is reminiscent of another such initiative a decade earlier, when Foreign Ministers Jobert and Scheel explored the possibilities of closer military cooperation. The politico-military situation was rather similar then: the United States and the USSR had just concluded the SALT I agreement and had shortly thereafter signed an agreement on the Prevention of Nuclear War. These agreements were interpreted both in Germany and France as evidence for a trend in which the two superpowers would engage in détente even at the expense of Western European security interests. They caused Jobert to refer to the treaties as the superpowers' attempt to degrade Europe to the status of condominium.[1] The Reykjavik meeting between General Secretary Gorbachev and President Reagan caused similar frustrations. Former Chancellor Helmut Schmidt, for example, complained that 'neither Michail Gorbachev nor Ronald Reagan thought it necessary to consult their respective allies before the meeting. The Europeans were treated like clients, that is clients in the old Roman sense of the word.'[2] Schmidt drew the conclusion from this analysis that France and Germany had to become the core of a revitalized Europe.

Whereas Germany's interests are primarily military and strategic, France has strong political interests in cooperating. The INF debate increased French fears that Germany would falter on its commitment to deploy INF missiles under severe Soviet political pressure and turn onto a more accommodating or neutralist course. The political benefit to Germany of increasing cooperation with France was to strengthen the European pillar in NATO and thus demonstrate publicly a greater degree of independence from the United States.

This chapter will review these attempts to improve Franco-German military cooperation. It is structured into seven sections centering on the following set of questions:

- What are the politico-military motivations and constraints for improved cooperation?
- What are the German perceptions of the nature of the French force structure and modernization plans?
- What are the perceived strengths and weaknesses of French conventional forces?
- What are the major problems of these forces from the perspective of a German planner?
- How might France contribute to the strengthening of West German capabilities to sustain conventional operations?
- How might France employ its forces to conduct combined operations with West German forces, in particular, and NATO forces in Germany, more generally? What do military exercises indicate to date on this issue?
- How far has actual planning for combined operations actually proceeded?
- What political implications does Franco-German cooperation have for the FRG?

We also examine the attitudes of uniformed military and civilians in the MoD, other government agencies, as well as the *Bundestag* and outside experts. Regarding actual planning, we review evidence from exercises of French and German forces in Germany.

At the outset it should be noted that publicly available material on Franco-German military cooperation is very limited. The reasons have to do with a greater degree of official secrecy, the small size of the strategic community, a less investigative media, and the sensitivity of the subject.

POLITICO-MILITARY CONSIDERATIONS

Germany has two broad political interests in improving cooperation with France. First, for domestic political and strategic reasons it would like to be assured about French participation in the conventional defense of Germany, and see the nuclear threshold raised. This poses questions for Germany regarding the criteria and timing of the French conventional involvement. Second, for foreign policy reasons it is opportune to Germany to strengthen the 'European pillar' in the Alliance, become less dependent on American political moods, threats of troop withdrawals, and the weakening of the US nuclear guarantee. Such an improved West European identity, it is believed, might increase the motivation for defense and decrease public criticism of NATO strategy.

The change of government in 1982 did not result in a change in these basic interests. The coalition agreement of the CDU/CSU/FDP in 1982 noted that the future government would 'pay special attention to close cooperation with France on the basis of the Franco-German treaty'.[3] Chancellor Kohl's first policy statement to the *Bundestag* on 25 November 1982 underlined that during his visit to France on the day of his election, he and President Mitterrand had brought into effect the provisions of Article II B of the Elysée Treaty regarding security cooperation. The Chancellor stressed that this cooperation was to strengthen the Atlantic Alliance as a whole and was not intended to replace or undermine relations with the United States.[4]

Germany has a particular interest in decreasing the uncertainty of French participation in the defense of West Germany. This entails information about the decision-making process, as well as criteria for the employment of French conventional and nuclear forces in case of a Warsaw Pact attack. In the conventional field, Germany has an obvious interest in seeing French forces participating in forward defense and going beyond arrangements for their being an operational reserve for NATO. In the nuclear field, Germany seeks information and consultation about employment concepts and targeting practice. Official German requests for extended French nuclear deterrence are not made explicitly, and implicit requests are at best ambiguous. The then head of the Planning Staff, Konrad Seitz, for example, wrote in 1982:

Nobody can expect that France will give a formal nuclear guarantee for its non-nuclear West European allies. However one thing is clear: the more official declarations emphasize that the French deterrence umbrella reaches beyond France's own territory, the greater is the additional deterrent effect in favor of the whole of Western Europe.[5]

Yet officials realize that Germany cannot *participate* in the decision of the French President to authorize a nuclear attack, although statements by high-ranking German officials sometimes give reason for the French government to clarify old principles.[6] The formula on the basis of which the two countries have agreed is that

[w]ithin the limits imposed by the extreme rapidity of such decisions the President of the

French Republic is prepared to consult the Chancellor of the Federal Republic of Germany on the possible use of French pre-strategic weapons on German territory. He reminds us that in this matter, the decision cannot be shared.

The President of the Republic announces that he has decided with the Chancellor of the Federal Republic of Germany to set up the technical means for immediate and reliable consultation in times of crises.[7]

In the conventional area Germany would like to see more detailed planning on possible contingencies that would allow the introduction of French troops in the battle for Germany. It should not be underestimated how much doubt and sometimes resentment German officials might still have. To some, continued French adherence to its nuclear strategy is evidence that Franco-German cooperation is only aimed at strengthening France's conventional *glacis*. Retired Deputy SACEUR General Guenter Kiessling noted that Schmidt's proposals for a joint force under French command could only mean that the French would have the decisive say in operations to which 'as a German' he could only answer 'No thanks!' Not even the 'justified distrust *vis-à-vis* the United States should tempt us to seek our salvation from a different leadership.'[8]

Germans realize that there are two other limits to Franco-German security cooperation beyond the apparent contradictions between NATO's strategy of flexible response and France's independent nuclear strategy which is essentially based on massive retaliation. The first constraint comes from the French drive for independence and its attempt to retain the status of a (nuclear) world power. Germany, because of its dependence on the United States, is seen as having only limited room for maneuver. Another limiting factor for closer cooperation is the perceived attempt by France to dominate armaments productions. Differences of interest regarding arms exports and perspectives on the Third World further complicate a comprehensive coordination of security policy and limit it essentially to the central region.[9]

GERMAN PERCEPTIONS OF THE NATURE OF THE FRENCH FORCE STRUCTURE AND MODERNIZATION PLANS

There is relatively little detailed public knowledge about the French force structure and budgetary planning in Germany. Only a handful of academic and outside analysts work on French military policy. Indicative of this fact is that the most detailed recent German-language article about the relationship between resources and strategic choices in France was written by an Englishman.[10] The article is representative for the level of understanding of French defense options:

- It demonstrates the realization that there is an internal French debate over the role and importance of conventional and nuclear forces dating back to the presidency of Giscard d'Estaing.
- The creation of the FAR in 1983 is seen as a politico-military gesture by the

Socialist government to reassure the Federal Republic about a French contribution to the defense of Germany.

* Giving up the notion of a German glacis is interpreted as the minimum price that France had to pay to make any progress in European defense cooperation.[11]
* There is a realization of French resource constraints that have, from a German perspective, led to an unhealthy competition between nuclear and conventional programs.

There is concern about the fact that the creation of the FAR stripped existing units of important mobility assets. Moreover, the Germans realize that nuclear modernization has been given a clear priority in the French programming laws. The German Minister of Defense pointed out in an interview that despite the apparent nuclear emphasis in the plans, he was little concerned about the apparent trade-off between nuclear and conventional forces because the French were planning to create the mobile FAR, increase the firepower of the French II Corps and leave personnel levels in Germany unchanged.[12] Germans realize that part of the restructuring of the French First Army and the creation of the FAR were the result of budgetary constraints and the will to gain flexibility in the conventional field at the same time. It was noted that the restructuring of the French I Corps in eastern France meant that the Corps lost two of its divisions to the FAR. Although the II Corps was somewhat strengthened by the restructuring, Germans are not certain about the net balance of these changes, because the I Corps was depleted from four to two tank divisions, to be replaced by an infantry and training division, and with the employment of the FAR remaining uncertain. Although the consolidation of assets into the FAR at the expense of existing corps increased mobility, the multi-purpose character of these troops as well as the weakening of the remaining corps in terms of tank, reconnaissance and helicopter assets is not viewed without ambivalence.

The net effect of these changes is militarily dubious from a German perspective because the French did not seek to *optimize* the solution for their counter-offensive mission in Germany but created an additional mission, i.e. to participate in countering a breakthrough in the forward area. The critical question thus is whether the I and II Corps can relieve the FAR quickly and effectively enough after only a few days' fighting, even though these Corps have themselves been weakened through the creation of the FAR.[13]

Nevertheless, the decision to create the FAR is seen as a qualitative and quantitative departure in the possible French participation in defensive operations in the CENTAG area, because the force has a greater logistics range and can more quickly be mobilized. Germans realize, however, that the crucial point remains the political decision to commit the force. The political leadership is aware that the FAR will not take over a slot in border defense.[14]

German officials are sensitive to the internal debate in France over the relationship of the nuclear and conventional components and noticed that in the first years of the Mitterrand presidency, talk about extending French nuclear deterrence over Germany, and the strengthening of the conventional component, receded compared to the period of Giscard's presidency. The French government's statements at the beginning of the 1980s were reminiscent of the Michel Debré 1972 White Paper in terms of emphasis on an independent strategy and the growing priority that needs to be given to nuclear forces.[15]

There is only circumstantial evidence regarding the specifics of German assessments of French modernization and restructuring. As the previously cited interview by Manfred Woerner suggests, the German MoD must have noted with interest the restructuring of the French army which decreased the number of tank divisions from eight to six by increasing equipment holdings of the remaining units. Of special importance from the point of view of allowing for French conventional operations independent of the nuclear element are the plans to create a special tactical nuclear artillery division equipped with *Pluton* and later *Hades* missiles. This unit will be under the direct command of the NCA.

To summarize, German views of French modernization plans are neither highly sophisticated nor well-informed. There is a general awareness of French priority for nuclear weapons and the underlying trade-off against conventional forces. The FAR is nevertheless seen as a worthwhile improvement of political and operational significance to the FRG. However, French forces are seen as weak in terms of mobility, firepower and logistical support. The restructuring of the First Army is believed to have advantages and disadvantages. No clear picture has emerged on whether the strengthening of the III Corps near Lille, for example, is seen as beneficial. There are no references in German sources to this north-eastern defense line and its potential utility to NATO and the NORTHAG area.

MAJOR PROBLEMS WITH FRENCH FORCES FOR GERMAN PLANNERS

The major problem for German planners is the lack of certainty regarding the timing and place of French force commitments. In the past, the First Army has merely had the role of an operational reserve to draw a defense line for France which, once crossed, would trigger a French nuclear response. It was not equipped to fulfill the counter-attack functions expected of it. To overstress the point slightly, these forces did not have much more responsibilities/capabilities than a second tripwire after NATO forces had been crushed. They were configured to deal with minor incursions and thus designed to avoid an 'all-or-nothing' dilemma. The forces were not intended to sustain longer engagements. This concept limited their employment in the forward line of defense in which they would release their delayed trigger function.[16]

However, the delayed trigger function is not the only purpose of these forces. A series of bilateral and multilateral agreements exists which specify, though in a general and not always unambiguous way, the conditions and principles governing the cooperation between French and German as well as French and NATO forces. The first Franco-German agreement dates back to 1957 in which certain joint logistics and training activities were specified.[17] A decade later the French had concluded an agreement with SACEUR General Lemnitzer regarding the operational principles of French conventional employment within a NATO context.[18] This agreement laid down the role of the I Corps either as an operational reserve for a NATO counter-offensive directed against a threat from the south-east (i.e. a Warsaw Pact advance through Austria) or as a force that would attack the flank of an agressor in the north. In 1974 there was a second agreement between then Chief of Staff of the French First Army, General Valentin, with the Commander-in-Chief of Allied Forces Central Europe (CINC-AFCENT), General Ferber. This agreement extended this counter-offensive role to the entire First Army.[19] Both agreements were then incorporated into a general agreement between the French Chief-of-Staff and CINC-AFCENT in 1978. There are contradictory statements with regard to the question whether the agreements envision the assignment of French forces under a NATO commander, a move that could be considered to run counter to the principle of French autonomy. The documents lay out principles of cooperation and assumptions under which these principles would be applied. German sources indicate that communications and traffic control problems as well as 'other logistic support' are outlined in agreements between French and German offices.[20] It can also be taken as read that the degree of commitment of the French First Army is laid out. Yet there is also little doubt that France would not participate in the defense of the German border but rather sees these forces as a reserve.[21]

Some political leaders have little patience with and are scornful of what they perceive as a convenient and chauvinistic French position on nuclear deterrence and conventional French commitments in reserving the right to remain ambiguous. One CDU member of the Defense Committee of the German *Bundestag*, Willy Wimmer, reportedly confronted French participants with his view to the effect that

[c]oncerning German participation in nuclear decisions, deterrence was better provided by the British and Americans than by the French because in France's case it was unknown when and where it would use its nuclear bombs. If a French *Pluton* fell on Stuttgart because France saw its own interest at stake there, Germans would have to ask themselves today whether it was worth to *mourir pour Paris* [to die for Paris]. Once the situation had developed that far, it might be better, to turn *Bundesbahn* train signals to green so that the Red Army could pass through to Brest right away.[22]

Although it may be desirable from the West German point of view to obtain clarification about French planning, it is recognized that this is probably infeasible to a full extent. As then Deputy Secretary of Defense Lothar Ruehl pointed out, Germany may have to adjust to the fact that full-fledged security guarantees may not be expected from France.[23] Although this statement referred primarily to nuclear weapons, it is also applicable to a considerable degree to the conventional field.

If declaratory statements about the automaticity and extent of French support in the battle of Germany are not forthcoming and for political reasons cannot be expected, it is nevertheless necessary to analyze the practical possibilities of a French conventional component.

As was mentioned before, one problem from the perspective of forward defense is the deployment pattern of the French forces. The II Corps is stationed in the Rhine valley (one division in Freiburg, and Corps headquarters in Baden-Baden), and west of the Rhine in the Palatinate (one division in Landau) and the Mosel region (one division in Trier), approximately 300–400 km behind the inner-German border. German planners consider the logistical reach of these forces as too short and mobility assets too small for a deployment far forward. Moreover in their opinion, the divisions are too light to engage full-strength Soviet or East German divisions. The French face major equipment weaknesses from the German point of view and could not be expected to sustain combat for very long.

Another concern is that the weakening of the I Corps in eastern France in favor of the III Corps in the north-east of France as well as the FAR reduces heavier resources available near the Rhine and thus for forward employment.

German officers also note that although the French First Army is a powerful resource, it would take considerable time to mobilize and deploy it. This requirement limits its utility for rapid reaction. Another concern is that the logistical reach of the force is too limited and thus calls into question whether the counter-attack mission could be implemented. Although coordination of support functions, air defense and close air support is believed to be adequate, German operational planners question the procedures to coordinate tactical nuclear fire of French forces with their neighboring forces, if the situation were to warrant it. While NATO nuclear fire support for the French forces would be decided under the existing NATO release procedures, there remains the question of coordinating NATO and French nuclear fire in an operational way.[24] The existing Franco-German bases of consulting if time permits does not appear to go into the detailed operational planning aspects. In practical terms this would be likely to warrant at least staff exercises that may be politically too sensitive.

HOW MIGHT FRANCE CONTRIBUTE TO THE STRENGTHENING OF WEST GERMAN CAPABILITIES TO SUSTAIN CONVENTIONAL OPERATIONS?

It was noted earlier that Germany has an interest in seeing French forces more closely involved in forward defense. While this desire might not go as far as calling for French responsibilities of a sector at the inner-German border, it does imply, first, an earlier commitment of French forces for NATO tasks, and secondly, employment further forward than suggested by their present deployment in the south-west of Germany. German officials also mention the possibility that the French government could show greater willingness to facilitate American reinforcements for Europe through logistical cooperation.[25] That the Germans are unlikely to seek French participation *immediately at the border in the first hours* of a conflict is plausible because there is an acknowledged lack of operational reserves. By contrast, German military professionals seem to be rather confident about NATO's ability to hold initially. Thus the role of French forces from a German perspective would be for NATO to be able to draw on French reinforcements in the forward battle after a few days, thus allowing both time for a French political decision and mobilization.[26]

Despite this apparent confidence to halt an initial assault, German planners are very much concerned about the possibility of a Warsaw Pact surprise attack. To many, the increased mobility of the FAR even at the expense of firepower therefore appears attractive:

It is this threat [of a surprise attack] in which quick reaction capability and the flexibility of some units of the FAR are of greatest operational importance. This is true especially for the 4th airmobile division (*division aeromobile*) and, with some limitations, the 6th light tank division (*division legère blindée*). General Fricaud-Chagnaud has emphasized another operational advantage of the 4th airmobile division with its significant fighting power of 90 anti-tank and 30 fire-support helicopters: the capability for fast termination of an operation and quick regroupment of the forces. That is, the emphasis on their flexibility in comparison to large combat units, which, once engaged in a counter-attack, cannot be easily withdrawn. It is these two elements, rapid availability and great flexibility, which enable the FAR to have a stabilizing effect for the defense especially in the initial phase of an aggression.[27]

These views explain why Germans attach an important deterrent value to the FAR. Its early commitment would demonstrate to an aggressor Western cohesion and resolve. The flexibility of the FAR is also the reason why it would be most advantageous from the German perspective to see the FAR's employment not limited to predetermined Corps sectors and to familiarize *all* relevant commanders with its potential. There is thus a need from the German point of view to coordinate FAR employment within the NATO framework. Germany also realizes that deploying FAR needs to be supported by German (or other) forces in terms of traffic flow, communications links, mass consumption goods, medical and even transport support. This is considered a more difficult issue, possibly requiring additional funds and extensive bilateral consultations.[28]

The interest in increased French 'participation in forward defense' needs to be further qualified. German officials are aware that a deployment of French forces on the border is politically as well as militarily unfeasible, however desirable it might be. A forward deployment in peacetime would be tantamount to a French return into the integrated military structure, an option which the French have repeatedly excluded. In practical terms it would require a redeployment of French forces in Germany involving outlays of some half a billion marks per brigade. Moreover, if such French units had tactical nuclear weapons with them and France continued to see their role as 'pre-strategic', their employment would contradict flexible response.[29] Finally, the equipment structure and combat strength of the French forces is significantly weaker than that of her Western allies. French responsibility for a Corps sector would raise the question whether it could cover it adequately with its exisiting resources.[30]

The most provocative proposal for the possible French contribution to the defense of West Germany came in June 1984 from Helmut Schmidt. On the basis of joint operational plans (the Ailleret-Lemnitzer and subsequent agreements), Schmidt argued, the mobilization potential of West Germany (18 divisions) and France (12 divisions) should be sufficient for a successful conventional defense of West Germany. Acknowledging that much of the equipment was lacking to mobilize, equip and sustain these forces Schmidt argued that the bulk of the resources needed should come from giving up the dual-capability of the army and most of that capability of the German air force. He also noted that this would require a French reorientation of its budgetary priorities from the nuclear to the conventional component. Furthermore, it would require German co-financing of joint weapons developments.[31]

In the context of the constraints outlined above, Schmidt's proposals are more of a visionary character than realistic prescriptions for action in the short term. However, his proposals may have an important catalytic effect on the ongoing debate in challenging conventional wisdoms and established policies. They also delineate the parameters and motivations of the internal discussions in the FRG and are thus an indicator of the state of Alliance relationships.

THE POSSIBLE EMPLOYMENT OF FRENCH FORCES: SOME OPERATIONAL EXPERIENCES OF COMBINED OPERATIONS

During their meeting 27–28 February 1986 President Mitterrand and Chancellor Kohl reaffirmed their willingness 'to strengthen the already close ties which bind the two countries'. Regarding operational cooperation and cooperation between the armed forces, the statement noted that the two countries would seek closer ties and pointed out:

With a view to increasing efficiency in strategy and inter-operability, the President of the French Republic and the Chancellor of the Federal Republic authorize the pursuit of studies relating to the improved use of French forces in Germany, and in particular the *Force d'Action Rapide*. From 1986–7 appropriate joint manoeuvres will be held to realize this agreement.

The two maneuvers that emerged from this to date were held in the autumn of 1986 and 1987 respectively. The first – *Franconian Shield* – was the first exercise with French participation at division level on German soil. The German government welcomed the French participation and interpreted it as 'strengthening our common security in a way visible to all and it strengthens deterrence.'[32]

Exercises are probably the best peacetime yardstick to test doctrinal statement and war plans. The analysis of such exercises has to weigh also the politico-military function of such maneuvers. Presently, information on French operations with German or NATO forces is sketchy at best. The reasons have only partially to do with the lack of published accounts. The main factor is that only two large joint exercises have taken place on German soil so far; only one of them involved troops from a third nation (the US). Both have been conducted under German command to avoid the impression of a NATO maneuver. Thus many questions must remain unanswered.

It is difficult to fathom the exact amount of exercise activities involving French forces in some sort of Allied role. The increase in exercise activities between France and Germany beyond the small units that previously took part in them seems to have begun in 1984 when German units of the III Corps went to France (Verdun).[33] There is also some evidence that approximately 100 French aircraft took part in the fourth

ATAF (NATO) exercise 'Central Enterprise' at the beginning of June 1984. On the last day of the maneuvers aircraft from the fourth ATAF flew sorties side by side with French *Mirages* over eastern France in an effort to test the French air defense system which, in its early warning component, is linked to the NATO network.[34]

Franconian Shield 1986

This first Franco-German exercise involving French forces at brigade strength took place in late September 1985. Arranged in the area of Wuerzburg, 100–150km east of Frankfurt, this exercise involved the 5th and 12th German tank division, the 1st American infantry division and components of the 1st French tank division. Altogether 50,000 personnel, 14,000 vehicles and 650 tanks were involved in the maneuvers.[35] The participation of the American forces was made possible by assigning the exercise command to the German forces and placing the exercise specifically outside the context of NATO's autumn force maneuvers. Relationships between the German 5th, American 1st and the French 1st divisions reportedly have been very close for two decades and officers call their units informally the 'first interallied corps'. There are frequent exchanges of companies. The maneuver was prepared by several war games and staff exercises.

The general scenario context for the maneuver could not be developed from available sources. Yet it is clear that the French units provided rear support for a German brigade that started a counter-attack through joint Franco-German lines ('*relevé par dépassement*'), an operation that is reported to require a special amount of coordination and communication. The forces used their own networks for internal communications; a special electronic interface had been built to connect the German 'Autoko' with the French 'Rita'. Language difficulties would have made communications complicated on the battlefield but because the frequencies used were different anyway, all communications had to be directed to the batallion level. The similarities of tactical symbols and tactics was reported to have facilitated cooperation at this level. The weak points were the company and platoon leaders, the majority of whom were not bilingual.

Bold Sparrow 1987

From 20–24 September 1987 French and German forces exercised for the first time at Corps level. The scenario underlying the exercise was not new to them. Two years earlier, maneuvers were held at the sub-brigade level involving 3100 German, 1500 French ground troops and several hundred American air force troops. Those maneuvers were attended both by French and German Ministers of Defense who noted that this was the largest such maneuver on German soil to date.[36]

The Bold Sparrow exercise increased French participation to 20,000 men. The most significant aspects of this exercise were:

- France sought to avoid a scenario in which it could be interpreted as participating in *Allied* forward defense. Instead it came to 'support' Bundeswehr units that had come into 'operational crisis' when being enveloped on its flanks by Red units.
- The exercise emphasized conventional support. The FAR involvement was

interpreted as an additional forward conventional defense line serving as a buffer to the nuclear-equipped II Corps. This underlines the point that France would like to stress possible conventional contributions while at the same time sticking to its definition of national strategy.

- The exercise was several hundred kilometers to the east of the bases of the II Corps, suggesting a French willingness to participate in forward operations. The exercise was also to test the mobility of the FAR by bringing in units from as far away as 800 km.

The scenario envisaged that units of the German II Corps were enveloped by Red units south of Augsburg. The FAR was brought in as an operational reserve from its main operating bases in France and was to relieve retreating Bundeswehr units from their positions. After a consolidation phase, French forces were to start a counter-attack pushing adversarial forces back behind the border. In this effort they were to be later supported and then replaced by regular units of the First Army.

The exercise has to be seen primarily as a peacetime demonstration of solidarity, not necessarily simulating war-time decisions. Whereas German officials emphasized the forward deployment of French forces as a demonstration of France to participate in forward defense, French military officers repeatedly made it clear that the FAR was the spearhead of the First Army. The French distributed press material outlining the task of the First Army which left little doubt about French intentions and war-time planning. These documents stated that the 'primary task' of the First Army was to force the enemy to commit its forces in such a way that it would become clear whether its intentions were directed against France and 'to insure sufficient time for a decision on a possible nuclear counter-attack'.[37]

The French insisted on the bilateral nature of the exercise to the point of setting the German Ministry of Defense up for embarrassment. Although the French had reportedly agreed to an invitation list including Generals Galvin and Altenburg in their NATO capacities, they withdrew their consent requiring that the two officers not attend. Problems such as these overshadowed other symbolic, positive aspects, e.g. the operational command of the FAR (while in Germany) by a German general.

German officers were reported to have summarized the exercise with 'almost nothing works'. The French units seem to have suffered from a critical lack of reconnaissance assets. Communications both between French units themselves as well as between French and German units was extremely difficult. A Red attack performed by the German 12th tank brigade proceeded 'unexpectedly' fast for hours without being engaged by the 6th light tank division which was delayed in arriving from a staging area near Stuttgart. Helicopters were seen hovering in the area without engaging.

Analyses of the maneuver emphasize that the exercise was not very realistic because the FAR, due to a lack of heavy equipment, could not be expected to initiate a counter-attack east of the border as envisaged in the scenario. The assets needed for that were provided in the exercise by the shifting sides from Red to Blue by the German 24th tank brigade. FAR units would probably only sustain engagements by operational maneuver groups for several days.

To summarize these maneuvers experiences: Franco-German security cooperation is under political pressure to show results despite its being intensified only recently and despite French insistence on sticking to the core of its traditional strategic and operational convictions. The contribution of the FAR as a rapidly mobilizable operational reserve remains limited because of the lack of heavy equipment. Communications, reconnaissance, mobility and sustainability would have to be significantly increased to give these units a more reasonable prospect of defending against heavy-armor Warsaw Pact forces. The same holds true for the forces of the French II Corps. As the political problems regarding visits by SACEUR General Galvin and CMC General Altenburg suggest, France is very determined to emphasize the bilateral and political element of these exercises.

PLANNING AND INITIATIVES TO IMPROVE COMBINED OPERATIONS

Franco-German cooperation is still at a very early stage in terms of planning for combined operations. Despite a considerable amount of traditional cooperation in training and logistics matters, activities are still at an embryonic stage if measured against war-time requirements of fully integrated activities. Moreover, several proposals have been tabled by the political and military leaders in the past months and years, so it is still rather early to determine what the cooperation has achieved beyond the discussions already outlined.

The crucial question that any analysis of French involvement in Allied defense has to answer is to what degree French involvement is real as opposed to serving only political purposes, such as reassuring the FRG. Except for the few exercises which had heavy political components, only rhetorical declarations and statements of intent have been made. This section begins by reviewing planning efforts prior to 1982 to give a perspective on the magnitude of changes and the proposals that have been made.

Logistical support arrangements
As has been pointed out before, both French logistical support for the reinforcement of the central region as well as the support for its own forces has been found to be inadequate. It is interesting to note that since the late 1950s Germany has had a steady though low-level cooperation with France on logistical matters. The FRG maintains a small logistics liaison staff in France with about 55 officers in peacetime. This office, under the command of the 'German Logistics Representative in France', would triple in size during war. It was set up in 1957, only two years after the creation of the Bundeswehr, on the basis of a bilateral agreement and initially located in Fontainebleau, next to the CINC-AFCENT. The purpose of the staff is to control the small number of German depots in France and to coordinate logistical cooperation in the areas of medicine and training. Thus, it assists German troops exercising in France. The German navy, for example, uses firing ranges south of Bordeaux, German helicopter pilots train in the Pyrenees, and there is a bombing range that may be used by German air force pilots in Suippes in the Champagne.[38]

The French also maintain a small logistics liaison office in Paris under the name

'Liaison Office for the Support of Allied Armies' which is the point of contact for the German Logistics Representative in France. These offices plan logistics exercises that take place every two years under the name *Forte*. In 1982, for example, 20 German tanks plus an additional 900 tons of material came by ship from Canada to La Rochelle where it was unloaded by 300 German and 500 French soldiers, as well as civilian personnel, and sent by rail to Germany. While politically not unimportant, this small exercise which took about five days, cannot be interpreted as providing the core of a rapid expansion of French lines of communications for the reinforcement of the Central Front. Yet it is indicative of the nature of long-standing Franco-German ties which survived the French withdrawal from the command structure.[39]

Regarding German logistical support for French forces operating forward in Germany, there appears to be a consensus that the FRG can and should help to overcome current impasses. Given the way French conventional forces are structured, German officials are aware of the need to provide logistical support as well as groundfire support and tactical air support. In the words of former Deputy Secretary Ruehl:

The working group on 'military security' [of the coordinating committee] has been striving since 1983 to define the conditions for a joint operation of French and German troops in Germany, possible logistics organization for mutual support and Franco-German exercises outside from NATO maneuvers. The discussions are also concerned with the employment of the large units of the FAR as well as operations of the 1st French army on German soil. The units of the FAR need to be supported not only logistically, but also need fire support from heavy weapons and the air force because an employment of the FAR further forward would make it increasingly dependent on such battlefield support.[40]

It is clear then that these support functions might have to come from other allies as well if French FAR operations, for example, were to be conceivable for Corps sectors other than German. This, however, would necessitate further NATO coordination.

Training

Another area of cooperation between France and West Germany is training. During their spring 1986 meeting, Chancellor Kohl and President Mitterrand agreed to have a joint officers training program. The goal of the initiative was to bring a number of general staff officer candidates to the respective military academies of France and Germany. Arrangements about joint training on a smaller scale date back to 1957. In 1960, German tank crews arrived at Sissonne for training and German parachutists 'took' an exercise field in Mourmelon. Until the 1980s these exercises remained at low personnel levels. Moreover, units of the German mountain division exercise in France, and vice versa. In 1985 approximately 65 partnerships existed between French and German units, involving personnel exchanges of perhaps German 1500 men and 1000 French soldiers.[41] Germany and France have had an exchange of army and navy officers since 1956, allowing a small number to participate in the general staff course of the other country. In 1968 this agreement was extended to include air force officers.[42] After France left the integrated military structure in 1966, field training activities were significantly reduced in size. Previously German units up to brigade size trained at various French facilities. The Franconian Shield and Bold Sparrow exercises show that, in the interest of demonstrating solidarity in forward defense, there is a high priority for joint exercise on German soil.

For completeness purposes it is worth adding that Mitterrand and Kohl also agreed that in future the exchange of officials is also to be extended to the Foreign Offices of the two countries.[43] Starting in 1986, diplomats from the planning and CSCE staffs have been exchanged. The French Foreign Minister Roland Dumas pointed out in a radio interview (given in German!) that the ideal goal would be that all French and German diplomats should be able to speak the other country's language within 15–20 years.[44]

Discussions about the creation of a joint brigade
In the summer of 1987, Chancellor Kohl proposed that France and Germany should set up a jointly manned brigade which according to later discussions should initially be under a French commander. The German Minister of Defense Woerner supported the idea as providing an opportunity to improve mutual understanding about command structures, training, equipment needs and operational concepts. Because of the differences between France and Germany, however, such an effort raises important questions regarding the relationship of this unit to the NATO command structure, and the strategic and operational underpinnings of its employment.[45]

Not least because of these complications but also because of internal MoD criticisms by high-ranking officers, German thinking has since moved away somewhat from the idea of a jointly manned brigade. The new proposals suggest joint Franco-German combat training at a training school in Hammelburg near the inner-German border. The school's capacity is roughly of brigade size and it is reasonable to expect that in the event of an emergency a combat unit would be assembled from its equipment and personnel assets. The proximity of the school to the bloc border and the implications of a French presence there during times of crisis might be a major factor for French reluctance to accept the proposal. On the other hand, if France did accept, it would be of significant symbolic value and underline the significance of Franco-German cooperation. The development of the debate on the brigade or joint combat training is thus an important indicator for the future development of Franco-German security cooperation.

Inter-operability
One approach to improved cooperation is improved standardization and inter-operability of weapons systems and joint procurement. Unlike the 1950s and 1960s, the 1970s were a decade of significant decreases in Franco-German joint programs. The joint tank project was cancelled in 1980 and several other programs were cancelled or experienced great delays and cost over-runs. There was therefore significant political pressure in 1983 for the FRG to respond positively to an industrial proposal for the joint development of an anti-tank helicopter (*Panzer-Abwehr Hubschrauber, PAH-2*) based on a common frame with three derivatives

which would fulfill the previously mutually exclusive national requirements. Because of the political significance of this joint program as a first pragmatic attempt to demonstrate the greater degree of Franco-German cooperation, the German army had to give up its goal to introduce a new helicopter for night combat at the end of the 1980s and give up its hope to purchase the heavier American Apache AH-64.[46] Introduction was planned for 1992 but lacking specificity of requirements will cause at least a several year-long delay.[47]

The institutional dimension

German observers were skeptical from the outset that the WEU could be a forum to improve Western European defense cooperation. They noted that Germany remained an active key member of NATO that had agreed to make operational arrangements with SACEUR, thus not having an opportunity to parallel or replace these arrangements with anybody else, except in the sense of bilaterally reinforcing and strengthening these NATO arrangements.

Toward that goal of improving bilateral relations, France and Germany created a coordinating committee in the autumn of 1982 in which officials at the state secretary level of the respective Foreign and Defense Ministries are represented. The committee has three working groups.[48] Initial work focused (1) on a concrete assessment of the military threat faced by the two countries in Europe; (2) the formulation of 'answers' and the determination of requirements and 'suitable military means'; and (3) the examination of possibilities for joint solutions in the framework of armaments cooperation.[49] In order to avoid frictions stemming from the FRG's role in NATO, Germany proposed and France agreed to include other European allies as well as the United States as far as possible. What concrete progress can be made in this group beyond the development of exercises remains to be seen. With the role and importance of the coordinating committee still unclear it is an expression of political symbolism that a new proposal for a new institution has recently been tabled.

At the conclusion of the Bold Sparrow exercise, Chancellor Kohl and President Mitterrand announced their intention to create a joint defense council. According to President Mitterrand, the council is to 'coordinate decisions and harmonize analyses in the areas of security, defense, research, armaments, the organization and deployment of joint units'. The formal creation was announced in the context of the 25th anniversary of the Elysée Treaty in January 1988. Mitterrand maintained that such a council could serve as the core of a joint European defense that could be opened to other counties as well. Spain and Italy were specifically mentioned and other countries not excluded. Such a council might make it easier for France and Germany to pursue military cooperation by working around existing NATO institutions on bilateral matters.[50] It is questionable, however, what positive practical impact the creation of the defense council might have in the short and medium term that could not have been produced by the coordination committee. It is also conceivable that the French wanted to table a proposal that had a wider implication for European integration. The work of the council will need to be observed carefully in order to discern whether this was a substantive or merely another symbolic move.

DOMESTIC POLITICAL DEBATES OVER FRANCO-GERMAN SECURITY COOPERATION

Increased Franco-German cooperation raises important questions regarding the FRG's orientation in foreign policy. There has been a traditional tension between Germany's European orientation and cooperation with France and its alliance with the United States. The prime example of course was the failed European Defense Community concept in 1954, due to the French parliament's refusal to ratify the treaty, and the resulting association of Germany with NATO. During the 1960s and the trans-atlantic debates over the adoption of the MLF and later the flexible response strategy, France again encouraged greater distance between Washington and Bonn, trying to force Germany to choose between the two countries. Yet Bonn opted to choose Washington, to a large degree because of the perceived unreliability and egotism on France's part.

During this period the SPD leadership was solidly in favor of preferring Washington over Paris, while the Christian Democratic Union was split between Atlanticist and Gaullist and the CSU toying with the idea of a European nuclear force. That traditional line-up no longer holds today.

The CDU still has a small Gaullist group which supports a reorientation of German security policy toward France, including the request for extended French nuclear deterrence. Earlier this year, in the context of disillusionment about the possibility of a double-zero solution for INF systems, the caucus leader of the CDU, Alfred Dregger, for example, called for some sort of a French nuclear guarantee for West Germany in the context of a 'Franco-German security community'.[51] His proposals included giving the post of SACEUR to a French officer. Internally, however, these proposals were heavily criticized as demanding something from Paris that France was known to be unwilling to deliver and for sending the wrong signals to Washington. The Chancellor has repeatedly stated that a 'French option' did not exist for Germany, and that Franco-German military cooperation was to strengthen Germany's NATO ties and not weaken it. An examination of Germany's policies confirms this view.

The visit to Paris by Alfred Dregger in the spring, for example, must be seen within the traditional context of the CDU's internal debate as well as coalition politics with the Free Democrats (FDP) rather than indicative of a strategic reorientation. Dregger sought to rally French support for a German decision against a zero solution for INF systems with a range of 500–1000 km (300–600 miles). Foreign Minister Genscher of the FDP publicly supported a second zero solution, while the majority of the CDU/CSU rejected it. Dregger's visit was an attempt to find tactical support in Paris for his party's views, and the security policy spokesman of the CDU caucus, Volker Ruehe, sought support in London.[52] Although the Chancellor has not done much to constrain Dregger's calls for a Franco-German alliance, it is reasonable to expect that the reason for this behaviour is *not* an underlying interest in a strategic reorientation of the FRG's foreign policy.

Within the SPD there has been considerable interest in France since the beginning of the 1980s. To a large degree this was related to the coming to power of the Socialist Party in 1981. With traditional reference to the concept of socialist solidarity, the SPD had been pushing the socialists to review the underlying principles of French security policy in terms of the possibility of closer cooperation with Germany. Much attention was therefore paid to Jacques Huntzinger's speeches regarding the possibilities for closer nuclear cooperation and extending the French notion of 'vital interests' to include the FRG.[53] Helmut Schmidt's proposals for closer cooperation are probably the best-known examples. Yet his proposals do not reflect mainstream thinking regarding the future course of the party and the role of France in Germany's foreign and defense policy. The former executive director of the SPD, Peter Glotz, noted in a recent article that Schmidt's motivations for proposing the strengthening of the European pillar in the Alliance through improved Franco-German ties resembled those of the left wing as represented by Oskar Lofontaine, for example. Both men, he argued, are interested in increasing the legitimacy of Germany's security through greater independence from the United States:

From year to year it becomes more difficult to explain to young Germans that the defense of the Federal Republic rests to a large extent on American troops and nuclear weapons the employment of which is decided by the American president. This is especially true in times in which the Americans face stronger isolationist tendencies and the country elects presidents who neither distinguish themselves through special interest nor special sensitivity for the Old Continent.[54]

The proposed prescriptions to achieve a greater legitimacy vary greatly. Whereas the left wing of the party favors a German withdrawal from NATO's integrated military structure and the party as a whole has endorsed the concept of a nuclear-free zone in Europe, Helmut Schmidt seeks to raise the nuclear threshold through improved conventional forces and a restructuring of NATO nuclear capabilities that would be contributed by German forces. The left wing of the party, on the other hand, looks at France almost with romantic envy as a model of independence (though without proposing a nuclear element for Germany) regarding that country's decision to leave NATO's integrated military structure. The motivation of that segment of the SPD is nationalistic in the same sense that France's decision to leave NATO was nationalistic. The reason for envy is the degree of autonomy that France appears to enjoy. There is rather little realistic assessment that this autonomy rests on the questionable assumption about the adequacy of the nuclear deterrent and German glacis. Since Germany would have neither a national nuclear option, nor a galcis solidly anchored in NATO and protected by the US, however, the 'French model' necessarily implies a more neutralist course for West Germany. Schmidt's design, on the other hand, seeks to change the security policy principles under which *France* is operating. It is a pro-NATO proposal with a focus on strengthening the Alliance's European component.

Sentiments against the 'artificial' division of Europe is considerable in the SPD and was a basic underlying motivation for *Ostpolitik*. Through a stable core relationship with Eastern European countries, Central Europe was to be made less vulnerable to fluctuations in the superpowers' relationship. A hoped-for by-product was to strengthen trends to increase independence of Eastern European states from the USSR. At the same time, West European integration was to create the platform from which Germany, strengthened and at the same time controlled by her allies, could pursue this policy. The relationship to France (but also to Britain) was a cornerstone in this design. The recently re-emerged concept of *Mitteleuropa* develops the notion of a gravitation of Germany (and possibly its immediate western neighbors) as well as East Germany, Czechoslovakia, Poland and Hungary toward realizing joint interests against their respective protective superpower on the basis of a stabilized East-West relationship.[55]

It is more than doubtful, and alert sympathizers of left-wing positions realize it, that France would play a part in supporting Germany's shift to a more neutral course. The very precondition of French interest to strengthen the partnership is the fear that Germany might drift away from NATO. It is inconceivable that France would allow it to be used in a first phase of creating a European pillar more independent of the United States in order to permit Germany in a second phase, under changed conditions, to pursue an independent, neutralist policy *vis-à-vis* the East. The left wing of the party will have to realize that or accept an indefinite status as opposition party. The SPD position that French nuclear assets should be accounted for in US–Soviet nuclear agreements as well as the SPD trend to move away from nuclear forces as a source of deterrence put the party fully at odds with established and reconfirmed French policies.[56]

CONCLUSIONS

Although there has been a considerable increase in Franco-German cooperative activities since 1982, German officials doubt whether the French moves toward including the security of the FRG in its definition of vital interests and granting consultations about nuclear employment is a significant shift from earlier positions. As before, France considers the question of using nuclear arms as 'indivisible' and the decision to employ its conventional forces as a purely national issue. Aside from rhetorical changes, France, on the whole, remains ambiguous about its wartime strategy. French resource allocation decisions seem to underline this ambiguity. Thus German questions about the reliability of French support persist despite the appreciation of rhetorical changes and exercise experiences.[57]

At the level of concrete planning, there has been some progress in terms of joint Franco-German exercises. These have provided opportunities to check weaknesses and go into operational details. Regarding the future possibility for closer coordination of French and German as well as Allied operations, exercises, doctrinal developments as well as resource allocation will need to be closely studied.

Until now, the stickiest issues in Franco-German cooperation remain on the agenda. These include, among others, the declaratory statements about the independence of French wartime decision-making, the possibility for French forces to be assigned to NATO command in war-time, and the availability of lines of communication through French territory for the reinforcement of Germany. Important indicators of future changes will be exercise activities, the volume of staff talks, and French moves on the role of the tactical nuclear component. If the frequency of tabling new proposals remains as high as in recent months the question arises how substantive these proposals can be.

The public dimension of increasing Franco-German cooperation may have political repercussions for the FRG's relationship to Washington. Above all, the request for an extended French nuclear deterrence sends the wrong signals to the US concerning the true interests of Germany. Most German officials realize that relations with the US, despite setbacks, anxieties and sometimes distrust, are the most important basis for German security which cannot be replaced by any other European power. Observers in the US should not be fooled into believing that the internal discussion of (sometimes radical) alternatives already constitutes a decision for a reorientation. Almost 40 years after the creation of the FRG, it is timely to reflect on the conditions of its existence. Although trans-atlantic discords played a significant role in motivating greater Franco-German cooperation and thinking about a 'European pillar', US policy can make an important contribution in demonstrating that increased European cooperation does not have to be driven by discord only.

NOTES

1. Minister Jobert and Minister of Defence Leber referred to the need to both strengthen conventional defense and increase West European cooperation as a result of the agreement.
2. See Helmut Schmidt, 'Deutsch-franzoesische Zusammenarbeit in der Sicherheitspolitik,' *Europa-Archiv,* no. 11 (1987), pp. 303-12 (303). Translation by the author.
3. See 'Niederschrift der Koalitionsgespraeche/Ergebnise zwischen CDU/CSU und FDP zur Regierungsbildung am 1.10.1982,' Bonn: Bundespress- und Informationsamt, 7 October 1982.
4. See Helmut Kohl, 'Erklaerung der Bundesregierung zur Aussenpolitik,' *Bulletin der Bundesregierung,* no. 118, 26 November 1982, p. 1070.
5. See Konrad Seitz, 'Deutsch-franzoesische sicherheitspolitische Zusammenarbeit,' *Europa-Archiv,* no. 22, 1982, pp. 657-64 (661).
6. An interview given by General Inspector Altenburg to the newspaper *Die Welt* prompted the French Ministry of Defense to issue a communique the next day stressing the requirement for speed in such consultations. Altenburg had stated that 'consultations mean that French pre-strategic weapons will not be used until the French side has heard the view of the German government.' He added that the consultation mechanism with France was to be similar to that existing in NATO. See 'Hoehere Glaubwuerdigkeit unserer Abschreckung,' *Die Welt,* 1 April 1986, p. 1; and Jochen Thies, 'Verstaerkte Zusammenarbeit zwischen Frankreich und der Bundesrepublik Deutschland,' *Europa-Archiv,* no. 9, 1986, p. D 233. Thus, President Mitterrand's emphasis in a press conference in March 1986 that the French principle of autonomy in its nuclear decision

was not addressed by the Germans, has to be taken with a pinch of salt: 'That [principle], in fact, is unchallenged and there is no request on the Federal Republic of Germany's part to alter this state of affairs. However, it is better said than unsaid.' See 'Press conference of François Mitterrand, President of the Republic of France' (Excerpts), 7 March 1986, *Survival*, Vol. 28 (4), 1986, p. 367.

7. See 'Franco-German summit statement, 27–28 February 1986,' *Survival*, Vol. 28 (4), 1986, pp. 366-7 (366).

8. This is only to illustrate that there are elements in Germany that have a deep sense of distrust and sometimes resentment against the French. The quote might be discounted for coming from an officer who is known for strong, sometimes chauvinistic opinions; yet the fact that the national newspaper *Die Welt* carried the editorial indicates that the comment is playing to existing feelings. See Guenter Kiessling, 'Gedankenspiele des Strategen Schmidt,' *Die Welt*, 12 April 1987, p. 15.

9. See Hans-Gert Poettering, 'Deutschlands und Frankreichs Interesse an einer europaeischen Sicherheitspolitik,' *Aussenpolitik*, 37th year, no. 2, 1986, pp. 175-85 (181). (Poettering is a security policy spokesman of the CDU/CSU caucus in the European Parliament.)

10. The German equivalent of *Foreign Affairs*, the journal *Europa-Archiv*, published a translation of an English article that appeared simultaneously in *The World Today*. See Jolyon Howorth, 'Begrenzte Mittel und strategische Optionen: Frankreichs Verteidigungspolitik am Scheideweg?' *Europa-Archiv*, no. 9, 1986, pp. 256-72.

11. The long time between the public denial in 1983 that the creation of the FAR would imply an *automatic* support of West Germany in wartime and Minister Hernu's talk of the FRG and France 'sharing common security interests' was interpreted as an indicator for the tensions within France.

12. See the transcript of Woerner's interview with the *Suedwestfunk* radio station provided by the Bundespresse- und Informationsamt, Ref. II R 3, no. 105, 6 June 1983, p. 22 ff. See also journalists' questions to that effect during the press conference by President Mitterrand in Baden-Baden where he announced the possibility of Franco-German consultations on nuclear employment. Cf. 'Pressegespraech des franzoesischen Staatspraesidents François Mitterrand, anlaesslich seines Besuchs bei den franzoesischen Truppen in Baden-Baden am 16. Januar 1986' (Excerpts), *Europa-Archiv*, no. 9, 1986, pp. D234-D235.

13. That the FAR has in fact a new mission in the defense of Germany emerges from the description of General François Valentin, 'Deutsch-franzoesische Zusammenarbeit in Europa- Mitte,' in Karl Kaiser and Pierre Lellouche (eds), *Deutsch-franzoesische Sicherheitspolitik*, Bonn: Europa-Union Verlag (1986), pp. 142-9 (144/145). See also Gerard Turbe, 'Die franzoesische Schnelleingreiftruppe FAR,' *Internationale Wehrrevue*, no. 8, 1987, pp. 1023-26.

14. See the article by Deputy Secretary of Defense Lothar Reuhl, 'Der Aufschwung der sicherheitspolitischen Zusammenarbeit seit 1982,' in Kaiser and Lellouch, *op. cit.*, pp. 27-47 (38).

15. These views are drawn from a summary of a Franco-German conference on security matters at Haus Rissen: 'Deutsch-Franzoesische Kolloquium ueber Verteidigungsfragen,' *Rissener Rundbrief*, no. 2 (1984). A German participant was quoted as referring to the nuclear element in French strategy as a new 'Maginot-thinking in which the defensive wall is created by American missiles in the Federal Republic.' See also the review of French armaments programs by Felix Mueller, 'Frankreichs Ruestung zwischen Wunsch und Wirtschaftszwaengen,' *Armada International*, no. 6 (1984), pp. 16-28.

16. For an American analysis see David Yost, *France's Deterrent Posture and Security in Europe*. Part I: *Capabilities and Doctrine*, London: IISS (Adelphi Paper No. 194) (Winter 1984/85, pp. 62-4.

17. See Jean Collin, 'Franzoesiche-deutsche Verteidigungskooperation,' *Truppenpraxis*, vol. 30 (6) (1986), pp. 514-16 (515). For details see below.

18. This agreement is known as the Ailleret-Lemnitzer Agreement. Gen. Ailleret was then the French Chief of Staff.

19. This information is drawn from two high-ranking officers who have recently retired. See the article by the former Chief of staff of the First Army, François Valentin, in Karl Kaiser and Pierre Lellouche, *op. cit.*, p. 144 and the former CINC-AFCENT, Franz-Josef Schulze, 'Die Notwendigkeit unverzueglicher gemeinsamer Abwehrreaktionen,' in Kaiser and Lellouche, pp. 150-9 (154).

20. See Schulze, *op. cit.*, p. 154.

21. This is based on an article by the senior defense correspondent of the *Frankfurter Allgemeine Zeitung*. See Karl Feldmayer, 'Frankreich kann der Bundesrepublik den Nuklearschirm nicht bieten,' *Frankfurter Allgemeine Zeitung*, 21 December 1985, p. 3.

22. This is not a direct quote but a translation of the report. See the report on a conference by the conservative Hanns-Seidel Foundation by A. Graf Kageneck, 'Euphorie ueber Frankreichs Sicherheitspolitik schwindet,' *Die Welt*, 17 July 1985.

23. See Ruediger Moniac, 'Verstaendnis fuer Pariser Position,' *Die Welt*, 18 July 1985.

24. See Schulze, *op. cit.*, p. 155.

25. See the article by Konrad Seitz, 'Deutsch-franzoesische sicherheitspolitische Zusammenarbeit,' *loc. cit.*, pp. 660f.

26. The call to strengthen operational reserves is a longstanding issue on NATO's agenda. For similar reasoning see Peter Schmidt, *Die deutsche Debatte ueber die nuklearen und konventionellen Streitkraefte Frankreichs und ihre Auswirkungen auf die deutsch-franzoesische militaerische Kooperation*, Ebenhausen: Stiftung Wissenschaft und Politik (SWP-AP 2476), pp. 14ff.

27. Schulze, *op. cit.*, pp. 157-8.

28. See ibid., p. 158.

29. Schulze, *op. cit.*, pp. 156f.

30. See Peter Stratmann, *NATO Doctrine and National Operational Priorities: The Central Front and the Flanks*, Ebenhausen: Stiftung Wissenschaft und Politik (SWP-LN 2447), 1985.

31. See Helmut Schmidt, 'Speech before the Bundestag on 28 June 1984,' *Informationen der Sozialdemokratischen Bundestagsfraktion*, no. 1257, 28 June 1984, pp. 10ff.

32. See the speech by then State Minister Juergen Moellemann before a Goethe Institute audience in Colmar: 'Deutsch-franzoesische Beitrag zu einem vereinten Europa,' *Bulletin der Bundesregierung*, no. 144, 26 November 1986, pp. 1205-6.

33. Since 1962 parachute units trained together in exercise 'Colibri' and the German navy was allowed to use shooting ranges in French territorial waters. The German air force also had been allowed to train in eastern France for a number of years. See 'Nun prueft sich, was sich ewig bindet,' *Bundeswehr Aktuell*, 22 July 1987, p. 3.

34. See Siegfried Thielbeer, 'Franzoesische Truppen ueben die Vorneverteidigung,' *Frankfurter Allgemeine Zeitung*, 16 August 1987.

35. French forces were comprised of two rank regiments, one mechanized regiment, an artillery regiment and support troops. The information presented here is drawn from Siegfried Thielbeer, 'Ich wollte, es wuerde Nacht und die Franzosen kaemen,' *Frankfurter Allgemeine Zeitung*, 1 October 1987, p. 5; Henri de Bresson, 'La 1re division blindée engagée devant le Main,' *Le Monde*, 27 September 1987, p. 4; Ulrich Mack-

ensen, '"Fraenkischer Schild" mit Deutschen und Franzosen,' *Frankfurter Rundschau*, 26 September 1986, p. 16; 'Manoever sind unverzichtbar' (interview with Army Chief of Staff Gen. von Sandrart), *Frankfurter Rundschau*, 25 September 1987, p. 4; and Siegfried Thielbeer, 'Franzoesische Truppen ueben die Vorneverteidigung,' *loc. cit.*

36. See Hans-Peter Oschwald, 'Der Schulterschluss auf Schwabens Alb,' *Aachener Volkszeitung*, 21 June 1985. The exercise did not receive much publicity.

37. This account of the experience in the Bold Sparrow exercise is drawn from these sources: 'Frankreichs Elitetruppen in Bayern – Politische Demonstration der Einsatzbereitschaft,' *Neue Zuericher Zeitung*, 25 September 1987, p. 3; Karl Feldmeyer, 'Beim Manoever "Kecker Spatz" klappt fast nichts,' *Frankfurter Allgemeine Zeitung*, 24 September 1987, p. 6; Jacques Isnard, 'M. Mitterrand et M. Kohl aux manoeuvres "moineau hardi",' *Le Monde*, 24 September 1987, p. 2; Karl Feldmeyer, 'Viel Wirbel um die Uebung "Kecker Spatz",' *Frankfurter Allgemeine Zeitung*, 23 September 1987, p. 14; Maurice Schmitt, 'Demonstration guter Kooperation,' *Die Welt*, 18 September 1987, p. 8; Jacques Isnard, 'La manoeuvre Franco-allemande "Moineau hardi" permettra de tester la capacité de la FAR a secourir la Bundeswehr,' *Le Monde*, 11 September 1987, p. 9; Detlef Phul, 'Der "Kecke Spatz" ist ein Novum in der Manoevergeschichte,' *Stuttgarter Zeitung*, 22 August 1987; and Seigfried Thielbeer, 'Keine Vorneverteidigung, wohl aber weit vorne und sehr schnell,' *Frankfurter Allgemeine Zeitung*, 13 July 1987, p. 11.

38. See A. Graf Kageneck, 'Diskret und erfolgreich: Logistische Kooperation,' *Die Welt*, 24 October 1985, p. 6.

39. See Thankmar von Muenchhausen, 'Kein Abenteuer, sondern militaerisches Ueben neuer Techniken und Organisationsformen,' *Frankfurter Allgemeine Zeitung*, 7 December 1982, p. 6.

40. See Ruehl, *op. cit.*, pp. 38-9.

41. These soldiers stay for up to two weeks in their host units. See Jean Collin, 'Franzoesische-deutsche Verteidigungskooperation,' *loc. cit.*

42. See Jean Collin, 'Franzoesische-deutsche Verteidigungskooperation,' *loc. cit.* For a full review of exchange programs and training activities, see Rolf Maginot and Ralf Cugaly, 'Grenzueberschreitende Kontakte,' *Informationen fuer die Truppe*, no. 6 (1987), pp. 42-50.

43. In a speech to the German equivalent of the Council on Foreign Relations, the *Deutsche Gesellschaft fuer Auswaertige Politik*, the Chancellor stated that, against the background of the two countries' history, it was more than a marginal achievement, if by the end of the century German and French Generals would emerge from a joint German-French general staff training. See Helmut Kohl, 'Leitlinien und Grunduebrzeugungen deutscher Aussenpolitik,' *Bulletin der Bundesregierung*, no. 78, 1 July 1986, pp. 657-63 (659).

44. See Jochen Thies, 'Verstaerkte Zusammenarbeit zwischen Frankreich und der Bundesrepublik Deutschland,' *Europa-Archiv*, no. 9 (1986), p. D 233. For details of the exchange agreements and statements about higher frequencies of meetings between the Foreign Ministers, see part 4 of the communiqué of the 26–28 February 1986 meeting, *loc. cit.*, p. D236F.

45. See Karl Feldmeyer, 'Das Umfeld einer gemeinsamen Brigade,' *Frankfurter Allgemeine Zeitung*, 22 July 1987, p. 8; Jacques Isnard, 'La brigade franco-allemande aurait pour mission d'aider l'armée française a s'engager outre-Rhin,' *Le Monde*, 19 July 1987, p. 6.

46. Cf. the statement by Chancellor Kohl during the November 1983 Franco-German consultations to that effect; 'Erklaerung des deutschen Bundeskanzlers, Helmut Kohl, zum Abschluss der 42 deutsch-franzoesischen Konsultationen in Bonn am 25 November 1983,' *Europa-Archiv*, no. 2, 1984, pp. D48-D49 (D49). High-level German planners expect that the smaller Franco-German helicopter in the end will be more expensive than the AH-64. This underlines the political significance associated with the PAH-2 program.

47. The Chief of Staff of the Army, LG Hans-Henning von Sandrart in December 1985 was not willing to even speculate about an IOC date. See interview with Hans-Henning von Sandrart, 'Die Ruestungsplanung des Heeres steht,' *Wehrtechnik*, no. 12 (1985), pp. 10-16 (11f). Some German sources estimate that the program will cost up to 2–3 times the amount initially authorized by the Bundestag. See 'Panzerabwehrhubschraub (PAH II): Politische Flexibilitaet muss erhalten bleiben,' *Wehrpolitische Informationen*, vol. 31 (18), pp. 9-12 (10).

48. The working groups center on politico-strategic questions, bilateral military cooperation, and armaments. See Seitz, *op. cit.*, p. 657 and Ruehl, 'Der Aufschwung der sicherheitspolitischen Zusammenarbeit seit 1982,' *loc. cit.*, p. 37.

49. See Ruehl, *loc. cit.*

50. See 'Manoeverbesuch von Mitterrand und Kohl,' *Neue Zuericher Zeitung*, 26 September 1987, pp. 1-2. See also James M. Markham, 'Paris, Bonn propose military council,' *International Herald Tribune*, 26 September 1987, pp. 1-5.

51. See 'Dregger variiert seine Vorstellungen,' *Sueddeutsche Zeitung*, 25 June 1987, p. 6; Karl Feldmeyer, 'Dregger: Die Bundesrepublik soll sich unter Frankreichs Nuklearschirm stellen,' *Frankfurter Allgemeine Zeitung*, 19 June 1987, p. 2.

52. See 'Union setzt auf Unterstuetzung Frankreichs im Bonner Streit um Raketen-Abbau,' *Sueddeutsche Zeitung*, 14 May 1987, pp. 1-2.

53. See for example *Frankfurter Allgemeine Zeitung*, 4 July 1985, p. 4.

54. See Peter Glotz, 'Die franzoesische Option. Eine Auseinandersetzung mit Helmut Schmidts' Strategie des Westens,' *Die Neue Gesellschaft*, 34th year, no. 4 (1987), pp. 292-6 (295).

55. Indicative of these thoughts are the writings of Peter Bender. See for example, his *Die Entideologisierung des Zeitalters* (Berlin: Siedler, 1982) and 'Mitteleuropa- Mode, Modell oder Motiv?' *Die Neue Gesellschaft*, 34th year, no. 4 (1987), pp. 297-8.

56. See, for example, the interview of the SPD newspaper *Vortwaerts* with Hermann Scheer, a Member of Parliament for the party: 'Auf neue Ruestung nicht mit neuer Ruestung antworten,' *Vorwaerts*, 10 May 1985, p. 19.

57. This is also the summary of a December 1985 Haus Rissen Conference on Franco-German cooperation. See 'Deutsch Franzoesisches Kolloquium: Die Zusammenarbeit Frankreich – Bundesrepublik Deutschland im Bereich der Sicherheit und der Verteidigung,' *Rissener Rundbrief*, no. 2 (1984), pp. 45-8.

Appendix A: Franco–German defense cooperation chronology

1955–57	Agreements for joint licensed production of aircraft. Contracts for licensed production of *Noratlas, Fouga Magister*.
March 1958	Agreement to establish joint institute for research and development in weaponry.
1959	MBB, Aerospatiale, and VFW formed 'Transall Group' to develop and produce C-160 aircraft. (Formal Memorandum of Understanding 1965.)
1963	Formal Memorandum of Understanding to govern licensed production. Coincides with signing of Franco-German treaty.
22 January 1963	Adenauer and de Gaulle sign the 'Treaty between the French Republic and the Federal Republic of Germany' (Appendix B). The treaty provides for regular consultations between the two heads of government and contains provisions for cooperation in security matters.[1]
October 1964	Initial Memorandum of Understanding (MOU) on *Roland* air defense missile system (France, FRG and US).
1965–78	MILAN, HOT and *Roland* systems developed and marketed.[2]
21 December 1966	Agreement on stationing and status of French troops in FRG.
1968	Mission Technique de L'Armament RGA established; FRG Defense Research Attaché to Paris.
1970	Armaments program offices created: Bureau de Programmes Franco-Allemand (BPFA) at Rueil-Malmaison; Franco-German Program Office (Ottobrunn). Common Procurement program [Programme d'Approvisionnement en Commun (PAC)] MILAN, HOT, *Roland*.
July 1970	Decision to produce *Alpha Jet*. Delivery of first production aircraft in December 1975.
August 1972	Agreement to develop rapid land mine-clearing device.[3]
1975	FRG determines need for night-capable helicopter. France

	selected as partner country. Aerospatiale and MBB conduct feasibility studies.
March 1977	Initial MOU on joint development of CL 298 reconnaissance.
July 1979	Initial MOU on MARS/MLRS basic system (with participation of France, FRG, UK, US; later Italy).
16 October 1979	Initial MOU to begin definition phase of PAH-2 helicopter.[4]
3–5 February 1980	Franco-German consultations in Paris: Giscard, Barre, Schmidt, and other ministers. Topics include Franco-German arms cooperation. The two Defense Ministers sign a statement of intention to develop a battlefield tank for the 1990s.[5]
June 1980	FRG and France sign initial MOU on *Roland 2* air defense missile system.
11–12 July 1980	Franco-German consultations in Bonn: Giscard, Schmidt, Barre, and other ministers. Security issues discussed.
December 1980	No agreement on PAH-2 helicopter. Discussion of projects reverts armaments directors.[6]
5–6 February 1981	Franco-German consultations in Paris: Schmidt and Giscard.[7]
12–13 July 1981	Franco-German consultations in Bonn: Schmidt, Mauroy, Mitterrand, and other ministers.[8]
24–25 February 1982	Franco-German consultations in Paris: Schmidt, Mitterrand, Mauroy, and other ministers. Ministers discuss possible joint production of aircraft and a battlefield tank. Hernu sets 31 March deadline for FRG tank decision. 'In the spirit of the Franco-German treaty of 22 January 1963', they agree to closer consultation in foreign policy and a 'more intensive exchange of views on security matters'.[9]
April 1982	Date of initial MOU on mine laying system 85 (Belgium, France, FRG, Netherlands).
Spring 1982	Joint battlefield tank project fails.
4 October 1982	Days after taking office, Kohl makes his first foreign visit to Paris to meet with Mitterrand. As suggested by Mitterrand in February 1982, security policy consultations are scheduled to take place on 21 October, the date of the next regular summit.[10]
21–22 October 1982	Franco-German consultations in Bonn: Kohl, Mitterrand, Mauroy, and other ministers. Kohl and Mitterrand agree to activate the portion of the Elysée Treaty calling for cooperation in security issues (Appendix C). Other topics of discussion include joint arms projects and the cost of French troops stationed in the FRG.
20 January 1983	Mitterrand visits Bonn on the 20th anniversary of the

	Franco-German treaty. Speaking before the Bundestag, Mitterrand expresses support for the NATO dual-track decision, and says that cooperation between France and the FRG must be intensified.[11]
21 January 1983	Kohl goes to Paris to mark the 20th anniversary of the Elysée Treaty. His speech seems intended to assuage French concerns that the FRG is not 'wandering' between East and West.[12]
February 1983	Agreement between France, FRG and UK to build third-generation anti-tank missile (PARS).
16 May 1983	Franco-German consultations in Paris. Genscher and Woerner precede Kohl to meet for security consultations. Woerner announces that 'good progress' has been made with regard to the joint production of an anti-tank helicopter gunship. The German delegation reported that a decision on the joint production of 300 helicopters will be taken in a few weeks, but uncertainties over financing and technical details remain. Armaments directors are to work out outstanding problems.[13]
20 July 1983	Mitterrand and Kohl meet informally to discuss INF.[14]
24–25 November 1983	Franco-German consultations in Bonn. Security issues predominate.[15] Agreement to begin development phase of PAH-2 helicopter.[16]
7 December 1983	First meeting of Franco-German steering committee. Chairmen: Dr Lothar Ruehl and M. Heisbourg.[17]
December 1983	Chiefs of Staffs of air forces of France, FRG, Italy, Spain, and UK sign 'Outline Staff Target for Future European Fighter Aircraft' (EFA).[18]
May 1984	MOU on development and production of type 124 frigate (with Canada, France, FRG, UK, Italy, Netherlands, Spain and US).
29 May 1984	Final agreement on development phase of PAH-2 helicopter. Three versions of the helicopter will be built.[19]
4 June 1984	Formal MOU between Kohl and Mitterrand on development phase of PAH-2 helicopter.
9 July 1984	Defense Ministers (UK, France, FRG, Italy and Spain) sign an agreement on feasibility study for European fighter Aircraft (EFA).
Autumn 1984	FRG breaks off discussions on Franco-German replacement for *Hawk* air defense system.
31 October 1984	Franco-German consultations. Kohl and Mitterrand agree on closer cooperation in research and technology, including European participation in US manned space station and the further development of the *Ariane 5* rocket. No commitment from Bonn on *Hermes*. Financial difficulties in

	the FRG may arise.[20]
January 1985	European Space Agency (ESA) agrees to participate in US *Columbus* program and to development of *Ariane 5*.[21]
1 March 1985	Franco-German consultations: Kohl, Mitterrand, Genscher, Dumas, Woerner, Hernu; Kohl and Mitterrand announce that studies on joint production of a fighter aircraft and anti-tank helicopter continue; and that joint military maneuvers will be held for the next two years. SDI is discussed as well.[22]
April 1985	Paris proposes the creation of a European Research Cooperation Agency (EUREKA).
23 May 1985	Genscher meets with Mitterrand in Paris. Talks focus on SDI and the European technology project, EUREKA. Genscher expresses his strong support for EUREKA. The Defense and Foreign Ministers from both countries are to meet to discuss SDI and the strategic consequences for both countries.[23]
28 May 1985	Franco-German consultations in Constance. Kohl and Mitterrand discuss SDI. Research ministers from both countries will meet soon to discuss participation in EUREKA.[24]
20 June 1985	Woerner and Hernu meet at the largest Franco-German 'alliance' troop maneuvers near Muensingen. The joint maneuvers involved a total of 4600 French and German soldiers and were the longest, most intensive, and largest joint maneuvers so far.[25]
26 June 1985	French and German Foreign, Defense and Research Ministers meet to discuss SDI and Eureka. Ministers are said to discuss the joint production of a reconnaissance satellite. The latter would be intended to make Europe less dependent on US intelligence, but would cost up to DM 10 billion over the next 8-10 years. No financing plan had been prepared.[26]
3 August 1985	Plans for French participation in EFA collapse.
24 August 1985	Kohl and Mitterrand meet to discuss EUREKA and defense matters, including the production of the EFA, and a European reconnaissance satellite.
8 October 1985	MoD state secretary Lothar Ruehl outlines measures to strengthen Franco-German military cooperation, including joint maneuvers in 1986 (150,000 French and German troops); and maneuvers of the French RDP in the FRG, scheduled for 1987, but possibly earlier.[27]
7 November 1985	Franco-German consultations: Kohl and Mitterrand, Defense and Foreign Ministers. Topics include European and East–West relations, defense cooperation and arms production, and European technological cooperation.

	Results: joint military maneuvers will be held in 1986 with the participation of the RDF; Mitterrand announces the 'symbolic' participation of France in the EFA project; the FRG rejects French proposal to build reconnaissance satellite. The Foreign and Defense Ministers discuss arms control negotiations in Geneva, SDI, French defense strategy and arms cooperation.[28]
17 December 1985	Kohl meets with Mitterrand in Paris. Defense cooperation is the central point of the discussion. General Inspector W. Altenburg and French General Chief of Staff, Jean-Michel Saulmer meet to discuss future defense planning, the inclusion of the French RDF in German defense, and joint training of general staff officers. Kohl suggests that Paris postpone *Hermes* in the hope of finding European financing plan.[29]
31 December 1985	Original contract for definition phase of PAH-2 ends. No final agreement on production. Problems of cost, production scheduling, and military requirements are unresolved.[30]
7 January 1986	Genscher meets with French Foreign Minister Dumas. The two announce that 1986 will be the year of Franco-German relations. The Foreign Ministers will meet quarterly; foreign office division heads for economics, politics, and culture will meet monthly. Discussions on *Hermes* will continue at the highest level.[31]
16 January 1986	Franco-German consultations in Baden-Baden: Mitterrand, Kohl, and the Defense Ministers and representatives of the general staffs. Mitterrand stresses that France retains national control over its nuclear forces but he supports consultations with the FRG. A consultation system must be developed for any situation involving military conflict on German soil. The French space shuttle *Hermes* is not discussed. They announce plans for joint maneuvers and training of high-ranking officers.[32]
28 January 1986	Genscher and Dumas make a joint appearance before the opening of the next round of negotiations of the CDE in Stockholm. Their joint statement refers to the importance of Europe's contribution to the détente process.[33]
28 February 1986	Franco-German consultations in Paris: Kohl, Mitterrand, Foreign and Defense Ministers. A new military accord is reached, which calls for greater operational cooperation between their armed forces (Appendix D). The FRG refuses to commit on a financial contribution to *Hermes*. There is no agreement on plans for the PAH-2.[34]
17 April 1986	Kohl meets for the first time with Chirac. Genscher is to

	meet in May with his French counterpart and leading officials from the Foreign Ministries to discuss the first exchange of personnel.[35]
12 May 1986	The French Defense Minister meets for the first time with Woerner. Both express their intention to intensify military cooperation further. Discussions cover arms cooperation, joint exercises and training.[36]
22 May 1986	Genscher meets with new French Foreign Minister, Jean-Bernard Raimond. Genscher reports that Paris and Bonn will consult more closely before international conferences and that a joint appearance is planned before the CSCE follow-up conference in Vienna (November).[37]
17 June 1986	Franco-German consultations. Topics include nuclear power, East–West relations, and the upcoming European summit. The deadlock on the joint construction of a combat helicopter is not broken, but Kohl remains 'optimistic' that the requirements of the two general staffs can be reconciled.[38]
25 July 1986	Giraud and Woerner meet to discuss the joint helicopter project. They announce that two studies will be completed by the respective directors for armaments in hopes of reconciling respective military requirements. Giraud presents Woerner with a proposal for a new tank co-production project.[39]
Autumn 1986	Joint maneuvers (*Frankischer Schild*) with 150,000 French and German troops.
28 October 1986	Franco-German consultations. Topics include European participation in space research and security issues. Kohl agrees to a 30 per cent participation in the financing of *Hermes* (DM 32 million). The two leaders sign a bilateral agreement on arms cooperation; mutual consultations on arms control, conventional and nuclear, are to be intensified. Kohl underscores the importance of French participation in negotiations on reductions of conventional forces.[40]
October 1986	Because of delays in PAH-2 program, Paris and Bonn order new feasibility study, due in December 1986.[41]
February 1987	Results of PAH-2 feasibility study published. Decision on project expected April/May 1987.[42]
19 June 1987	Kohl proposes the creation of a Franco-German combat unit.[43]
July 1987	Woerner meets with Giraud in Paris. Decision is taken to abandon first MOU on helicopter; a new agreement is to be signed at autumn Franco-German summit. Agreement on night vision sight will require a separate MOU. A working group is created to study Kohl's combat bri-

gade proposal.[44]

21–22 September 1987   Joint maneuvers (Bold Sparrow) near Ulm. RDF partici-
pates.[45]

24 September 1987   At the conclusion of joint maneuvers, Mitterrand announces that negotiations are under way to create a joint
military council, to be composed of senior ministers and
officers.[46]

See Appendix E for sources.

Appendix B: Treaty between the French Republic and the FRG on Franco–German cooperation

(EXCERPTS) 22 JANUARY 1963: DEFENSE

In the area of defense the following goals shall be pursued:

1. In the area of strategy and tactics, the authorized agencies of both countries shall strive to reconcile their views in order to arrive at shared concepts [of strategy]. Franco-German institutes for operations research shall be established.
2. The exchange of personnel between the armed forces shall be strengthened; this applies in particular to the instructors and pupils of the general staff academies; the exchange may also include the temporary delegation of entire units [to foreign command]. To facilitate this exchange, both parties shall make an effort to provide language instruction for the appropriate personnel.
3. In the area of armaments, both governments shall make an effort to organize joint projects, beginning with the initial project development phase and continuing through the preparation of financing plans.

For this purpose, a joint commission shall examine armaments-related research projects and take up a comparative study. It [the commission] will provide the ministers with [project] proposals, which shall be examined at their tri-monthly meetings, and for which they [the ministers] shall provide the necessary instructions for implementation.

The governments shall review the prerequisites to initiate Franco-German cooperation in civil defense.

['Der deutsch-franzoesische Vertrag vom 22. Januar 1963,' *Europa-Archiv* 18, no. 4 (25 February 1963): D85.]

Appendix C: Reactivation of the Elysée Treaty. The October 1982 Franco–German summit

At a joint press conference following the routine autumn summit, Chancellor Kohl and President Mitterrand announced the formal reactivation of the Elysée Treaty's security clause. Kohl described the decisions taken in the area of defense:

Particular prominence was given in our talks to security policy questions. After 19 years we have activated for the first time an agreement under the German-French friendship treaty which very pointedly refers to the development of a common security policy.

I can announce to you that in execution of the mandate given by the heads of state and government at the German-French summit in February 1982, the foreign and defense ministers of the two countries met yesterday for a first extensive exchange of views on questions of defense and external security. The FRG and France are both members of the Atlantic alliance. Although their situations concerning defense problems are different, they do have common concerns regarding their security and are therefore of the opinion that closer coordination in these questions would be in their common interests. These talks permit the application of the regulations of the 1963 German-French treaty concerning defense, which aim at bringing the views of the two countries closer together and formulating common concepts. . . .

The president of the republic and I have agreed to the proposal of the four ministers – the two foreign and the two defense ministers – to continue the extended exchange of views. We have also arranged for a coordinating group consisting of high-ranking representatives of the four ministries to get together between these meetings and to prepare for these meetings. This coordination group will convene with groups for special questions.

Foreign Broadcast Information Service (Western Europe) 25 October 1982, J3-4.

Appendix D: Franco–German agreement on defense cooperation – February 1986

Following two-day consultations in February 1986, Chancellor Kohl and President Mitterrand issued a joint statement outlining specific provisions for cooperation between the FRG and France in the area of defense. In the agreement the two leaders agreed to new measures in conventional defense cooperation, including the holding of joint maneuvers with the participation of the FAR; and Paris pledged to consult the Chancellor of the FRG before the use of 'pre-strategic' nuclear weapons on German territory.

STATEMENT ON THE AGREEMENT BETWEEN THE CHANCELLOR OF THE FEDERAL REPUBLIC OF GERMANY AND THE PRESIDENT OF THE FRENCH REPUBLIC (EXCERPTS)

1. The Chancellor of the Federal Republic of Germany and the President of the French Republic discussed at length problems of security and defense which are of concern to the FRG and France. They called special attention to their agreement, within the framework of the Elysée Treaty of 22 January 1963, to promote measures that could contribute to the already strong ties between the two countries in this area.

2. **Operational cooperation, cooperation between the armed forces**
    The governments of the two countries announced their consent to expanded operational cooperation between their armed forces. With a view to greater efficiency in the areas of strategy and operational cooperation, the Chancellor of the Federal Republic and French President are authorizing the continuation of studies on the more effective deployment of the French armed forces in Germany, in particular the rapid deployment force (FAR). Appropriate joint maneuvers to begin in 1986–87 will concretize this agreement.

3. **Training**
    In addition, the Chancellor of the Federal Republic and President of the French Republic approved proposals for joint officer training. During the first phase, which may include subsequent measures, joint courses of instruction for

officers will be provided. Courses will begin in 1986–87 and will be held on an alternating basis in the Federal Republic and France.

4. Consultations

The President of the French Republic declared his willingness to consult with the Chancellor of the Federal Republic about the possible use of French prestrategic weapons on German soil, within the limits posed by the extraordinary rapidity with which such decisions must be taken. He recalled, however, that decisions in this matter cannot be divided. In this regard, the President of the French Republic called attention to a resolution taken with the Chancellor of the Federal Republic to create the technical means necessary for immediate and reliable consultations in crisis situations.

Europa-Archiv 41, no. 9 (1986): D235-6.

Appendix E: Sources

1. *Europa-Archiv* 18, no. 4 (25 February 1963), D83.
2. Lars Benecke, Ulrich Krafft and Friedhelm Meyer zu Natrup, 'Franco-West German technological cooperation,' *Survival* (May/June 1986), pp. 235-6.
3. Wolfgang Flume, 'Ruestungskooperation mit Frankreich,' *Wehrtechnik*, vol.16, no.2 (February 1984), p. 33.
4. 'PAH-2/HAP/HAC-3G,' *Wehrtechnik*, vol. 17, no. 1 (January 1985), p. 21.
5. *Europa-Archiv* 35, no. 5 (10 March 1980), Z43; 'Bonns Interessen am "politischen Gleichklang" mit Paris,' *Frankfurter Allgemeine Zeitung* (*FAZ*), 24 February 1982, p. 5.
6. 'PAH-2 Deutsch-franzoesische Kooperation oder?,' *Wehrtechnik*, no. 4 (April 1981), p. 74.
7. *Europa-Archiv* 36, no. 7 (10 August 1981), D203.
8. *Europa-Archiv* 36, no. 15 (10 August 1981), Z150.
9. *Europa-Archiv* 37, no. 6 (25 March 1982), Z53; 'Gemeinsame Erklaerung des Praesidents der Franzoesischen Republik, François Mitterrand, und des Bundeskanzlers der Bundesrepublik Deutschland, Helmut Schmidt, anlaesslich der 39. deutsch-franzoesischen Konsultationen, in Paris, am 24 und 25 Februar 1982,' *Europa-Archiv* 37, no. 7 (10 April 1982), D194-5.
10. 'Bonn: die Gespraeche waren freimuetig,' *FAZ*, 6 October 1982, p. 3.
11. *Europa-Archiv* 38, no. 4 (1983), Z30; James M. Markham, 'Mitterrand, on Bonn visit, warns against effort to divide the West,' *The New York Times*, 21 Januar 1983, pp. 1, 9; 'Rede des franzoesischen Staatspraesidents, François Mitterrand in Bonn am 20. Januar 1983 anlaesslich des zwanzigsten Jahrestags der Unterzeichnung des Vertrags ueber die deutsch-franzoesische Zusammenarbeit' *Europa-Archiv* 38, no. 5 (1983), D145-62.
12. 'FRG Chancellor Kohl's 21 January speech in Paris,' *FBIS* (Western Europe), 21 January 1983, K1-2; 'Kohl in Paris: Wir haben die gleichen Sorgen und die gleichen Einschaetzungen,' *FAZ*, 22 January 1983, pp. 1-2; 'No drift toward neutralism, Kohl tells the French,' *The New York Times*, 22 Januar 1983, p. 4; 'Rede des Bundeskanzlers, Helmut Kohl, in Paris am 21 Januar 1983 anlaesslich des zwanzigsten Jahrestags der Unterzeichnung des Vertrags ueber die deutsch-franzoesische Zusammenarbeit,' *Europa-Archiv* 38, no. 5 (1983), D145-62.

13. 'Agreement in sight for joint construction of helicopter,' *FBIS* (Western Europe), 20 May 1983, K3-4; 'Chancellor Kohl leaves for Paris talks 16 May,' *FBIS* (Western Europe), 17 May 1983, J1; 'FRG Chancellor arrives for summit talks,' *FBIS* (Western Europe), 17 May 1983, K1-2; 'Mitterrand, Kohl, hold working session 17 May,' *FBIS* (Western Europe), 18 May 1983, K1-2.

14. John Vinocur, 'Kohl and Mitterrand meet on missiles,' *New York Times*, 20 July 1983, A3.

15. *Europa-Archiv* 39, no. 2 (1984), D43-49; 'Erklaerung des deutschen Bundeskanzlers, Helmut Kohl, zum Abschluss der 42. deutsch-franzoesischen Konsultationen in Bonn am 25 November 1983,' *Europa-Archiv* 39, no. 2 (1983), D48-49; 'Gemeinsamer Wille,' *FAZ*, 26 November 1984, p. 1; 'Mitterrand beim Bundeskanzler,' *FAZ*, 25 November 1983, pp. 1-2; 'Staatspraesident Mitterrand heute bei Bundeskanzler Kohl,' *FAZ*, 24 November 1983, pp. 1-2; 'Tischrede des deutschen Bundeskanzlers, Helmut Kohl, aus Anlass der 42. deutsch-franzoesischen Konsultationen in Bonn am 24 November 1983,' *Europa-Archiv* 39, no. 2 (1983), D43-46.

16. 'FRG, French Defense Ministers sign declaration,' *FBIS* (Western Europe), 29 November 1983, K3.

17. Wolfgang Flume, 'Weapons development with France – growing European orientation,' *Wehrtechnik* (February 1984): 23-117.

18. Benecke, Krafft, and zu Natrup, p. 238.

19. 'PAH-2/HAP/HAC–3G.'

20. 'Further on Kohl–Mitterrand summit meeting,' *FBIS* (Western Europe), 31 October 1984, J1-2; 'Mitterrand-Kohl summit yields few results,' *FBIS* (Western Europe), 14 November 1984, K2.

21. Benecke, Krafft, and zu Natrup, p. 241.

22. 'Kohl, Mitterrand agree on military maneuvers,' *FBIS* (Western Europe), 1 March 1985, K1; 'Mitterrand, Kohl adopt "European Stance",' *FBIS* (Western Europe), 5 March 1985, K2-4.

23. 'Genscher "encouraged" by talks with Mitterrand,' *FBIS* (Western Europe), 24 May 1985, J1-2; 'Genscher zeigt sich in Paris ermutigt,' *FAZ*, 24 May 1985, p. 6; 'Genscher backs technical cooperation with France,' *FBIS* (Western Europe), 28 May 1985, J1-2.

24. *Europa-Archiv* 40, no. 12 (1985), Z99-100; 'Bonn: Das Konstanzer Treffen bestaetigt die Zusammenarbeit,' *FAZ*, 30 May 1985, pp. 1-2; 'Kohl, Mitterrand discuss "Star Wars", Eureka,' *FBIS* (Western Europe), 29 May 1985, J1-2; James M. Markham, 'Kohl meets with Mitterrand,' *The New York Times*, 29 May 1985, p. 8.

25. 'Woerner, France's Hernu on joint troop maneuvers,' *FBIS* (Western Europe), 21 June 1985, J2.

26. 'Bonn und Paris bekraeftigen den Willen zu technologischer Zusammenarbeit,' *FAZ*, 28 June 1985, p. 2; 'Genscher, Woerner meet French counterparts,' *FBIS* (Western Europe), 27 June 1985, J1.

27. 'Greater military cooperation with France noted,' *FBIS* (Western Europe), 8 October 1985, J3-4.

28. 'Kohl, Mitterrand meet for consultations,' *FBIS* (Western Europe), 8 November 1985, J1-2; 'Kohl und Mitterrand vorsichting und zurueckhaltend. Zwei Entscheidungen beim bonner Gipfel,' *FAZ*, 9 November 1985, pp. 1-2; 'Lange Themenliste fuer den 46 deutsch-franzoesischen Gipfel,' *FAZ*, 7 November 1985, pp. 1-2; John Tagliabue, 'Paris and Bonn set accord on projects,' *The New York Times*, 9 November 1985, p. 41.

29. 'Mitterrand hosts talks with FRG's Kohl in Paris,' *FBIS* (Western Europe), 18 December 1985, K1.

30. 'PAH-2/HAP decision postponed until fall,' *Aviation Week and Space Technology*, 23 June 1986, p. 29.

31. 'Bonn und Paris wollen 1986 zum Jahr der deutsch-franzoesischen Beziehungen machen,' *FAZ*, 8 January 1986, p. 1.

32. 'Kohl, France's Mitterrand meet in Baden-Baden,' *FBIS* (Western Europe), 17 January 1986, J2-3; 'Pressegespraech des franzoesischen Staatspraesidenten, François Mitterrand, anlaesslich seines Besuchs bei den franzoesischen Truppen in Baden-Baden am 16 Januar 1986,' *Europa-Archiv* 41, no. 9 (1986), D234-5; 'Kohl und Mitterrand in Baden-Baden,' *FAZ*, 17 January 1986, p. 5.

33. 'Deutsch-franzoesische Zusammenwirken bekraeftigt,' *FAZ*, 29 January 1986, pp. 1-2.

34. Paul Lewis, 'Paris-Bonn military accord is reached,' *New York Times*, 2 March 1986, p. 3; 'Mitterrand, Kohl begin 47th summit in Paris,' *FBIS* (Western Europe), 28 February 1986, K1; 'Summit statement on military cooperation with FRG,' *FBIS* (Western Europe), 5 March 1986, K10; 'Gemeinsame Erklaerungen des Bundeskanzlers der Bundesrepublik Deutschland, Helmut Kohl, und des franzoesischen Stattspraesidenten, François Mitterrand, in Paris am 28. Februar 1986 nach zweitaegigen bilateralen konsultationen,' *Europa Archiv*, 41, no. 9 (1986), D235-7; 'Kohl und Mitterrand beschliessen engere militaerische Zusammenarbeit,' *FAZ*, 1 March 1986, pp. 1-2.

35. 'Kohl, France's Chirac meet in Bonn 17 April,' *FBIS* (Western Europe), 18 April 1986, J1-2.

36. 'French Defense Minister Giraud pays 1-day visit,' *FBIS* (Western Europe), 13 May 1986, J1.

37. 'Fuer internationale Nuklear-Konvention,' *FAZ*, 25 May 1986, p. 2.

38. '*Le Monde* views "Friendly" Summit with FRG,' *FBIS* (Western Europe), 23 June 1986, K3.

39. 'Giraud, Woerner talk further on helicopter plan,' *FBIS* (Western Europe), 31 July 1986, K1.

40. 'Deutsch und Franzoesen feiern in Frankfurt die Freundschaft zweier Voelker,' *FAZ*, 28 October 1986, pp. 1-2; 'Bonn und Paris vereinbaren engere militaerische und sicherheitspolitische Zusammenarbeit,' *FAZ*, 29 October 1986, pp. 1-2.

41. 'Germans, French to study substitute for PAH-2 helicopter,' *Aviation Week and Space Technology*, 20 October 1986, pp. 38-9.

42. 'French, West Germans consider combining helicopter versions,' *Aviation Week and Space Technology*, 23 February 1987, p. 27.

43. Robert J. McCartney, 'Kohl proposes joint German-French combat unit,' *Washington Post*, 20 June 1987, A20; James M. Markham, 'Paris and Bonn start to think of a special alliance,' *The New York Times*, 24 June 1987, p. 3.

44. 'Gemeinsame Entwicklung eines deutsch-franzoesischen Hubschraubers,' *FAZ*, 17 July 1987, pp. 1-2.

45. 'Keine Vorneverteidigung, wohl aber sehr weit vorne und sehr schnell,' *FAZ*, 13 July 1987, p. 5.

46. 'Paris and Bonn negotiating a joint military council,' *The New York Times*, 26 September 1987, p. 7; 'Bonn und Paris planen Verteidigungsrat,' *Sueddeutsche Zeitung*, 25 September 1987, p. 2.

Index